Social Formalism

SOCIAL FORMALISM

The Novel in Theory from
Henry James to the Present

Dorothy J. Hale

Stanford University Press
Stanford, California
1998

Stanford University Press
Stanford, California
© 1998 by the Board of Trustees of the
Leland Stanford Junior University
Printed and bound by CPI Group (UK) Ltd, Croydon, CR0 4YY

CIP data appear at the end of the book

For Jeffrey

Acknowledgments

Much of the pleasure I have derived from writing this book has come from the conversations it has occasioned; I am profoundly grateful to my family, friends, colleagues, and students for their willingness to enter into the issues and problems of *Social Formalism*. Their generous response has influenced the project from start to finish, and their willingness to be interested—or at least cleverly to feign interest—has provided intellectual sustenance and impetus, without which I can't imagine having brought this book to completion.

My study of the theory of the novel was inspired by the scholarship and teaching of my graduate advisor, Ralph W. Rader. His intellectual integrity and generosity remain a model to me of professional and personal character; I feel privileged to have enjoyed his incisive critical judgment, his astute advice on all professional matters, and his ready wit. The groundwork for *Social Formalism* in particular was laid in graduate classes that I had at U.C. Berkeley with Ralph Rader, Carolyn Porter, and Seymour Chatman. Their thinking and teaching shaped the intellectual terms of this project in more ways than I probably even know—and I hope in ways that they may not regret. I am deeply appreciative for their penetrating responses to my work, for their willingness to read so much of it, and for their unflagging support over the years.

Samuel Otter, Nancy Ruttenburg, Lynn Wardley, and Cindy Weinstein have all read the pages of this book almost as many times as I myself have read them. Their insights have been invaluable—and their camaraderie has made everything seem possible. I don't know how we were able to have so much fun while working so hard together, but I do know that the book is, as I am, the better for it. I am also greatly indebted to those who read parts of the manuscript at different stages of its development: Elizabeth Abel, Charles Altieri, Oliver Arnold, James Astorga, Richard Brodhead, Charles Berger, Deirdre D'Albertis, Paul Frye, Stephen Greenblatt, Susan Hegeman, Steven Knapp, Mark Maslan, Susan Maslan, Eric Sundquist, and the members of the Bay Area Americanist Reading Group. The anonymous readers who reviewed my manuscript in its penultimate form prompted the revisions I have made over the past year. My research assistants, Luciana Herman, Benjamin Widiss, and Joseph Jeon, have provided not just the precise execution of nitty-gritty detail work, but ongoing intellectual companionship. I am indebted to them for their reliability and keen judgment as well as for their unfailing good cheer. I would also like to express appreciation to Jonathan Freedman, a reader for the Press, and to my editor, Helen Tartar.

Chapter 5 of the book is a revised version of "Bakhtin in African American Literary Theory," an essay that appeared in *English Literary History* 61 (1994) and is reprinted here in its modified form with the journal's permission. Some of the ideas in this book were refined through their presentation as talks: my thanks to participants at the International Bakhtin Conference in Mexico City; the meeting of the Western Humanities Center in Seattle; and the Madison, San Diego, Park City, and Gainesville meetings of the International Conference on Narrative Literature. Thanks as well to audiences at U.C. Santa Barbara and the California Institute of Technology. I owe a special debt of gratitude to the Humanities and Social Sciences Division of Caltech for the productive and stimulating term I spent in residence there.

Fellowships from the American Council of Learned Societies, the University of California, and the Doreen Townsend Humanities Center materially contributed to the completion of the book by making possible uninterrupted time in the library and in front of the computer.

Nan Elliot, Doreen Klein, Elisabeth Garst, Walter Greenblatt, Raluca Iuster, John Nash Hale, William Hale, Susan Vernon, Lynn Ward, and Henry Wigglesworth all were willing to discuss my book with me even when they were most entitled to be thoroughly sick of it. I regret that, after sharing so much in it, Dorothy Long Hale and John Heald Hale could not witness the finished product.

Jeffrey Knapp's contribution to this project cannot be measured. Intrepid reader, ingenious problem solver, reluctant but cajolable bibliographer, he has seen *Social Formalism* through from beginning to end, from high theory to lowly punctuation point. If my laptop computer risked spoiling one or two vacations over the years, Jeffrey's unstinting interest and encouragement are what in fact determined me to keep at it and made it all seem worthwhile.

D.J.H.

Contents

Social Formalism

Introduction

Novel Theory and Ideology

The refinements of the art of fiction have been accepted without
question, or at most have been classified roughly and summarily—
as is proved by the singular poverty of our critical vocabulary, as
soon as we pass beyond the simplest and plainest effects. The expressions and the phrases at our disposal bear no defined, delimited
meanings; they have not been rounded and hardened by passing
constantly from one critic's hand to another's.

—Percy Lubbock, *The Craft of Fiction* (1921)

Anyone who has begun the study of fiction has encountered terms
like *point of view, flashback, omniscient narrator, third-person
narrative.* One can't describe the techniques of a novel without
such terms, any more than one can describe the workings of a car
without the appropriate technical vocabulary. But while someone
who wanted to learn about cars would have no trouble finding a
manual, there is no comparable work for the student of literature.

—Jonathan Culler, Foreword to Gérard Genette,
Narrative Discourse (1980)

These essays take the nineteenth-century novel seriously by not
treating it as privileged—by directing attention, in other words, to
the language and systems of representation that it shared with the
wider culture, and to the more or less open ways in which it participated in that culture. If the authors are not as obviously engaged
with the poetics of fiction as they might have been a decade ago,
they are perhaps more alert to the fictiveness of discourse generally,
and to the anxieties that any fiction may manipulate and conceal.

—Ruth Bernard Yeazell, *Sex, Politics, and Science
in the Nineteenth-Century Novel* (1986)

Narratology is, after all, as I hope I have made clear, here and
there, just another narrative, not only extradiegetic, metalinguistic,
transtextual, paratextual, hypotextual, extratextual, intertextual,
etc. but also, yes, textual, all at the same time. Nevertheless, the
study of narratological phenomena became, as so often happens,
an endless discussion about how to speak of them.

—Christine Brooke-Rose, "Whatever Happened to
Narratology?" (1990)

W̲H̲A̲T̲ ̲W̲A̲S̲ ̲N̲O̲V̲E̲L̲ ̲T̲H̲E̲O̲R̲Y̲? Born in the attempt to articulate the distinctiveness of the novel as a literary form, novel theory now seems either dismissed or ignored as literary critics become cultural critics, turning their attention from text to social context, from poetics to ideology. At the beginning of the century, the novel gained new
prestige as an art form when critics granted it a unique technical complexity; now the novel's value is defined by its ideological typicality. As
debates about the novel circulate around the question of cultural function, critics seem to be left with little interest in or need for what at the
beginning of the century was considered by many to be the point of literary analysis generally and the mission of novel theory in particular:
the isolation and description of the generic features that not only distinguished one literary object from another but defined the literary as a
logical category.[1] Formal and generic descriptions of the novel have increasingly been subsumed by the almost hermetically sealed field of narratology, which, from its structuralist inception, has ardently pursued
the increasingly rarified business of nomenclature. Narratologists may
debate amongst themselves about the relative merits of terms like
"focalization" and "filter"; they may work to characterize "narrative
speed and its canonical tempos," to differentiate among "posterior, an-
terior, simultaneous, and intercalated" narrative structures, and to detect a variety of "implied" narratorial agents; but cultural critics seem to
find the old-fashioned vocabulary of plot, character, point of view, and
exposition entirely adequate to their interpretative purposes.[2] If any-

---

[1] In 1952 John Aldridge claimed that a poetics of the novel was imminent: "We
have not yet formulated it or codified its insights or dignified it with a term, as we
certainly shall do, and as we have already done with the criticism of poetry"
(*Critiques*, iv). As late as 1961, however, Robert Scholes could introduce a collection of essays on the novel by declaring that "up to now, no one work has been
written which we can point to as a Poetics of the Novel" (*Approaches*, v). By 1967
novel study was prolific enough to have a journal, *Novel*, devoted exclusively to its
own study, and the 1984 volumes of that journal might be regarded as a watershed
in the rise and fall of novel theory. Devoted to the question of "why the novel matters," this series of issues reflected the shifting criteria for artistic merit. The literary
status that so many theorists and critics sought to confer upon the novel was suddenly a liability; the less literary an art work was, the more "real" it could be. In
their introduction to the essays collected from the series, the editors of *Novel* ask,
"Why *do* novels matter, after all, at a time when criticism seems to protect us *from*
literary fictions by exposing their hazardous social codes or, conversely, by confin-
ing them in various ways to 'the prison house of language'?" (Spilka and McCracken-Flesher, *Why the Novel Matters*, 198).
[2] Prince, "On Narrative Studies," 271. While such debates are ubiquitous, numbers 2 and 4 of *Poetics Today* (1990) provide an important estimation of narratol-

thing, it is the narratologists who feel their criticism is undertheorized. Cultural critics may not miss a technical terminology that details the inner workings of the novel, but narratologists have felt compelled to expand their study of the novel to describe the ideological work the genre performs.[3]

---

ogy by founders of and practitioners in the field. For the debate within narratology about the status of "implied" agents, as well as a defense of the implied author, see Chatman, *Coming to Terms*.

One might compare the proliferation of terms that Prince cites as one of narratology's chief contributions with the account of "narrative procedure" in *Bleak House* offered by D. A. Miller. Miller's brilliant reading of the "form" of *Bleak House* is inseparable, as I will later discuss, from an account of the novel's generic identity; however, his discussion of the operation of plot, characterization, narration, and description have more need for the technical concepts offered by Foucault's account of the operation of social power than for the specialized vocabulary of narratology. See *The Novel and the Police*, 58–106. For an excellent brief overview of narratology, see Claudia Brodsky, *The Imposition of Form*, 3–16.

[3] Feminists were among the first to imagine that ideology presented a challenge to the discipline of narratology. As early as 1981, Susan Sniader Lanser critiqued narratological accounts of point of view for attempting to be "value free." See her *Narrative Act*, 42. More recently, in her "Shifting the Paradigm: Feminism and Narratology" (1988) and "Toward a Feminist Narratology" (1991), Lanser generalizes the feminist political "objective" as the exercise of a critical vision made possible by woman's identity as a social subject, specifically her oppression by male hegemony. In contrast to the scientist who works to establish objective models of inquiry, feminists, according to Lanser, embrace instead a political objective, an objective that, as she formulates it, is itself a point of view: women's social condition of "outsiderness" qualifies them "to provide [an] outside perspective upon all fields of intellectual inquiry" ("Shifting," 54). Robyn Warhol's version of a feminist narratology attempts a revisionist reading both of the ideological significance of nineteenth-century narrative technique and the "gender bias in literary theories that have overlooked the engaging narrator as a convention central to realist fiction" (*Gendered Interventions*, 24).

The shift from formal studies of the novel to studies of the novel as ideology can be seen more generally in the work of American critics who began the 1980s investigating problems of narrative form and ended the decade considering the novel as a cultural discourse. James Phelan, for example, follows *Worlds from Words: A Theory of Language in Fiction* (1981) with *Reading Narrative: Form, Ethics, Ideology* (1989). D. A. Miller's *Narrative and Its Discontents: Problems of Closure in the Traditional Novel* (1981) is followed by *The Novel and the Police* (1988).

For an optimistic account of how narratology might not be superseded by but rather might meet and further ideological interpretation, see Elizabeth Wright's "An Ideological Reading of Narrative," a 1990 omnibus review of recent trends in narrative theory. See Prince, "On Narratology (Past, Present, Future)," for a more extended account of the challenges posed to narratology by ideological critics. Prince singles out the work of Jean-Michel Adam and Marie-Laure Ryan as well as Lanser and Warhol. See, too, his most recent debate with Lanser ("On Narratology: Crite-

Yet if novel theory began to wither at the moment of its flowering, novel studies have never been more robust. "Deprivileging" the literary object as such has only raised the stock of novels generally, making not just the "literary" novel but any novel at all an object of serious critical attention. The novel seems to be revenging itself on the academy. For two centuries it was deemed unworthy of its own poetics; now that such a poetics appears to be dead, the novel remains, dancing on its grave. This new triumph of the novel is, of course, a paradoxical phenomenon. The novel has become a preferred object of literary study precisely because it is treated as the genre that is "least" literary—distinguished (if that is the term) by its ordinariness, its popularity, its derivativeness from other cultural discourses.[4] The very features that for two centuries made it aesthetically disreputable are now considered the source of its cultural power.

A "new" investment in the novel as the most social of literary forms was, however, as crucial to novel theory as to the cultural studies that has supposedly replaced it—which suggests that the reports of the death of novel theory may have been greatly exaggerated. It will be a central contention of *Social Formalism*, in fact, that cultural studies has been deeply influenced by a tradition of theory about the novel whose origins lie in the formalist criticism of Henry James. By showing that cultural studies is more dependent than it knows upon novel theory, *Social Formalism* will also attempt to prove that novel theory is not exactly the formalism we have taken it to be.

Perhaps the quickest way to grasp the general connection between formalist and cultural approaches to the novel is to consider the theoretical difficulties that cultural critics have encountered in justifying their studies of the novel. Many of these critics have posited a special relation between the ideology of literary form and what we might call the literary form of ideology. Eve Kosofsky Sedgwick's *Between Men: English Literature and Male Homosocial Desire* (1985) is a highly influential case in point. Sedgwick explicitly asks—and then indirectly answers—why her study of "the homosocial continuum" should be a "*literary* question" (5; her emphasis).

---

ria, Corpus, Context," and Lanser, "Sexing the Narrative").

   [4] Wallace Martin, for example, records in his survey of narrative theory the attitudes that correlate the novel's status as the least "artistic" of genres with its capacity to provide "a record of the problems confronting individuals in a stable social structure, given their circumstances and class origin, or the problems they face when confronted with social change" (*Recent Theories*, 18).

Her explanation begins with a discussion of a best-selling American novel, *Gone with the Wind*. In calling *Gone with the Wind* an "ideological blockbuster of white bourgeois feminism," Sedgwick implies that novels are worth attending to because they are popular—and thus ideologically influential—cultural forms (8). But in this book about the English literary tradition from Shakespeare to Dickens, it is certainly not American and barely British sociocultural detail that interests Sedgwick. Nor is her topic best-sellers. What makes *Gone with the Wind* a blockbuster for Sedgwick ultimately has to do less with its sales figures than with its formal power. In her account, the portrayal of the social in *Gone with the Wind* may be taken to be so *thoroughly* symptomatic of the society in which it was written that the novel ends up constituting a self-sufficient representation of the ideology it reflects: it is an "ideological microcosm" (10). Thus Sedgwick does not feel compelled to go outside of *Gone with the Wind* to study, for example, the cultural "discourse of rape" that the novel instantiates.[5] If the novel in Sedgwick's criticism is no longer a formalist world apart, it nonetheless retains much of the representational autonomy it enjoyed under the old newcritical regime that Sedgwick has helped to supplant: the cultural critic who has dedicated herself to depriviling the novel on aesthetic grounds finds herself reinstating the novel's formal privilege on the grounds of its social representativeness.[6] Such a belief that the novel can formally both encapsulate and fix a social world is, I want to argue, the strongest link between the new cultural study of the novel and the formalist tradition of novel theory from which it so much wants to depart.

Only by examining this link, which I call social formalism, can one explain how other, subsidiary themes of novel theory have come to retain a commanding position in the critical vocabulary of recent ideo-

[5] Sedgwick construes American ideology and culture so broadly that she deliberately chooses to treat both the novel and film version of *Gone with the Wind* as interchangeable cultural artifacts.

[6] Sedgwick's conception of novels as "ideological microcosms" justifies for her not only the study of literature per se but also the methods of analysis that modern critics have applied to literature—specifically, the new-critical practice of close reading. If an entire ideological discourse can be packed into a novel such as *Gone with the Wind*, the resulting fine print can be deciphered only through the most detailed engagement with the literary work's representational strategies: "It is of serious political importance that our tools for examining the signifying relation be subtle and discriminate ones" (*Between Men*, 10). Cf. Carolyn Porter's critique of New Historicism, in which she argues that the "social text turns out to be read as we have been trained to read a literary text, that is, in traditional formalist terms" ("History," 257).

logical scholarship. One such theme is point of view. In 1921 the Jamesian disciple and novel theorist Percy Lubbock declares, "the whole intricate question of method, in the craft of fiction, I take to be governed by the question of the point of view"; in 1985 the cultural historian Jane Tompkins presents point of view as the key to the whole intricate question of ideology:

> Because I want to understand what gave these novels force for their initial readers, it seemed important to recreate, as sympathetically as possible, the context from which they sprang and the specific problems to which they were addressed. I have therefore not criticized the social and political attitudes that motivated these writers, but have tried instead to inhabit and make available to a modern audience the viewpoint from which their politics made sense.[7]

Why does Tompkins assume that the best way to understand past novels is to inhabit the point of view of their original audience? As she herself stresses, this scholarly posture sacrifices any critique of past "social and political attitudes." What's more, the imaginative inhabitation of alien and anachronistic view points would seem particularly difficult for a critic who maintains that she herself is firmly anchored in the cultural interests that constitute her own point of view.[8] As Tompkins puts it,

[7] Lubbock, 251; Tompkins, xiii.

[8] Sedgwick is decidedly less anxious than Tompkins about the mediation of past ideology by present point of view; she frankly admits that she holds both "historicizing and dehistoricizing motives": "As a woman and a feminist writing (in part) about male homosexuality, I feel I must be especially explicit about the political groundings, assumptions, and ambitions of this study in that regard, as well. My intention throughout has been to conduct an antihomophobic as well as feminist inquiry" (*Between Men*, 16, 19). But it turns out that dehistorization and historization are after all remarkably compatible pursuits; the political values that Sedgwick holds are fully compatible with the picture of history she provides. The self-sufficiency of the literary microcosm seems to give Sedgwick both the fix on past ideology and the external standard by which to gauge present ideology that she requires.

Paul Ricoeur's characterization of Althusser makes clear how the marxist faith in scientific objectivity also helps to dispel the anxiety about ideological mediation: "[Althusser's] claim is that while no Marxist can say anything that is not ideological concerning the roots of distortion in some more imaginary layer, he or she may still speak scientifically of the ideological apparatus within which the distortion works" ("Althusser's Theory," 62). But although Sedgwick may be implicitly indebted to such larger marxist methodological consolations, this particular argument is not one that she explicitly invokes, preferring to find, it seems, objectivity in literary form itself.

It is interesting to note that Jonathan Arac, like Sedgwick, defines the problem of present ideology in terms of contemporary politics. But he is more pessimistic about

"any reconstruction of 'context' is as much determined by the attitudes and values of the interpreter as is the explication of literary works; my reading of the historical materials as well as the textual analyses I offer grow directly from the circumstances, interests, and aims that have constituted me as a literary critic" (*Sensational*, xiii).[9] And yet Tompkins insists that, to grasp the force of novels "for their initial readers," a critic must to some degree become those readers.[10] The assumption that to fathom a novel is to inhabit a point of view seems an inheritance from novel theory that Tompkins has uncritically absorbed. Another such inheritance, I hope to show, is the logical as well as ethical bind she faces in attempting to mediate between the point of view with which she sympathizes and the point of view from which she sympathizes.

In general, the problem that social formalists seek to address is how

---

the kinds of politics that are available to academics: "As cultural intellectuals we are participating in a hegemonic practice, more deeply than we can ever fully know, yet we also understand ourselves in our activities as teachers, scholars, and writers to be doing 'counter' work that not only aims but somewhat succeeds at making an opening where alternate views and practices may emerge" ("Rhetoric," 174).

[9] Ruth Bernard Yeazell shares Sedgwick's and Tompkins's belief that historical accuracy need not be compromised by the necessary projection onto the past of contemporary cultural identity. Yeazell wants to assert that the account of culture offered by the essays in her volume is superior to past accounts because the analysis is more inclusive—and thus, presumably, more accurate—and yet she also suggests that accuracy is irrelevant since any contemporary critical unanimity expresses not an objective truth about the past, but the objective truth of present desire: "Refusing to isolate the writing of fiction from other forms of representation, the authors contribute to an analysis not only of the nineteenth century's novels but of the culture as a whole. The very convergence of their arguments in a compelling diagnosis of nineteenth-century anxiety, however—even their success in identifying such anxiety—might prompt us to ask what anxieties of our own this new habit of reading seeks to manage and control" (*Sex*, xii).

[10] Tompkins's "sympathy" thus seems the post-structuralist version of the novelistic "imagination" extolled by Brooks and Warren in their *Understanding Fiction*: "This whole textbook is devoted to the accomplishments (and occasional failures) of the fiction writer's imagination as he attempts to present the truth about human life" (514). Note, too, the compatibility of the premium Tompkins places on cultural alterity with Van Ghent's humanistic claim that novels "extend our lives in amplitude and variousness" (*English Novel*, 7).

David Minter's recent study of the American novel similarly assumes the value of alterity as a generic imperative: "In teaching us how language and culture work, novels carry us into handsome drawing rooms and down into the mean streets of the city slums. . . . They give us a sense of how lives lived in other times and places differed from our own. They challenge us to register voices whose moral and cultural resonances—or gendered and racial resonances—differ from our own" (*Cultural History*, xv–xvi).

objective interpretation can be accomplished in a world where meaning is necessarily subjective, dependent on one's point of view. So strong is the belief among social formalists that there is no meaning beyond subjectivity that subjectivity itself becomes in this tradition the only possible meaning. But because social formalists are equally committed to a moral belief in the intrinsic good of alterity—that humans are most fulfilled when they come to know sympathetically persons who are substantially different from themselves—they have a stake in mitigating the radical relativism of their ontological position. They thus ascribe to certain representational forms the power to fix and limit subjective mediation through the concretization of identity: they imagine in particular that the form of the novel can accurately instantiate both the identity of its author and the identity of the subject the author seeks to represent. If this definition of the social seems so minimalist as to barely warrant the term, that is exactly my point. What is remarkable about the tradition that I am tracing is that this subjectivist literary formalist account of identity, representation, and interpretation becomes, as I hope to show, the underpinning of one of the most influential "social" theories of the twentieth century.

Although it is certainly true that, in the tradition I am analyzing, the concept of the social is severely compromised by the formalism of its theorists, it is not my intention to claim that every literary-critical or literary-theoretical invocation of the social need be formalist.[11] The confusion of sociohistorical and formalist critical aims that I have described is not logically inevitable. There is nothing inherently social-formalist to the questions about the novel and society that have been asked by such important historicist critics as Nancy Armstrong, Nina Baym, Cathy Davidson, Richard Brodhead, Philip Fisher, Catherine Gallagher, Sandra Gilbert and Susan Gubar, and D. A. Miller—questions, for instance, about what made the novel "rise," what caused *this* particular cultural discourse to be produced, and what ideological work, in given periods, the novel performed.

Nonetheless, it is surprising to see how often the historically specific answers these critics unearth not only take the same shape as, but strikingly mirror the novel theorist's conception of the novel: regardless

[11] There is such a variety of excellent sociohistorical studies of the novel that it seems invidious to hold up any one as paradigmatic, but Michael Gilmore's "The Book Marketplace I" certainly serves as an example of the kind of social study that discusses novelistic form without reifying it.

of period or national origin, the novel's primary ideological work turns out to be the promotion of sympathy. In her study of antebellum American novels, for instance, Nina Baym argues that novelistic sympathy, encouraged through the manipulation of character and point of view, worked as a subversive social force, challenging cultural authorities.[12] Richard Brodhead, on the other hand, contends that the sympathy inspired by novels contributed to the invention of "disciplinary intimacy," the consolidation of "the emotional bond between the authority figure and its charge" that effected the decline of corporal punishment and became the "self-identifying badge" of the nineteenth-century American middle class (*Cultures*, 17–19). In her examination of eighteenth-century British fiction by women, Catherine Gallagher has recently argued that the novel's "very specificity and particularity of realist representation" helped to fashion the middle class subject as an economic subject: the novel, according to Gallagher, helped foster in the reader not just sympathy but sympathetic "appropriation" (*Nobody's Story*, 173), a psychological and emotional capability that became "one among many modes of facilitating property exchange and investment in the period, of creating the speculative, commercial and sentimental subject" (194). Gilbert and Gubar believe that the novel produces not a class-based but a gendered-based social subject. They argue that the novel's narratorial structure, specifically its capacity for telling a story from one or more points of view, promoted an authorial "selflessness" that was congenial to nineteenth-century women who had been taught by a patriarchal culture "to speak indirectly rather than directly" (*Madwoman*, 548), to constitute their own identities, in other words, through the achievement of alterity.

It is not just the belief in the novel's special power to arouse sympa-

---

[12] Baym's study documents antebellum culture's theorization of the novel as socially subversive: "In gratifying the self, novels foster self-love and a tendency to self-assertion that make the mind ungovernable and thus jeopardize the agencies of social and psychological control" (*Novels*, 39). Although her study is interested in the historical definition of the novel's generic power, Baym sometimes seems to be arguing ahistorically for the "inherent power of the form to generate reader excitement" (43).

Cathy N. Davidson also argues the position that the novel posed a threat to antebellum American culture. Davidson also seems to feel that the novel's capacity for social subversion is not simply historically specific but generically inherent: "The reader is 'present at the conversation' and becomes imaginatively part of the company. Whether an esteemed political leader or a lowly printer's apprentice, the reader is privileged in relationship to the text, is welcomed into the text, and, in a sense, *becomes* the text" (*Revolution*, 52).

thy that links these critics to an older tradition of novel theory, however; it is also the tendency of these critics to attribute social efficacy to the form as well as the content of novels. This tendency is perhaps least apparent in Nancy Armstrong, who in her account of eighteenth-century British domestic fiction argues that the novel's distinctive generic feature, its representation of character as psychologically complex, was one of many social forces that helped to produce a distinctively "modern" social subject (*Desire*, 3–8). Yet other historicist work is more ambiguous about the novel's status as a causal force. When D. A. Miller, for example, reads the intricate plot structures of Victorian novels as fostering a "liberal" social subject, or when Philip Fisher presents the lack of intricacy and reliance on cultural stereotypes in the nineteenth-century American historical and sentimental novel as performing the "radical work" of deradicalizing cultural change, are we to conclude that the novel is a social discourse like any other?[13] Or, if we should understand the novel as exceptionally powerful in generating the sociality that comes to define a given period, what are we to think makes the novel so exceptional, other than its form?

The temptation to regard the novel as *formally* producing social change is most attractive to cultural historians who have been strongly influenced by marxism. In his recent introduction to *Marxist Literary Theory*, Terry Eagleton sees the notion of an ideology of form as the key to avoiding, on the one hand, "mere formalism" and, on the other, "vulgar sociologism": "The wager here is that it is possible to find the material history which produces a work of art somehow inscribed in its very texture and structure, in the shape of its sentences or its play of narrative viewpoints, in its choice of a metrical scheme or its rhetorical devices" (11). (Eagleton cites approvingly the work of Walter Benjamin, Lucien Goldmann, and Theodor Adorno as contributing to the advancement of the study of ideological form; and surely Raymond Williams with his notion of a "structure of feeling" and Fredric Jameson

[13] For Miller's full statement about the respective social agency of the novel's formal, thematic, and market values, see *Novel*, x. For Miller's specific discussion of the cultural function of the Victorian novel's formal intricacy, see esp. 81–106.

Philip Fisher argues along similar lines that the American nineteenth-century novel's formulaic plots and stereotypical characters accomplished the "radical 'work'" of fostering cultural change. According to Fisher, the readability that made the novel popular also allowed it to stage a "psychological rehearsal that creates an ordered resignation that lets a group 'face' . . . [what] they have already chosen and set in motion, but have not yet morally or psychologically passed through" (*Hard Facts*, 18–19).

with his belief that novels make visible the "master code" of a particular culture should be included in his list, whether or not we want to name Althusser as the most influential social theorist in this tradition.)[14] Yet, as Catherine Gallagher has pointed out, Eagleton and his teachers can uphold art's traditional epistemological privilege only by granting art a material rather than an ideological autonomy: "Williams and Eagleton retain the 'idealist' emphasis on the irreducibility and autonomy of art, its specific aesthetic nature, but redefine this autonomy as itself material" ("Materialism," 643).[15] Gallagher's claim is borne out by Pierre Macheray, who shows how, for literary marxists, a social value that is derived causally from extrinsic factors can collapse into an intrinsic feature of the art work: "To explain the work is to show that, contrary to appearances, it is not independent, but bears in its material substance the imprint of a determinate absence which is also the principle of its identity" (*Literary Production*, 79–80). In the very act of demonstrating the art work's dependence on society, Macheray finds a new source for artistic autonomy: the materiality of the art work itself contains an "imprint" that makes its social character both legible and self-sufficient.

[14] Like Eagleton, Jameson explicitly champions the notion of the "ideology of form" (*Political Unconscious*, 76).

Jameson's own Percy Lubbock, William C. Dowling, implicitly makes the connection between post-structuralist accounts of the novel and the Jamesian tradition when he declares: "The problem raised by *Grammatology* and *The Political Unconscious* alike . . . is the problem of style as enactment: a way of writing that *shows* as well as *tells* what it is trying to get across" (*Jameson*, 11; Dowling's emphasis). Brodsky confirms Jameson's sense that "narrative is the literary form most generally understood to foster its own logical understanding" (*Imposition*, 3).

For Lucien Goldmann, the relation of novelistic form to society is less an ideological microcosm than an ideological homology, but the primacy of novelistic form in conveying the social meaning of the text is never in doubt: "The first problem that a sociology of the novel should have confronted is that of the relation between the *novel form* itself and the *structure* of the social environment in which it developed . . ." ("Introduction," 209; Goldmann's emphasis).

[15] See Mulhern (163–64) for a critique of Eagleton—one that he extends to Althusser and Macheray—that is compatible with Gallagher's. As other critics have observed, the larger problem of ideological autonomy is a theoretical crux in marxist theory: "Knowledge about social formations is achieved by juggling theoretically with 'relative autonomy' and 'determination in the last instance' rather than through empirical and historical research" (McDonnell and Robbins, "Marxist Cultural Theory," 160–61). E. P. Thompson is, of course, scathing in his critique of what he regards as Althusser's abandonment of what we might call "base" values to superstructural complexification: he claims that Althusser's structuralism causes him to "be silent (or evasive) as to . . . important categories, among them 'economic' and 'needs'" (*Poverty*, 5).

The vagueness with which Macheray treats materiality is an ambiguity that can be traced back to Marx himself. In *Capital*, Marx never clearly explains how "abstract human labor is objectified [*vergegenständlicht*] or materialized" in objects (*Capital*, 129). He describes labor, for example, as being "embedded" in a coat or "coagulating" into an objective form (142). The equivocality of these metaphors is echoed by Raymond Williams in his attempt to define the objective meaning contained within an art work's materiality: "Every specific art work has *dissolved* into it, at every level of its operations, not only specific social relationships . . . but also specific material means of production, on the mastery of which its production depends" (*Marxism*, 163; my emphasis).[16] Marxists such as Althusser do on occasion acknowledge that not all materiality is the same: "Of course, the material existence of the ideology in an apparatus and its practices does not have the same modality as the material existence of a paving-stone or a rifle" ("Ideology," 156). And yet Althusser's exclusive interest in the material that makes ideology legible quickly leads him to ignore the very distinctions he generates: "I shall leave on one side the problem of a theory of the differences between the modalities of materiality" ("Ideology," 159).[17] Gallagher spells out the theoretical slippages that such a laissez-faire attitude toward the differences among material "modalities" produces:

> When such solid, material objects as shoes and potatoes are themselves "read" as signifiers within complex signifying systems, the distinction be-

[16] See Simpson for a trenchant critique of the exceptionalist definition of art implied by Williams's notion of "the structure of feeling" ("Feeling," esp. 38–39 and 44).

[17] By contrast, Williams does attempt to sort out the different types of materiality that should concern a materialist. But in *Marxism*, his historical account of the way society has regarded art as material is in tension with his own theoretical account of art's materiality (see especially 159–62). The project of showing that different cultures treat art as more or less material does not necessarily advance the project of saying why the art work's materiality should be understood in (post) marxist terms. More often than not, he relies in his theorizing on what we might call a minimalist definition of the art work's materiality, invoking either the "biological processes, especially those relating to body movements and to the voice, which are not a mere substratum but are at times the most powerful elements of the work" (*Problems*, 113), or else, more particularly for literary works of art, "material notations on paper" (*Marxism*, 162). While few would deny that it makes sense to think of art as material in this elemental way, it remains unclear why, for example, "notation" should be thought of as "*embodying* many of the most intense and most significant forms of human experience": how, in other words, literary texts' status as objects allows us to read them as "specific objectifications" of social experience (*Marxism*, 162; my emphasis).

tween material and symbolic products breaks down. The physical object becomes a signifier, and the physical properties of conventionally-recognized signifiers (e.g. the aural and visual qualities of spoken and written words) are emphasized. Everything can then appear equally autonomous and dependent, determined and determining, referential and self-referential, symbolic and real. ("Materialism," 635)

It is this slippery materialism that creates a bridge, I want to argue, between marxist literary criticism and Anglo-American literary formalism. And to demonstrate how the theory of the novel has been vital in forging this connection, I have positioned my study of social formalism around two key figures: Henry James and M. M. Bakhtin. Although Anglo-American critics explicitly turned to Bakhtin in the attempt to move beyond Jamesian formalism, it is in fact the compatibility of Bakhtin with James that, in my view, prompted Anglo-American theorists to embrace Bakhtin with such enthusiasm. Far from rejecting James, in other words, recent novel theorists have only refined James's foundational recharacterization of the novel as the genre that does not simply represent identity through its content but actually instantiates it through its form.

NOVEL THEORISTS WERE, of course, not the first to praise novels for their ability to represent social life. Before James, however, discussions of the novel's social mimesis concentrated on content and characters; novelists and reviewers debated about the quality of authorial wisdom and morality in a novel and argued about how novels might influence social behavior.[18] But by the turn of the century, the increasing equation of novelistic realism with novelistic objectivity created a certain theoretical embarrassment about the novelists who happened to author these realistic portraits of society.[19] How could the novel be said to give an objective picture of social life when it was the product of only

---

[18] See Watt, whose study of the eighteenth-century novel relates the novel's generic particularity to "the individualisation of its characters and to the detailed presentation of their environment" (*Rise*, 18).

[19] See Auerbach, *Mimesis*, esp. 534–38, for a discussion of the development of modern skepticism about "the writer as narrator of objective facts" (534).
The nineteenth-century notion that novelistic realism provides an objective picture of life is famously critiqued by Sartre: "The error of realism has been to believe that the real reveals itself to contemplation, and that consequently one could draw an impartial picture of it. How could that be possible, since the very perception is partial, since by itself the naming is already a modification of the object?" ("Why Write?" 66).

one person's vision? Rather than abandon the project of defining novelistic realism as the objective representation of society, novel theorists
began to address the problem of the author's subjective partiality by
considering novelistic representation as itself a social experience.[20]

What immediately distinguished the novel theory of James and Lubbock from prior accounts of the novel was the strange abstractness with
which James and Lubbock treated the hitherto conventional view that
the novel is above all a representation of society. In the theories that
constitute what I am calling the social formalist tradition, sociality in
the novel is not defined as the beliefs, values, and behaviors that belong
to a group of characters, nor is it located in the representation of certain
political, legal, economic, or gender systems that influence the identities
and actions of characters. The social is, in short, barely defined themati-
cally—because any theme could so easily be reduced to the subjective
projection of an author. Instead, by narrowly characterizing the social
as the experiential interaction between human subjects, social formalists
treat this relationality as a formal property of the novel. The successful
novelist, for these theorists, is the virtuous one who is both willing and
able to maximize the novel's generic disposition to embody social relatedness; such an author profits in return, securing an objective representation of her own identity insofar as she allows the society of the novel,
and not her own intrusive ego, to represent her.

At the beginning of the social formalist tradition, its theorists try to
prove that novels instantiate social relations by reading from novels the
altruistic ties that they claim novels establish among author, narrator,
character, and reader. In later twentieth-century theory, this formal
view of social relations in the novel grows increasingly detached from
the novel itself—unsurprisingly, perhaps, since in this theoretical tradition the social has so little to do with the novel's content—and begins to
appear in accounts of narrative language generally, of language generally, of society generally, and finally, in a reversal of the universalizing
trajectory of this tradition, in accounts of subaltern social identities. As
social formalism evolves out of novel theory and into social theory,
some of its ethical implications are reexamined: the earlier, positive accounts of novelistic social relations as altruistic is challenged by a politi-

[20] The philosopher Martha Nussbaum offers a humanist version of the novel's
structural capacity to represent social identity: "For while they do speak concretely
about human beings in their varied social contexts, and see the social context in
each case as relevant to choice, they also have built into their very structure a sense
of our common humanity" (*Love's Knowledge*, 96).

cal critique that redefines altruism as a mask for the operation of hegemonic power. What is crucially retained from novel theory, however, is the belief that formal markers can not only express the intrinsically social character of one's identity but embody it too.

I am not, of course, arguing that the social formalist tradition I am analyzing is the only influential conceptualization of the novel offered in the twentieth century; yet as I hope to demonstrate, the scope of the tradition and the range of thinkers it includes attest to the weightiness and vitality of social formalism as a theoretical logic. It is certainly not unusual to place the thinkers who are the focus of my study—Henry James, Percy Lubbock, Wayne Booth, Gérard Genette, Roland Barthes, M. M. Bakhtin, Henry Louis Gates, and Barbara Johnson—on the same theoretical continuum. Customarily, however, this continuum is described teleologically: the move from Henry James to Henry Louis Gates is charted as a steady intellectual evolution out of quaint and belletristic formalism into sophisticated and highly technical post-structuralist accounts of language, literature, selves and societies. By revealing the social formalist subplot within the supercessivist account of novel theory's rise and fall, I hope to enhance our understanding of not only how the novel has been theorized in the twentieth century, but also why a novelized conception of social identity has outlasted the poetics that invented it.

My first chapter examines the roots of social formalism in the writings that have generally been regarded as the founding documents of Anglo-American novel theory: Henry James's Prefaces to the New York edition (1905–7) of his collected work. At first glance, nothing seems less committed to the value of social interplay than these Prefaces, which treat the expression of authorial point of view as an overriding generic imperative. Yet in the Jamesian version of the egotistical sublime, artistic point of view is strangely contingent. While James insists on the radical individualism of point of view, in other words, he also claims that the definitive attribute of the true artist is an endless capacity to be "interested" in the world. The specificity of an artist's point of view is thus indirectly defined through the nature and value of the objects that elicit his attention. According to James, the novel that strives to represent the artist's point of view directly has mistaken both the aims and the tokens of the true artist, which are inherently relational.

Chapter 1 concludes with the work of James's most influential disciple, Percy Lubbock, who, as he tries to extract a systematic theory of the novel from the Prefaces, paradoxically reduces James's general reflections on the interested artist into a formal prohibition against authorial self-representation. For Lubbock in *The Craft of Fiction* (1921), the generic imperative of the novel to represent the author's point of view is best met only when all tokens of authorial identity have been *eliminated* from the novel: to convey without distortion what the author sees, the novel must, in Lubbock's account, transform the objects of authorial interest into autonomous subjects—specifically, into characterological points of view. The poetics of vision that Lubbock derives from his revision of James thus inaugurates the preoccupation in novel theory with the ethics of the narrator's relation to his characters; where James's artist dedicated himself to the interest of his object, Lubbock's novelist dedicates himself to liberating his characters from his own projective power.

An attack on the Lubbockian poetics of vision unifies the work of what I call the second wave in novel theory. Focusing on seminal theoretical texts by Wayne Booth, Gérard Genette, Dorrit Cohn, Roy Pascal, and Roland Barthes, Chapter 2 demonstrates how these otherwise divergent thinkers were united in their commitment to dethroning the then-reigning Lubbockian aesthetic imperative that novels should present an objective rather than subjective vision of life, that they should "show" rather than "tell." According to the theorists of the second wave, novels always tell—and what they tell is the delusoriness of Lubbock's conception of novelistic sociality as an aesthetic world apart. The real change from one generation of novel theorists to the next is thus not the critique of "vision" as "voice"—novelistic vision for James as for Lubbock had always been linked to the subjective identity of authorial point of view—but the later theorists' more extended account of how human identity is socially mediated. Whereas James and Lubbock identify the novel's sociality exclusively with the interactions of author, character, and reader, the second wave of novel theorists maintain that the novel also manifests the operations of social mediations that are prior to the novel. For the second wave as for the first, however, the novel remains the most vivid objectification of social identity.

My third and fourth chapters take up the extraordinarily influential work of M. M. Bakhtin. Since Bakhtin claims to offer a philosophy of social identity that challenges the grounding assumptions of formalism, it is not surprising that Anglo-American cultural critics in the eighties believed they had found in Bakhtin's recently translated works a new direction for literary studies. Inspired by marxism, Bakhtin and his circle argued that language should be understood not as an abstract system of signification but rather as a fundamentally social phenomenon. Yet, as the enthusiastic reception of Bakhtin by such Anglo-American formalists as Wayne Booth suggests, the combination of Bakhtin's literary interests with his marxist stake in the primacy of material causes produces a complex reinscription of the formalism that his work explicitly sets out to attack. For Bakhtin, ideology is associated with two forms of materiality: the forms of production that shape it and the signs that express it. Confusing one kind of materiality with the other, Bakhtin comes to regard signs as the generators of ideology and thus assumes that social identity is embodied in literary form.

Yet this transferral of social identity from persons to texts does not empty out the category of individual agency for Bakhtin any more than it does for his Anglo-American contemporaries. If Bakhtin believes that the social identity of an individual inheres less in her putative subjectivity than in her palpable language, he also assumes that an individual can more or less maximize the sociality of her language by allowing the different voices in her words to speak. Like Lubbock, Bakhtin thus paradoxically accords a special fullness to the subject who is able to empty herself of any interest except the representation of others different from herself; and, assuming as Lubbock does that the novel is generically the most social art form, Bakhtin along with Lubbock decides that the ideal exemplar of this appreciative subject must be the novelist.

Chapters 3 and 4 thus attempt to chart the intersection between two distinct yet surprisingly correspondent schools of novel theory: the Jamesian tradition that defines the sociality of the novel in terms of the relations among authors, characters, and readers; and a marxist literary-critical tradition that defines the sociality of novels in terms of class, ideology, history, and culture. Because Bakhtin's novel theory cannot be divorced from his social theory, my analysis of Bakhtin considers the whole shape of his career, from the early "political" works such as *Marxism and the Philosophy of Language* to the later "literary" studies such as "Discourse in the Novel." Indeed, Bakhtin's career as a marxist literary theorist represents perhaps the fullest articulation in the century of a specifically "social" formalism—even as it renders marxist social imperatives strangely insubstantial.

These chapters focus on Bakhtin's theories in such detail because it is his work—and not, say, Lukács's or Jameson's—that has made social formalism a vital concept in contemporary theory. In my final chapter I explore the latest development of social formalism: the influence exerted by the Jamesian tradition, with its new Bakhtinian inflection, on identity studies. How, recent identity theorists have asked, can one preserve the notion of a distinctive subaltern cultural identity without resorting to a racist or sexist essentialism? In response, literary critics such as Henry Louis Gates and Barbara Johnson, in some of their most influential essays, have turned social formalist claims about the novelist into a description of the subaltern subject: like Bakhtin's novelist, the subaltern subject of Gates and Johnson possesses a special capacity to represent alterity and thus represent herself objectively. But this strategy of minority empowerment is, I argue, disadvantageously predicated on a reductively linguistic account of social relations: the theory, adapted from Bakhtin, that subalterns can battle hegemonic oppression merely by expressing their "never-ending self-difference" through language.

From James to Johnson, then, the social formalist maintains that individual identity is radically constituted by its interpersonal relations and that this relational subjectivity can be objectified in representational forms. A tradition that begins with the definition of subjectivities as points of view and culminates in the definition of languages as subjectivities is based on the enduring desire to imagine that even de-essentialized identity can have stability, that the "characters" of both people and literary genres can be recognized through their material manifestations in language. For formalists, the inherently social work of the novel is only superficially accomplished by the novel's depiction of fictional characters; the novel's deeper social power lies in its capacity to objectify points of view.

The theorists whom I have chosen to analyze in *Social Formalism* are offered both as representatives and as major shapers of the social formalist tradition. My intent has not been to construct a family tree for novel theory that would catalogue all its trends and chart their interrelationships, nor has it been to give an exhaustive account of a tradition that I see as profoundly rich and complex. I have striven to consider an exemplary rather than an exhaustive list of theorists in order to assess the logic of a particular theoretical tradition as well as to explain how this logic has gained a purchase on current theory. My aim is to have identified such a tradition, to have documented its surprising range and influence, clarified its logic, and evaluated both the premises and the consequences of that logic.

In rewriting the history of the theory of the novel, I hope I will have successfully motivated the study of larger philosophical issues, which might profitably lead to the clarification of theoretical assumptions about the novel that extend beyond the strict bounds of the social formalist tradition. How seriously, for instance, should we take the supposition that the novel as a genre is specially able to represent alterity? And how much moral as well as aesthetic weight do we want to give to a novelist's ability to represent alterity? Does it make sense even to think of a novel's characters as others whom a novelist could liberate or oppress? If these questions sound oddly old-fashioned, that may be because they have not been adequately addressed by contemporary theory, or it may be that, despite the truths we think we have learned from post-structuralist theory, we still believe in the ethical imperatives that made social formalism so enduring in the first place. To isolate these imperatives, and define the theoretical tradition they have inspired, is the first step in the reevaluation of novel theory, and that is what I have undertaken here. The pursuit of answers to these questions is work for future theorists, who will either defend or revoke the novel's status as the most social of literary forms.

1

Henry James, Percy Lubbock, and the Formalist Vision of the Novel

> The successful application of any art is a delightful spectacle, but
> the theory too is interesting.
> —Henry James, "The Art of Fiction" (1888)

IN ENGLAND at the end of the twenties, the poetics of the novel had come sufficiently into its own to invite pragmatic skepticism. If E. M. Forster had entirely disapproved of the efforts of Henry James and his followers to change the public's belief that "a novel is a novel, as a pudding is a pudding, and that our only business with it could be to swallow it," he would never have written his own *Aspects of the Novel* (1927); but Forster thought that the Jamesians had gone too far:

> Zealous for the novel's eminence, they are a little too apt to look out for problems that shall be peculiar to it, and differentiate it from the drama; they feel it ought to have its own technical troubles before it can be accepted as an independent art.[1]

For Forster, the problem with the Jamesians was not only that, in attempting to elevate the novel as an art form, they had saddled it with an unnecessary "apparatus" of "principles and systems"; what particularly bothered Forster about the desire to make novel criticism more of an "exact science" was the objectivity this view presupposed in both the novel and the critic.[2] By insisting on the importance of technique, the Jamesians had fundamentally misrepresented the power of the novel to "bounce" a reader, which in Forster's eyes had far less to do with logical "formulae" of any theory than with the workings of "the human heart" (*Aspects*, 23).[3]

[1] James, "The Art of Fiction," 4; Forster, *Aspects*, 79.

[2] Forster, *Aspects*, 23; James, "Preface to *The Awkward Age*," in *Art*, 118; hereafter referred to as Prefaces.

[3] Ian Watt's estimation of novelistic realism suggests a representational reason for the novel's belated evolution into a form of high art: "Since the novelist's pri-

Forster's own meditations on the novel were accordingly "unscientif-
ic and vague" (24); and no doubt it was this eschewal of a technical vocabulary that has given Forster's theories—especially his concept of
"flat" and "round" characters—such longevity in the plain speech tradition of Anglo-American literary criticism. Critical hostility toward the
"scientific" impulse in novel theory has in fact only grown since Forster's day, although "cultural work" has taken the place of the human
heart as the true source of the novel's interest. But attacks on or dis-
missals of Jamesian theory have, I want to argue, been too quick to endorse Forster's characterization of that theory as dedicated above all to
the question of novelistic technique. When Scholes and Kellogg, for instance, write that James's disciples have "erected" from his Prefaces to
the New York edition of his works "a system of rules, dealing primarily
with the management of point of view, by which they propose to judge
all narrative writing," they drastically narrow the role of "point of
view" in Jamesian novel theory.[4] For the Jamesians, I will try to show,
point of view is the name given not merely to a secondary technical consideration but also to the set of authentic interests that constitute a particular human identity. What's more, as I will argue in my subsequent
chapters, James and his followers constructed an ethics around the issue
of point of view—what I am calling the appreciation of alterity—that
has helped determine the course not just of novel theory but also of later
theories about literature and identity that have invoked the novel as a
privileged locus of evidence. This chapter examines the roots of this substantial theoretical tradition by discussing the role of point of view first
in James's Prefaces and then in the work of Percy Lubbock, the infa-
mous "codifier" of James whose *Craft of Fiction* (1921), Forster grum-
bled, would inspire others to believe that they too could "lay a sure
foundation for the aesthetics of fiction" (*Aspects*, 78).[5]

---

mary task is to convey the impression of fidelity to human experience, attention to
any pre-established formal conventions can only endanger his success.... [T]he
poverty of the novel's formal conventions would seem to be the price it must pay for
its realism" (*Rise*, 13).

[4] Scholes and Kellogg, *Nature*, 269–70. The interpretation of the Prefaces as the
elaboration of a system of rules goes back at least as far as 1918 when Beach lauded
James for articulating a *"mechanics of technique"* (*Method*, xiv; Beach's emphasis).

[5] The Anglo-American scholarly record is virtually unanimous in crediting James
and Lubbock as the forefathers of novel theory. Carl Grabo's declaration in 1928
that "James is the most technically aware, so to speak, of the great novelists, or has,
at any rate, left the most extensive and valuable comment on technical method"
(*Techniques*, v) is echoed by Mark Schorer in 1949: "The modern criticism of the

Point of View: Making Life Interesting

In "The Art of Fiction" (1888), Henry James appears to voice the conventional view of what distinguishes the novel from other literary genres:

---

novel begins in the modern novel, in the works of Flaubert, James, Conrad, among others, and in their utterances, especially James's about their works" ("Foreword," xii). For Arthur Mitzener in 1950, James's Prefaces are still "the best kind of talk about the novel we have" ("Novel," 2). Daniel Schwartz (1986) credits James not just for his talk, but for the way he talked: "They [James and Lubbock] focused attention on the art of the novel and gave their successors an example of systematic and rigorous thought about the genre" (*Humanistic Heritage*, 39). Mosher and Nelles (1990) deem James a formative figure not just for Anglo-American criticism but for novel theory generally. They refer to a "long golden age" in narrative theory, "marked by invention, debate, and revision, often said to begin with Aristotle but for our century, probably with Henry James, and developing with such Russian Formalists as Victor Shklovsky and Vladimir Propp, such French structuralists as Roland Barthes and Gérard Genette, as well as German theorists like Franz Stanzel and American critics like Wayne Booth" ("Guides," 419). Carroll (1982) maintains that the French return to James for a theory of the novel (*Subject*, 53). Sonja Bašić (1983) thus does not seem hyperbolic when she declares, "the formalists and structuralists have embraced his point of view; the phenomenologists and deconstructionists have consecrated his 'figure in the carpet.' No matter who wins, James remains" ("James's Figures," 214).

Of course, one of the testaments to James's influence was that his thinking was also the object of theoretical attack. Edwin Muir (1928) does not deny James's profound influence, but he is not as willing as later critics to laud Jamesian rigor: "James is the father of most of those question-begging terms; he was an incurable impressionist; and he has infected criticism with his vocabulary of hints and nods" (*Structure*, 15). Kathleen Tillotson (1959) also doubts James's theoretical contribution, debunking his "theory" as simply the anachronistic reading of novels written before his own: "Most novel-criticism now takes its criteria from the later Henry James, applying what might be called late Jacobean standards to Victorian and eighteenth-century novelists" (*Tale*, 12). But while Tillotson's objection is powerful, what is still more powerful is James's theoretical hegemony as late as 1959.

Given James's dominance in the formation of novel theory, it might be hard to believe James E. Miller when he bemoans in 1972 the lack of direct attention given to James's critical writings as a coherent body of work. Yet Miller is right; most theorists and critics, before and after James E. Miller, dip in and out of the Prefaces, quoting or paraphrasing what they want from James in order to mount theories of their own that are indebted to him but do not explicate him or even engage the Prefaces with any thoroughness. Anglo-American theories of fiction that were explicitly indebted to James include, chronologically: Hamilton (1908); Hughes (1926); Grabo (1928); Muir (1928); Roberts (1929); Edgar (1933); Gerould (1937); Brooks and Warren (1943); Wiesenfarth (1963); and Veeder (1975). Ward (1967), Asthana (1980), and, of course, Blackmur (1934), along with James E. Miller, do attempt an explication of the Prefaces.

> One can speak best from one's own taste, and I may therefore venture to say
> that the air of reality (solidity of specification) seems to me to be the su-
> preme virtue of a novel—the merit on which all its other merits (including
> that conscious moral purpose of which Mr. Besant speaks) helplessly and
> submissively depend. (14)

But while James subordinates the thematic content of the novel to its
"solidity of specification," to the objective weight of novelistic detail, he
also insists on the primacy of subjective judgment in assessing and, implicitly, composing a novel: "One can speak best from one's own taste."[6]
In his Prefaces, James clarifies his belief that the generic purpose of the
novel is not only to "reproduce life" but to make it "interesting"—and
for James the novel will prove interesting only to the degree that it successfully expresses the novelist's unique point of view:

> The question comes back thus, obviously, to the kind and the degree of the
> artist's prime sensibility, which is the soil out of which his subject springs.
> The quality and capacity of that soil, its ability to "grow" with due freshness
> and straightness any vision of life, represents, strongly or weakly, the pro-
> jected morality. That element is but another name for the more or less close
> connexion of the subject with some mark made on the intelligence, with
> some sincere experience. (Prefaces, 45)

James's emphasis on the artist's "prime sensibility" makes the intrinsic capacities of the artist sound crucial to the novel's reproduction of
life. Yet what in James's account distinguishes the artist from any ordinary person? His superior sensibility and intelligence do not mean that
the artist enjoys feelings and knowledge that are unavailable to the ordinary person, nor does his special "quality and capacity," the "kind
and degree" of his sensibility, result in the possession of specific virtues
that would make him qualitatively better than other people. What distinguishes the artist is, on the contrary, simply his ability to express his
own point of view authentically—"freshly" and "straightly." The "projected morality" of a novel is thus for James a function of the artist's
sincerity, her fidelity first to her own perspective and second to the
"mark" made on that perspective by "experience." In "The Art of Fiction" James declares that the sources of novelistic interest "are as various as the temperament of man, and they are successful in proportion as

---

[6] Michael Davitt Bell notes that James evaluates the success of other realists by
the criterion of subjective expression: "For James's Balzac . . . realism is a matter
not of faithful imitation but of personal expression; the authority of 'the real,' for
this Balzac, is its authority 'for his imagination'" (*Problem*, 78).

they reveal a particular mind, different from others. A novel is in its broadest definition a personal, a direct impression of life" (9). In his letter to the Deerfield Summer School (1889), James democratically assures the coed student body that "any point of view is interesting that is a direct impression of life. You each have an impression colored by your individual conditions; make that into a picture, a picture framed by your own personal wisdom, your glimpse of the American world."[7]

"*Any* point of view is interesting": this refusal to value one perspective over another is the cornerstone of a famous set piece in the Prefaces, the elaborate conceit of the "house of fiction." According to James, the house of fiction has "not one window, but a million—a number of possible windows not to be reckoned, rather; every one of which has been pierced, or is still pierceable, in its vast front, by the need of the individual vision and by the pressure of the individual will" (Prefaces, 46).[8] As James takes pains to emphasize, all that distinguishes one viewer from another in the house of fiction is the "need" and the "pressure" of the "individual will." No viewing position is privileged; no window offers a more accurate or more preferable understanding of life than another:

> He and his neighbours are watching the same show, but one seeing more where the other sees less, one seeing black where the other sees white, one seeing big where the other sees small, one seeing coarse where the other sees fine. And so on, and so on; there is fortunately no saying on what, for the particular pair of eyes, the window may *not* open; "fortunately" by reason, precisely, of this incalculability of range. (46; James's emphasis)

The passage implies that the artist need not worry about justifying his vision; at the same time, however, the mere act of seeing through a window does not entirely take the place of more ordinary conceptions of value in this account.[9] While James declares that it is "fortunate" that

[7] Henry James to the Deerfield Summer School (1889), 29.

[8] James's commitment to the relativity of individual identity is, as Wayne Booth has noted, reflected in the range of his critical admiration. He appreciates romance as much as realism; Stevenson, Fielding, and Scott as much as Flaubert, Balzac, and George Eliot. In his famous discussion of the difference between romance and realism, James argues that both must be accepted on their own terms, since an author's choice of one mode, or as James calls it, one "value," over the other is beyond his control; the decision is foreordained by who he is, which is for James always a matter of how he sees.

[9] For Mark Schorer, James's house of fiction conceit and his theory of the novel generally opened the way to elevate the novel to the status of poetry:

> The novel, written in prose, bears an apparently closer resemblance to discursive forms than it does to poetry, thus easily opening itself to first questions about

there is "no saying on what, for the particular pair of eyes, the window may *not* open," and thus makes it sound as if he values merely the incalculable particularity of individual perception, his preference for a view of "more" rather than "less" or of "fine" rather than "coarse" is unmistakable. Whatever his conceit implies, James cannot bring himself absolutely to neutralize the differences in sensibility among viewers by treating those differences as nothing more than accidents of perspective.[10] Yet his resistance in the Prefaces toward offering any more value-laden description of a superior artistic vision than that it sees "more" shows how James strives to preserve the relativity of perspective while also retaining a standard by which to judge artistic achievement.[11]

This ambivalence in James's conception of the novelist helps explain a related doubleness in his account of novelistic sincerity.[12] On the one

---

philosophy or politics, and, traditionally a middle-class vehicle with a reflective social function, it bears an apparently more immediate relation to life than it does to art, thus opening itself to first questions about conduct. Yet a novel, like a poem, is not life, it is an image of life; and the critical problem is first of all to analyze the structure of the image. Thus criticism must approach the vast and endlessly ornamented house of fiction with a willingness to do a little at a time and none of it finally, in order to suggest experiences of meaning and of feeling that may be involved in novels, and responsibilities for their style which novelists themselves may forget. (*World*, 24)

[10] For an account of the house of fiction as an allegory for James's hegemonic attitude toward culture, see Sara Blair, who reads "James's visual epistemology, and his acts of insight and recognition, [as constituting] a regulation of cultural forms" ("Henry James," 96). The implicit "imperialism" that Blair ascribes to James's epistemology is, as I will show, an explicit element of the Lubbockian version of Jamesian aesthetics.

[11] The same tension between relative perspectives and absolute standards figures in James's discussion of the "artistic subject." In the Preface to *The Portrait of a Lady*, James insists that we must grant the artist his choice of subject, that the "measure of the worth of a given subject . . . [is] is it valid, in a word, is it genuine, is it sincere, the result of some direct impression or perception of life?" (45). Yet in the Preface to *The Ambassadors*, James declares that "there are degrees of merit in subjects" (309).

[12] M. H. Abrams reads Jamesian sincerity as the "disengagement" from "associations both with spontaneity and with morality" that leads to a "specifically aesthetic conscience and integrity" that is the grounding of "*l'art pour l'art*" (*Mirror*, 320). While I certainly agree with Abrams that sincerity is the basis of Jamesian aestheticism, I would emphasize that Jamesian sincerity cannot be understood as anything but intensely engaged; if James's belief that the novel should be a vision of life can nonetheless inspire and resemble "*l'art pour l'art*," it is due, I will show, to the deconstructive logic that informs Jamesian wonder. See Freedman, *Professions of Taste*, esp. 245–54, for an account of the modernist "re-aestheticization" of James that would have prepared the ground for Abrams's views on James. See Brodhead,

hand, James maintains that, to succeed in conveying a direct impression of life, a novelist must only be true to what he possesses in common with all other people: an identity defined by a unique point of view. In "The Art of Fiction" James asserts that the "first aid" to writing good fiction "is a capacity for receiving straight impressions" (21); "the only condition that I can think of attaching to the composition of the novel is . . . that it be sincere" (26). Yet a novelist must also be true to the view as well as to the point from which he sees that view: he must experience life "directly," unmediated by any subjective partiality. Which, then, is the novel's proper subject: the viewer or the viewed? In the Prefaces, it seems, James outlines two competing ideals of novelistic authorship: on the one hand, the successful novelist is the one who most transparently expresses his unique "impression" of life; on the other hand, the successful novelist is the one who does not allow his own views to prevent life from making its "impression" on him. In the first case, the novelist is best when he projects his views; in the second, when he refuses to project them.[13]

Once we appreciate this tension between projection and reception in James's account of novelistic point of view, we can better understand why James sometimes describes novel writing as a process of self-expression that any person can undertake and at other times represents it as an art requiring uncommon sensibility. As his letter to the Deerfield students makes clear, James believes that the great accomplishment of "doing something from one's own point of view" is actually inseparable from the project of considering "life directly and closely" (29). When he counsels the "novice" author in his "The Art of Fiction" to " 'write from experience and experience only,' " James quickly adds that the mere uniqueness of one's experience is not enough to make it interesting; the novice must also " 'try to be one of the people on whom nothing is lost!' " (13).[14]

Faced with the conflicting demands of expression and impression that he thus places on the novelist, James supplements his ambiguous call for

---

School, esp. 114–69; and Ross Posnock, *Trial*, for other important socioliterary contextualizations of the Prefaces.

[13] My sense of the tension in James's notion of sincerity thus differs from Carroll's. For Carroll, the threat to James's theory of point of view comes from the "nonsynthesizable plurality" that contradicts its premises of a coherent phenomenological subject who is present to itself.

[14] See Rowe, *Theoretical Dimensions*, esp. 9, for an excellent discussion of the postmodern inheritance of the Jamesian theory of interest.

"sincerity" with the stipulation that the artist communicate his sense of "wonderment" too.[15] On the one hand, James attributes the capacity for wonderment to people on whom nothing is lost: "We care, our curiosity and our sympathy care, comparatively little for what happens to the stupid, the coarse and the blind; care for it, and for the effects of it, at the most as helping to precipitate what happens to the more deeply wondering, to the really sentient. Hamlet and Lear are surrounded, amid their own complications, by the stupid and the blind, who minister in all sorts of ways to their recorded fate" (Prefaces, 62). Hamlet and Lear are certainly not ordinary minds on ordinary days; their royal lineage suggests that, for James, the placement and trimmings of one's window might not, after all, be wholly irrelevant to an assessment of one's perspective, that sensibility may depend on the privileges of social position. But to underscore only the causal relation between status and vision implied by James's exemplars of prime sensibility would be to miss the greater oddity in his invocation of these particular Shakespearean heroes: James's spectacular lack of concern for any specific attribute or action associated with these characters. Beside the related virtue of sincerity, wonder is the only character trait to which James wants to limit his novelist.[16]

And wonder, as James describes it, necessarily diffuses an interest in the novelist's character by turning the act of novel writing into a negotiation between viewer and viewed that relies as much on the worthiness

[15] See Posnock, *Trial*, for a cultural and philosophical contextualization of Jamesian "wonder." See Jay for an overview of the philosophical distinction between curiosity and wonder in the Western tradition (*Downcast Eyes*, esp. 271).

[16] Charles Feidelson rightly connects the theory of artistic perception that is articulated in the Prefaces to Romantic antecedents, particularly to the "Wordsworthian Poetic Everyman" ("James," 336). But what Feidelson considers the "uneasy" and "precarious" relation in James between imagination and the world (352) is for James the positive condition of novel writing: rather than representing an interpretive impasse or "hermeneutic circle" (339), in other words, James's wondering "interest" in alterity is for him what inspires both his novels and his theories about them. The larger irony of Feidelson's interpretation is that, by equating the character Lambert Strether with James himself, Feidelson overlooks the major activity of the imagination for James: the writing of novels. In my account, imagination is structured by the productive tension between impression and expression. In describing James's representation of the "imaginative man" as the one who is "intrinsically unrepresentable in fiction," who "remained unrepresented while he fell back on 'other subjects' that he was more able to bring into focus," Feidelson himself comes close to describing the dynamic between representing self and represented other that I am arguing is the basis of Jamesian wonder and, more generally, novelistic alterity (335).

of the view as on the viewer's capacity to "see." In James's formulation, "excited wonder must have a subject, must face in a direction, must be, increasingly, *about* something" (253; James's emphasis). The view cannot be wonderful if the viewer thinks her sensibility makes it so; conversely, the viewer's sense that the view is so powerful as to transcend her comprehension of it always keeps her in "close connection" with the view. Such outward-directedness is, for James, the optimal condition for novelistic creation because it can express the viewer's sensibility while at the same time maintaining the integrity of the view.[17] It is the "subject" about which the artist wonders, James argues, that enables us to measure "his bias and his range":

> About what, good man, does he himself most wonder?—for upon that, whatever it may be, he will naturally most abound. Under that star will he gather in what he shall most seek to represent; so that if you follow thus his range of representation you will know how, you will see where, again, good man, he for himself most aptly vibrates. (253–54)

Paradoxically, the artist who most fully conveys this vibration of wonder to the reader is the least personal writer, insofar as he must remain true to his subject in order to vibrate "most aptly":

> The person capable of feeling in the given case more than another of what is to be felt for it, and so serving in the highest degree to *record* it dramatically and objectively, is the only sort of person on whom we can count not to betray, to cheapen or, as we say, give away, the value and beauty of the thing. By so much as the affair matters *for* some such individual, by so much do we get the best there is of it, and by so much as it falls within the scope of a denser and duller, a more vulgar and more shallow capacity, do we get a picture dim and meagre. (67; James's emphasis)[18]

---

[17] Carroll includes James's Prefaces in his description of phenomenological theories of the novel that attempt "a neutral description of the world free of all presuppositions in order to guarantee the immediacy of the relationship between subject and object, self and other, consciousness and reality" (*Subject*, 11; for the characterization of James as a phenomenologist, see 60).

[18] Although the connection between James's theory of novelistic technique and his theory of artistic point of view is a complex topic that I will treat in more detail in "Point of View: Materializing Identity" and "Literary Criticism as the End of Art," this passage from the Prefaces already suggests why James so often describes novel writing as, oxymoronically, picture making through narrative. Because for James the artistic process is predicated on the apprehension and expression of an interesting object's identity, he thinks of narrative as a development in the sense that a photograph might be said to "develop": an unfolding of latent potential rather than a transformation of identity in and through time. The "picture" of the subject that

A superior sensibility is revealed precisely to the degree that it "records" "dramatically and objectively," without, that is, the self-interest that would interfere with the appreciation of the subject's virtues.[19] By the same token, the more beautifully—which is to say, vividly and completely—the "thing" is represented, the more it bespeaks its indebtedness to the viewer/artist's own interests.[20] It is to the question of how this symbiosis between the artist and his subject produces specific novels that I will now turn.

Point of View: Materializing Identity

Only when we appreciate the full intricacies of James's point-of-view philosophy can we begin to understand why in James's fiction the "direct impression of life" seems so indirectly presented. If the artist should strive to convey "a personal, a direct impression of life" ("Art of Fiction," 9), then wouldn't an autobiography accomplish this goal most effectively? Or shouldn't his fiction at least strive to imitate autobiography? Shouldn't all novels, for James, be romans à clef? That James gives us *The Portrait of a Lady* rather than *The Portrait of the Artist as a Young Man* indicates how strongly he believes that the subject most worthy of artistic representation possesses its own independent sources

---

James says the wondering viewer perceives thus becomes the basis for the picture that James says the novel constitutes per se (see the Preface to *The Tragic Muse* for one of James's most sustained discussions of the novel as picture; the metaphorics of painting is incessantly invoked throughout all the Prefaces). The narrative that James tells of the artistic process underscores his sense of the evolutionary relation of artistic subject to novelistic character: whether characters in his novels change because of time or unfold in time (different novels imagine different fates), characters in general should not in any simple way be equated with the wonderful object that precedes and stimulates novelistic creation. James's tendency to refer to the novel as a picture while at the same time using "picture" more specifically as a technical term equivalent to "summary" (as distinguished from "scene") adds yet another layer of intricacy to the relation James establishes among artistic subject, the novel's generic character, and narrative technique. See the Preface to *The Wings of the Dove*, esp. 300, for an example of how James defines picture against scene; see the Preface to *The Portrait of a Lady*, esp. 57, for an example of how he delights in combining picture and scene without eliding their difference. For a more extended account of James's reliance on pictorial metaphor, see Bowden, *Themes of Henry James*.

[19] Posnock also describes Jamesian wonder as grounded in alterity: "Rather than subsuming the object, James imitates it, thus crystallizing and preserving its otherness" (*Trial*, 142).

[20] The larger Kantian influence on James's theory was apparent to Muir in 1928.

of interest; the artist's capacity for wonder best enables him to convey his "personal, direct impression of life" when he is sympathetically responding to the "value and beauty" that he perceives to exist outside himself. As we have seen, perception is always for James a matter of sensibility, the extent and quality of a person's capacity for appreciation. Yet James insists that the finest sensibility will express itself through what it records rather than invents; as radically formulated in the Prefaces, the crucial index of a novelist's character is his level of sincerity and wonderment—in short, his capacity for appreciation. Accordingly, James devotes a large proportion of the Prefaces to describing the process by which the "sharp impression or concussion" of experience led him to write.

As critics have noted, the Preface to *Spoils of Poynton* represents James's fullest attempt to trace the operation of artistic "vision" from its arousal in life to its fulfillment in art.[21] *Spoils* came into being, James tells us, when at a dinner party one night a guest, in "ten words" (Prefaces, 121) or so, alluded to an altercation that had estranged two devoted family members: a widow and her son had quarreled over the possession of valuable furniture left in a house that had been willed to the son by his father. Holding himself to the "habit of vigilance" (122) that he so often recommends to aspiring novelists, seeking as always to lose nothing from life, James intuitively senses that this brief scenario holds the "germ" of a "story" (119). The conversion of reality to fiction, of gossip to art, begins with James's feeling that the stream of life has cast up what he calls an "interesting particle," an object that irresistibly commands the artist's attention (119).[22] At the time, the social situation required that he hear more details about mother, son, and furniture—he even learned how their real life story unfolded. But these facts were, as James puts it, part of the "disjoined and lacerated lump of life" (120); they explained nothing about the elicitation of his interest and even threatened to "strangle it in the cradle" (121). The "ten words" that James heard thus derive their importance not from any meaning that "life" gave them, but from the meaning that they somehow independently and latently contained, waiting upon James's comprehension.[23]

[21] See, for example, Booth, *Rhetoric*, 345.
[22] See the Preface to *The Ambassadors*, esp. 307, for another instance of James's use of the term "particle" to describe the interesting object that generates the work of art.
[23] By comparing the Preface's version of his dinner experience with his Notebook

The niceness of this distinction (between the meaninglessness of life itself and the meaningfulness of interesting parts of life) becomes blurred as James attempts to explain how life can be both the origin and the antithesis of art. He sets up an opposition that is familiar to any reader of James's criticism: life, he proclaims, is "all inclusion and confusion," art "all discrimination and selection" (Prefaces, 120). James does not want to know what really happened to mother and son because, he believes, life inevitably fails to actualize the latent "value" of the situation. By grandly dismissing life, James of course also discards any ordinary determinants of value such as social, market, moral, or psychological forces. As he goes on to explain, "life" can never actualize value because it has no point of view, no appreciative capacity; it can yield an "interesting particle" only when something or someone in life matters *for* someone, when the object of interest becomes the "subject" of her inquiry. But if "life has no direct sense whatever for the subject and is capable, luckily for us, of nothing but splendid waste" (120), how does the interest of the object, which the artist transforms into her subject, amount to anything more than the artist's projection of a "sense" that life otherwise lacks?

James seems to acknowledge the projectedness of the value he perceives as he continues to outline the evolution of *Spoils*:

> I "took" in fine, on the spot, to the rich bare little facts of the two related figures [quarreling mother and son], embroiled perhaps all so sordidly; and for reasons of which I could most probably have given at the moment no decent account. Had I been asked why they were, in that stark nudity, to say nothing of that ugliness of attitude, "interesting," I fear I could have said nothing more to the point, even to my own questioning spirit, than "Well, you'll see!" By which of course I should have meant "Well, *I* shall see"—confident meanwhile (as against the appearance or the imputation of poor taste) that interest would spring as soon as one should begin really to see *anything*. That points, I think, to a large part of the very source of interest for the artist: it resides in the strong consciousness of his seeing all for himself. (122; James's emphasis)

On the one hand, the "bareness" and "littleness" of the "facts" suggest that their "richness" lies in their very blankness, the opportunity they

---

account of the same, we can clearly see how James's later description has been carefully reworked to fit the philosophy of artistic creation he puts forth in the Prefaces. See especially *Notebooks*, 79–80, 121–22, 131–36 to compare the Prefaces' streamlined account of both the finding and the representation of the artistic subject with the Notebook's profusion of detail.

present for a replete consciousness to project its full value on to them. But the blankness of the facts would, on the other hand, not explain why they catch James's attention to begin with. Although James at first cannot satisfy his own "questioning spirit" as to why he finds the facts interesting, even the "starkness" of their "nudity" reassures him, insofar as it highlights the *concreteness* of what he sees:

> Life being all inclusion and confusion, and art being all discrimination and selection, the latter, in search of the hard latent *value* with which alone it is concerned, sniffs round the mass as instinctively and unerringly as a dog suspicious of some buried bone. The difference here, however, is that, while the dog desires his bone but to destroy it, the artist finds in *his* tiny nugget, washed free of awkward accretions and hammered into a sacred hardness, the very stuff for a clear affirmation, the happiest chance for the indestructible. (120; James's emphasis)

Bareness turns to richness, a bone to a nugget of gold, as the artist first digs and then hammers the "hard latent *value*" of the facts into "a sacred hardness." The earlier ambiguity about whether the artist discovers or creates interest is washed away by the artist's growing certainty that he has been rewarded with a "clear," because "hard," "affirmation" of value.

In the Preface to *Spoils*, then, James preserves the definitive alterity of the interesting object only by attributing to artistic vision the creative power of materialization. Never is the process of recording the object's interest a passive operation for James's artist: "The particular case, or in other words his relation to a given subject, once the relation is established, forms in itself a little world of exercise and agitation" (*Prefaces*, 121).[24] But the artist's creative energies are based upon the objective foundations of interest that he had first sniffed out:

> He [the artist] has to borrow his motive [the object of interest], which is certainly half the battle; and this motive is his ground, his site and his founda-

---

[24] Whereas Sharon Cameron believes that James's representation of consciousness in his novels is more complex—and accurate—than his theoretical description of consciousness, my sense of James's definition of artistic interest as relational leads me to see a consonance between James's novelistic theory and practice. Cameron argues that in the Prefaces James articulates a notion of "consciousness as a unified phenomenon" but that his novels represent consciousness as "*inter*subjective," valorizing consciousness "just to the extent that consciousness can be separated from the confines of a self" (*Thinking*, 76, 77; Cameron's emphasis). Yet, as I will show, Cameron's description of consciousness in the novels is compatible with the theory of artistic interest put forth in the Prefaces.

tion. But after that he only lends and gives, only builds and piles high, lays together the blocks quarried in the deeps of his imagination and on his personal premises. He thus remains all the while in intimate commerce with his motive, and can say to himself—what really more than anything else inflames and sustains him—that he alone has the *secret* of the particular case, he alone can measure the truth of the direction to be taken by his developed data. There can be for him, evidently, only one logic for these things; there can be for him only one truth and one direction—the quarter in which the subject most completely expresses itself.[25] (Prefaces, 122–23; James's emphasis)

The desire to grasp the "secret" of what interests him does lead James to plumb the "deeps" of his "personal premises," but this self-excavation results in no psychological or self-reflexive knowledge, no autobiographical association, nothing that might be considered a positive term of Jamesian identity. If the artist discovers himself in the process of hammering his subject into a sacred hardness, that is only because he has been guided by his subject to an objective assessment of the material within him—and this material, when "quarried," manifests the identity of the subject as an independent entity. Indeed, the workshop of the artist's imagination is nothing other than the "quarter in which his subject most completely expresses itself." Just as he hammers his imagination into the "blocks" that fit and fill in the "hard" outlines of his subject, so the artist will ultimately verify the autonomous substance of what interests him by transforming that interest into a material objet d'art.[26]

The artist's desire to appreciate fully the intrinsic qualities that make the interesting object interesting thus is for James inseparable from the compulsion to represent; the artist's appreciative vision, his search to understand the autonomous value of the interesting object, "to get the best

---

[25] This passage has been adopted by many critics as the definitive formulation of Jamesian craft. See, for example, Leon Edel's paraphrase of the *Spoils* Preface in general and the language of construction in particular: "We are taken from the germ of a story, some odd little fact or remark at a dinner table, some brief incident or anecdote, into human behavior and human motivation. We watch James in his workshop building narratives brick by brick with a kind of Olympian mastery" ("Introduction," xi). For Percy Lubbock, as I will show, the artist's workshop evolves into readerly noetic materialism.

[26] I thus take to be more literally material what Carroll describes as a characterological possession: "The goal of the author-subject . . . is to be able to take on another form while remaining identical to himself, to disguise himself all the better to remain himself, to project himself into another in order better to be what he is. The unity of the form of the novel is intimately linked to the skill with which the author is able to possess and be possessed by a fictional other" (*Subject*, 56–57).

there is" of it, irresistibly turns a "particle" into a whole, the object of attention into an artistic "subject." The artist's "sense for the subject" thus ends up achieving the interesting object's own best representation; the artist's own subjective mediation becomes the material of alterity, the "quarter in which his subject most completely expresses itself."[27]

In James's account, then, the artist's interestedness is always a force of production; his capacity for alterity, his "sense for the subject," is literally constructive. In a radical formulation of artistic "wonder," the artist can know his subject fully only by instantiating that subject; objective knowledge is achieved through artistic materialization. The artist's "vision" of the fully manifested value of the artistic subject is simply the first step in that materializing process. The "ten words" James hears, the figurative object of his attention, begin to become something to be seen rather than heard as soon as James removes them from their original context and installs them in his imagination. Although he will refer to what interests him with a variety of terms—a case, an incident, a germ, a motive, etc.—artistic interest operates successfully only when a locus of value becomes objectified as an art object.

The artist maximizes the constructive value of his interest by creating an art "work" that, if successful, not only represents the artist's interest and the subject's interestingness, but also, as a coherent totality in its own right, possesses an independent value of its own. The artist's "vision of life" thus ultimately fulfills itself when it most distinguishes itself from life: when the object of interest is reconstituted as a form that "wastes" nothing, that is, in other words, wholly meaningful. James describes this productivity as "the sublime economy of art, which rescues, which saves, and hoards and 'banks,' investing and reinvesting these fruits of toil in wondrous useful 'works' and thus making up for us, desperate spendthrifts that we all naturally are, the most princely of incomes" (120). The most wondrous achievement of the artistic vision is the conversion of "toil" to "income"; the expense of interest leads to its capitalization, but since the artist is both laborer and consumer, the reification of interest in the art "work" is an alienation that leads to the better self-fulfillment afforded by objectification.[28] The concretizing of

---

[27] As Booth has pointed out, "subject" is a term that James allows a range of meaning (*Rhetoric*, 345). I would emphasize that the latitude of this term helps James to imagine the metamorphosis of the interesting object into a self-expressive subject.

[28] See Porter for a critique of what she terms the "economic mystification which sustains the artist's power" (*Seeing*, 131–32).

the artist's vision in and through the art object gives that vision an additional source of value derived from the internal relations established by the art work: the work's intrinsic ability to increase value through the way that it objectifies value.[29] As James puts it in another Preface, "economy is always beauty" (257); the "sublime economy of art" is thus not simply the materialization of "interest" into "works," but the maximization of interest within the work itself.[30]

As I have suggested, such accounts of meaning becoming materialized are frequent in James, and contrast markedly with his relative silence about the nature of the meaning that interests him. At one point in the *Spoils* Preface, however, it seems as if James might actually define the value that makes the object of his attention worthy of artistic representation. What James begins to "see" in the "ten words," is, fittingly, a critique not just of modern materialism but of the modern nostalgia for a past regarded as "more material." As James contemplates the "nugget" that he has found within the dinner party gossip, he considers

> the sharp light it might project on that most modern of our current passions, the fierce appetite for the upholsterer's and joiner's and brazier's work, the

[29] James's theorization of novelistic representation as economical is, of course, part of his bid to lobby against formless "baggy monsters." His persistent description of the novel as an art of portraiture indicates the essentially static view he has of narrative. In the Preface to *Roderick Hudson*, for example, James advises the novelist to establish a productive relation between the episodic and the pictorial:

> I was already consciously in presence, here, of the most interesting question the artist has to consider. To give the image and the sense of certain things while still keeping them subordinate to his plan, keeping them in relation to matters more immediate and apparent, to give all the sense, in a word, without all the substance or all the surface, and so to summarise and foreshorten, so to make values both rich and sharp, that the mere procession of items and profiles is not only, for the occasion, superseded, but is, for essential quality, almost "compromised"—such a case of delicacy proposes itself at every turn to the painter of life who wishes both to treat his chosen subject and to confine his necessary picture. It is only by doing such things that art becomes exquisite. (14)

The narrative artist seeks a delicate balance between procession and picture; the unfolding of "items and profiles" retains the heterogeneous integrity of narrative sequence while contributing to the representation of a larger whole. Summary and foreshortening do not diminish the subject of representation but, on the contrary, vivify its meaning by economically enlisting heterogeneous details into a unified image. See the Preface to *The Tragic Muse* (esp. 87), the Preface to *Daisy Miller* (esp. 278), the Preface to *The Princess Casamassima* (esp. 64), and the Preface to *The Ambassadors* (esp. 319) for related discussions of novelistic economy.

[30] See the Preface to *Roderick Hudson* (esp. 12–13) for discussion of the relation between the "interest of the subject" and the "exhibitional interest" of the art work.

chairs and tables, the cabinets and presses, the material odds and ends, of the more labouring ages. A lively mark of our manners indeed the diffusion of this curiosity and this avidity, and full of suggestion, clearly as to their possible influence on other passions and other relations. (Prefaces, 123)

Given the complicated account of artistic production that I have been tracing, this specification of James's subject matter seems refreshingly straightforward; it also appears to shed light on the passion for an object that has driven James's interest from the start. Yet a lust for antiques hardly seems to live up to James's description of the novelist on the same page as a "modern alchemist" who harbors "the old dream of the secret of life"; and indeed James quickly rejects this first conception of his subject matter as too crude an interpretation of his interest. It is only by suspending and then renewing his attention many months later that James is able to appreciate his true object, not to mention justify his necromantic conception of the artist, more fully. In describing the climactic moment when he at last unlocks the secret that will reward him with *Spoils,* James sounds like a Frankenstein bringing his creature to life: "the subject had emerged from cool reclusion all suffused with a flush of meaning" (124). Characteristically, James does not specify here what this fuller meaning is and how it differs from the social critique that had proven only a rough and partial interpretation of his object. Instead of specifying what he now knows, James instead emphasizes how he knows, which is, of course, what he sees. Once immersed in the alchemical workshop of his imagination, the "nugget" emerges as a meaningful "subject"; but now it also has the "flush" of independent life.

The artistic subject thus is a concept that for James registers the art work's particular identity—this novel is "about" something different from that novel—while serving to define that identity less as something nameable and more as presence itself: what the work is finally "about" is the successful instantiation of the interesting object's coherent identity. Finding the secret of the object of wonder, the "thing," transforms the interesting object into a subject—almost a subjectivity—capable of self-expression. For James, the appreciation of alterity is, then, not only an economy of relation between representer and represented but a sequence of transmutation: the artist's identificatory understanding has the power to turn the object of interest into an artistic subject—and then to recast that subject as a self-expressive art work. In the Jamesian version of the appreciation of alterity, the artistic subject is ultimately defined by its hybrid nature: the artistic subject is first of all both author and other, but is also person and thing; the artistic subject is experienced by James as both a subjectivized object and an objectifiable subject. If the artist's appreciation discovers the interesting object to be capable of humanlike self-expression, it is the objectiveness, derived from its objectness, of the artistic subject that allows James to believe that alterity can be instantiated through artistic form.

The laborious constitution of the interesting object as artistic subject is matched by what James experiences as the equally strenuous search for appropriate representational form. As he puts it in the Preface to *The Ambassadors*, "the subject is found, and if the problem is then transferred to the ground of what to do with it the field opens out for any amount of doing" (312). In the Prefaces James customarily describes these two acts of vision as discrete tasks, but if we follow the steps that he claims led him to *Spoils*, we can see how the two processes—the discovery of the artistic subject and the discovery of its "right" representational form—resemble one another, and we can also see why they resemble one another. In the same way that the artist's vision of life was both limited and concretized by its engagement with the interesting object, so too is it both limited and concretized, for James, by the power of specific narrative techniques to materialize identity. In other words, just as the artist's endlessly vibrating appreciation for "life" found focus and meaning through his belief in the knowable alterity of the interesting object, so too is the artist's "doing" productively limited to a relatively small selection of representational techniques that, in James's mind, most effectively materialize the artist's vision of the artistic subject, creating a form which, as a totality, will manifest the full value of the artistic subject. [31]

We can see the reciprocity between the two stages of the creative process—the apprehension of the interesting object's value and the expression of that value in and through the objective principles of novelistic art—in James's description of the liminal moment in the creative evolution of *What Maisie Knew* when the artistic subject begins to take form as a work of art. Here James describes the process of appreciative comprehension as developing like a photograph into an artistic composition:

[31] The techniques that James recommends are so well known that they barely need summarizing: they range from large-scale suggestions about narrative management (the use of a compositional center, how to alternate between scene and summary, the efficacy of third-person narration, the use of *ficelles*) to specific representational details (the advantages of a sentient protagonist, why dialect should be used sparingly, how best to represent historical personages, when to use real place names).

Sketchily clustered even, these elements gave out that vague pictorial glow which forms the first appeal of a living "subject" to the painter's consciousness; but the glimmer became intense as I proceeded to a further analysis. The further analysis is for that matter almost always the torch of rapture and victory, as the artist's firm hand grasps and plays it—I mean, naturally, of the smothered rapture and the obscure victory, enjoyed and celebrated not in the street but before some innermost shrine; the odds being a hundred to one, in almost any connexion, that it does n't arrive by any easy first process at the *best* residuum of truth. That was the charm, sensibly of the picture thus at first confusedly showing; the elements so could n't but flush, to their very surface with some deeper depth of irony than the mere obvious. It lurked in the crude postulate like a buried scent; the more the attention hovered the more aware it become [sic] of the fragrance. (Prefaces, 141; James's emphasis)

Just as value was latent in the interesting object, so too is representational form latent in the artistic subject. The "flush" of meaning that characterized the fully realized artistic subject now becomes the "flush" of a "pictorial glow" that, when fully developed, will illuminate the form that the artist's representation of his subject must take. By thus dictating the terms of its own representation, the interesting object retains its alterity even when translated into James's writing. Indeed, James rarely discusses his novelistic representations *as* writing; composition in the Prefaces is not a matter of word choice or style but of painting the very picture that the artistic subject has already "shown."[32]

The *Spoils* Preface records the succession of partial images through which James approaches the full portrait of his subject. At first James plans to analyze the "fierce appetite" of modern society for "the chairs and tables, the cabinets and presses, the material odds and ends, of the more labouring ages" by organizing his composition around the "things themselves." This strategy recommends itself to him when he still believes that the critique of modern consumerism latent in his dinner companion's gossip is the primary interest of his subject. His task will be to write a novel that will provide a portrait not of quarreling son and mother but of the furniture itself:

On the face of it the "things" themselves would form the very centre of such a crisis [the modern rage for antiques]; these grouped objects, all conscious of their eminence and their price, would enjoy, in any picture of conflict, the heroic importance. They would have to be presented, they would have to be painted—arduous and desperate thought; something would have to be done

---

[32] See note 18 for James's use of picture in the Prefaces as a whole.

for them not too ignobly unlike the great array in which Balzac, say, would have marshalled them: *that* amount of workable interest at least would evidently be "in it." (Prefaces, 123–24; James's emphasis)

At this stage of conception, objects, not the people who desire them, constitute the heroic center of the novel; a few pages later, James writes of the separate "identity" and "character" each "thing" possesses, which it is his job vividly to portray (126).[33] But such personification of things turns out to have distinct limitations, and it is the thinness or, in James's terms, the cheapness of the consciousness that James can impute to furniture that makes him change his mind about what the center of *Spoils* should be.[34] As James puts it,

> The spoils of Poynton were not directly articulate, and though they might have, and constantly did have, wondrous things to say, their message fostered about them a certain hush of cheaper sound—as a consequence of which, in fine, they would have been costly to keep up. (127)

Furniture is not normally thought capable of even indirect articulateness; only James's insistence on treating the source of his artistic subject as an independent object would lead him to envision things, and not the people who desire them, as his protagonists. But James finds that the personification of things looks too much like projection: as he remarks about the "elements" of novels in his Preface to "The Altar of the Dead," "these appearances [should] be constituted in some other and more colourable fashion than by the author's answering for them on his more or less gentlemanly honour. This is n't enough; *give* me your elements, *treat* me your subject, one has to say—I must wait till then to tell you how I like them" (255; James's emphasis). Thus the creative process culminates in James's replacement of impersonal with human "characters"; the flushed bride of immanent meaning materializes into the figure of Fleda Vetch:

> [She] marked her place in my foreground at one ingratiating stroke. She planted herself centrally, and the stroke, as I call it, the demonstration after which she could n't be gainsaid, was the simple act of letting it be seen she had character. (127)

---

[33] James's original title for *Spoils* emphasizes the objectness of his subject; the novella was first published serially in *Atlantic Monthly* (1896) as "The Old Things."

[34] Whereas Fleda's value lies in her outward-directedness, her capacity for appreciation, James describes the furniture as self-reflexive: "these grouped objects, all conscious of their eminence and their price" (42). Looking inward rather than outward, the furniture may be personified, but it does not thus possess, in James's sense, a point of view.

If the representation of furniture depended upon James's "answering for" the furniture, the human character that replaces the furniture as a compositional center possesses a "sense" so much her own that she reduces her author to the position of silent spectator, whose task is merely to "let it be seen" that Fleda has character. And this "character" easily generates the terms of the picture of life upon which James settles as the true portrait of his artistic subject: "I committed myself to making the affirmation and the penetration of [Fleda's understanding] my action and my 'story'" (Prefaces, 128). In the Preface to *The Portrait of a Lady*, James had described a similar focus on human characters as the practice of Turgenev, for whom the creative process almost always began

> with the vision of some person or persons, who hovered before him, soliciting him, as the active or passive figure, interesting him and appealing to him just as they were and by what they were. He saw them, in that fashion, as *disponibles*, saw them subject to the chances, the complications of existence, and saw them vividly, but then had to find for them the right relations, those that would most bring them out; to imagine, to invent and select and piece together the situations most useful and favourable to the sense of the creatures themselves, the complications they would be most likely to produce and to feel. (42–43)

James's statement in the Preface to *Spoils* that "a character is interesting as it comes out, and by the process and duration of that emergence" (127–28), seems to imply that the same search for "right relations" is what enabled the "growth and predominance of Fleda Vetch" (126).[35]

[35] James's discussion of Turgenev in the Preface to *The Portrait of a Lady* has led some critics to conclude that, for James, novel writing always begins with a vision of "some person or persons . . . interesting and appealing to him just as they were and by what they were" (Prefaces, 42–43). As Walter F. Wright has observed, however, the Jamesian recaptured "germ" is usually an "incident or situation, though a few stories began with a vague image of character" (*Madness*, 34). The coincidence in the *Portrait* Preface of the interesting object with a particular character (Isabel Archer) is in fact a short-circuiting of the creative process that James usually describes. See, for example, the Preface to *The Awkward Age* (esp. 99–100), the Preface to *What Maisie Knew* (esp. 140), and the Preface to *The Aspern Papers* (esp. 162) for more typical accounts of the transition from "life" to "art."
Even in the cases where a character does germinate a fictional work, James has, in comparison to Turgenev, a more formal notion of an author's subjective relation to the character or characters that inspire him. As Lawrence Holland notes, by refusing to identify the biographical source of his characters and instead, "returning repeatedly to the question of their origin," James defines his "relation to them as materials, chosen or given, for his novel" (*Expense*, 6–7). In the Preface to *Portrait*

But *Spoils* does not begin with a vision of persons; when James declares that "something like Fleda Vetch had surely been latent in one's first apprehension of the theme" (Prefaces, 126), he means (as the objectifying reference to the "it" of Fleda's "character" suggests) that Fleda is only a better "thing" than the furniture was, a more vivid personification of the artist's interesting object than the furniture could be.[36] This subordination of Fleda to the interesting object becomes clearer in James's discussion of the characters in *Spoils* who are subordinate to Fleda. In James's view, these secondary characters are "terms" for the "bringing out" of Fleda, what James in the Preface to *The Portrait of a Lady* famously calls *ficelles* (322). The value of Mrs. Gereth, like that of the furniture, is extrinsic to her character; her primary function, according to James, is to provide the painterly value of contrast, to throw Fleda's qualities into relief (130).[37] Just as Mrs. Gereth lends vivacity to Fleda, so Fleda lends vivacity to the interesting object.

What, then, does Fleda's all-important character finally manifest about the interesting object, what lively picture does it at last reproduce? To answer these questions, we should begin by noticing that, after James first assumes and then denies that the interest of his object lies in the lust of contemporary society for antiques, he does not again attempt to characterize the nature of the value that absorbs him. Fleda renders such formulations both obsolete and irrelevant, not only because she so

---

we can see how James's initial endorsement of Turgenev's characterological account of novelistic inspiration is quickly modified by James to suit his own author-based philosophy of point of view. James expands the definition of *disponible* to include the "given" of the artist's "prime sensibility," his "sincere experience" (45).

[36] This belief in Fleda's immanence is especially striking given James's remarks, in the Prefaces generally and in the Preface to *Spoils* particularly, about the variety of economic, institutional, and even environmental factors that have influenced his creative process. His own need to make his writing pay divided his attention among artistic projects, regulated the pace of his production, and compromised the autonomy of his creative process more than his philosophy of artistic creation generally allowed. His decision to discard the "things" as his focus is certainly linked to commercial concerns (since the spoils of Poynton were not "directly articulate," the public's love of dialogue would be ungratified and his editors would be unhappy), but these factors in exchanging the "things" for Fleda remain untheorized in the phenomenology of artistic creation that he puts forth.

[37] James introduces the term *ficelle* in the Preface to *The Portrait of a Lady* with this vivid figure: "Maria Gostrey and Miss Stackpole then are cases, each, of the light *ficelle*, not of the true agent; they may run beside the coach 'for all they are worth', they may cling to it till they are out of breath (as poor Miss Stackpole all so vividly does), but neither, all the while, so much as gets her foot on the step, neither ceases for a moment to tread the dusty road" (55).

fully embodies James's sense of his interest but because she embodies it as an action, a seeing rather than a knowing: "From the beginning to end, in *The Spoils of Poynton*, appreciation, even to that of the very whole, lives in Fleda" (129). At first glance, no resolution to the creative process, no "secret" of the case, could seem less committed to alterity than this one: the fully realized artistic subject mirrors back to the author the state of mind in which the creative process began. But, as an extraordinary passage from the Preface to *The American* makes clear, to embody wonder in character is, for James, to ensure the subordination of projection to discovery:

> If Newman was attaching enough, I must have argued, his tangle would be sensible enough; for the interest of everything is all that it is *his* vision, *his* conception, *his* interpretation; at the window of his wide, quite sufficiently wide, consciousness we are seated, from that admirable position we "assist." He therefore supremely matters; all the rest matters only as he feels it, treats it, meets it. A beautiful infatuation this, always, I think, the intensity of the creative effort to get into the skin of the creature; the act of personal possession of one being by another at its completest—and with the high enhancement, ever, that it is, by the same stroke, the effort of the artist to preserve for his subject that unity, and for his use of it (in other words for the interest he desires to excite) that effect of a *centre*, which most economise its value. (37–38; James's emphasis)

When James started quarrying his imagination into blocks to pile upon the foundation of his subject, he had begun construction on a house of fiction; the character is a window in that house, not the scene upon which the window looks. When James vampirishly takes "personal possession" of the character, he only projects himself, he believes, into a more refined position of "appreciation" than the one from which he began.[38] Indeed, as an embodiment of the wonder inspired by the interest-

---

[38] James imagines Fleda as an "other" who will be known when her interiority has been "penetrated" (128). He thus sets forth a model of authorial/characterological relation that is based upon interpersonal—even physically interpersonal—experience rather than authorial omniscience. In the Preface to *The Princess Casamassima* he specifically describes appreciation as intimacy:

> My report of people's experience—my report as a "story-teller"—is essentially my appreciation of it, and there is no "interest" for me in what my hero, my heroine or any one else does save through that admirable process. . . . I then see their "doing" . . . as, immensely, their feeling, their feeling as their doing; since I can have none of the conveyed sense and taste of their situation without becoming intimate with them. I can't be intimate without that sense and taste, and I can't appreciate save by intimacy. (65–66)

ing object, the character rescues James from the potential "waste" of novel writing by "preserving" his original wonder—with the difference, however, that James as the wondering subject has been removed, supplanted by a characterological subject position or "window" from which any reader can wonder at the interesting object as well.[39]

The advantage for James of replacing himself as wonderer with a character as wonderer is not only the appearance of objectivity that the character provides; the character, James believes, also stimulates wonder better than a representation of James as appreciator ever could. Over the course of explaining how Maisie's "wonder" constitutes the center of *What Maisie Knew*, James declares, "it is her relation, her activity of spirit, that determines all our own concern—we simply take advantage of these things better than she herself. Only, even though it is her interest that mainly makes matters interesting for us, we inevitably note this in figures that are not yet at her command" (Prefaces, 146). In the case of the *Spoils* furniture, a cheapness of consciousness had blocked James's interest by requiring him to involve his own consciousness too baldly in the creative process; with its greater autonomy, Maisie's "activity of spirit" instead "makes matters interesting" for James and

---

The vampirish quality of Jamesian intimacy lies not only in its physicality (the penetration of the body that veils feeling, the "sense and taste" he ascribes to feeling itself) but in its lack of reciprocality: in the logic of Jamesian alterity, the autonomy of characters—like the autonomy of the interesting object—is predicated upon their obliviousness to authorial intimacy. Geoffrey Hartman expresses a similar view: "James obstacles himself; he refuses simply to know. Every mind tends to be viewed through another, and the desire to know positively (and can even the artist escape it?) is always presented as a vampirish act" (*Beyond Formalism*, 70).

See Porter, *Seeing*, esp. 129–33, for an account of how James's conception of the artist as a participant observer of his characters relates to his depiction, within novels such as *The Sacred Fount*, *The Portrait of a Lady*, and *The Golden Bowl*, of the characters themselves as participant observers.

[39] Carolyn Porter argues for a causal connection between the vision of life expressed in *The American* and the aesthetic position expressed by its Preface: "But what had driven James finally to ground moral value in the artist's imagination is already apparent in *The American*, where the social ground of such value threatens to disappear" ("Gender," 43). Porter's discussion of the complexity with which *The American* depicts transcendent value as defined against but also in terms of cash value (43) explores a tension in James's thinking that is analogous to the one that I am tracing in the Prefaces. But if James in this early novel appeals to "the artist's imagination" as a ground for moral value, this ground turns out, in the Prefaces as a whole, to be itself unstable—in part because James's aesthetic concerns in the Prefaces cause him to emphasize the *relativity* of moral value. James's search for a more stable ground of value is what helps produce the metaphors of materiality that I have been analyzing.

his readers, but the human character retains a certain cognitive inadequacy as well—this time so that the *independence* of the character's consciousness will not block our interest either: thanks to the rich littleness of Maisie's consciousness, we "take advantage" of things "better than she herself."[40] The final assurance for James that our reading into the character will not amount to projection is that the character enables us to take advantage only of a point of view; the subject of our interest remains the object of our vision, which the independent consciousness of the character enables James to represent as hammered into richness by the character's appreciation:

> There was the "fun," to begin with, of establishing one's successive centres—of fixing them so exactly that the portions of the subject commanded by them as by happy points of view, and accordingly treated from them, would constitute, so to speak, sufficiently solid *blocks* of wrought material, squared to the sharp edge, as to have weight and mass and carrying power; to make for construction, that is, to conduce to effect and to provide for beauty. (296; James's emphasis)

The views "commanded" from the character-windows seem to James so objective that he can describe them as "solid *blocks* of wrought material." Their weightiness counterbalances the airy indeterminacy of the agent that has sculpted them: whether it is the artist, the character, the reader, or the artist's interesting object.

Literary Criticism as the End of Art

The Prefaces thus develop a theory of fictional point of view that is itself grounded in and authorized by authorial point of view: James, as an acclaimed and accomplished novelist, speaks with the authority of his own artistic experience when he describes how the expression of point of view serves as the motive and structure for novelistic representation. But one of the fascinating aspects of the Prefaces is that they enable James to regard his fiction from another point of view—a switch in positionality that, in accordance with the subjectivist logic that guides James's thinking, has significant theoretical ramifications. Asked to produce a definitive version of his work for the New York edition

---

[40] Georges Poulet finds the depicted relationship between viewer and viewed to be the heart of all James's novels: "The Jamesian novel . . . tends, despite all the windings and arabesques which mask the center, to establish . . . the simplicity of a unique object contemplated by a unique consciousness" (*Metamorphoses*, 319).

(1907–9), James finds himself looking at his fiction from the unique double point of view of an author who is compelled to reread his past publications. This double perspective, he believes, allows him to apprehend what as an author he could only hope to imply: the sincere character of his own interest. Thanks to his belief in the ability of the successful art work to objectify authorial point of view in and through the artist's representation of his subject, James's rereading of his oeuvre for the New York edition presents him with a rare opportunity for self-knowledge. In the first Preface, James declares that the "revision, correction, and republication" of his novels for the New York edition has opened his eyes to a new narrative recounted by his works: a story about the "continuity of an artist's endeavor, the growth of his whole operative consciousness" (Prefaces, 4). As the reader of his own fiction, James discovers the interesting object to be, it seems, nothing other than himself—or at least his "whole unfolding" as a novelist, which he now "fondly takes . . . for a thrilling tale, almost for a wondrous adventure" (4).

The Prefaces themselves do not appear to bear the burden of new artistic production in this regard; their part in James's literary autobiography is ancillary, wholly dependent upon the aesthetic success of the literary works collected in the volumes of the New York edition. Yet even with this proviso in mind, the reader who hefts the New York edition in pursuit of James's "thrilling tale" will sooner or later come to doubt either the sincerity or the relevance of the Preface's opening promise. Like the novels themselves, there is little or no reference in the Prefaces to the conventional matter of autobiography, the life events that stimulated the growth of James's artistic consciousness. When James does make personal references, they usually take the form of anonymous and abstracted vignettes—an anecdote, or more likely a remembered phrase—whose importance lies in their power not so much to advance James's consciousness as to germinate an art work. Where we might expect to learn of the external or internal factors—the people and doings or the thoughts and feelings—that enriched James's "whole unfolding" as an artist, we hear instead about the rooms and the cities that James chose as the scenes for his writing. Rather than sequential chapters in a story of development, the Prefaces seem more like autonomous rooms themselves, especially since most restrict themselves to the evaluation of the works discussed in the volume they introduce. What's more, James rarely indulges in the comparative evaluation of his artistic endeavors, which might put them more clearly in relation to each other and establish a narrative of artistic development. Not even when taken together do the separate critical judgments of each novel imply such a development: if James bemoans certain shortcomings of *Roderick Hudson*, for instance, he is also disappointed by features of *The Wings of the Dove*. Finally, James so much suppresses any detailed account of the relation of past to present that, if the Prefaces were her only source of information, a reader would never even realize the extent and scope of James's revisions.[41] The Preface to *The Portrait of a Lady* informs us that James enjoys Isabel's midnight vigil and regrets Henrietta's "superabundance," but judgments of this sort give the reader no indication of—let alone explanation for—the hundreds of textual changes that made James regard the New York volumes as the authoritative edition of his work.

The glaring absence of the promised "thrilling tale" of artistic development is highlighted by James's return to the topic of autobiographical retrospection in the final pages of the final Preface. The Prefaces end, that is, where they began, with James asserting his desire to tell the "history" of his artistic development as if he were mentioning the topic for the first time.[42] His suggestion that this important and interesting story deserves more space than he now commands shows how little he is burdened with the memory of his opening promise. The narrative of his artistic development seems to be a topic that retains its attraction by being postponed. The story of "his whole unfolding" remains the tale he thinks he has learned, wants to tell, and yet never brings himself to recount.

Though the Prefaces never deliver their promised story, the final Preface does at least eloquently explain the reasons for that story's deferral, by placing retrospective self-knowledge in opposition to retrospective autobiography.[43] As James describes it, the thrill and excitement that has

---

[41] See Horne, *Henry James and Revision*, for a discussion of the scope and extent of James's revisions for the New York edition. Cameron points out that while James emphasizes his "minute textual revisions," in fact, the New York edition, with its serial order and prefatory interpretations, accomplishes a revision so profound as itself to be a "reconception" of the novels (*Thinking*, 37).

[42] Robert Caserio argues that the Prefaces "attempt to unify more than thirty years of work, to suppress transitions and discontinuities for the sake of an appearance of consistency" (*Plot*, 199).

[43] Far and away the best reading to date of the Preface to *The Golden Bowl* is by J. Hillis Miller. But Miller's vow "to make James's text my law, . . . follow[ing] what he says with entire fidelity and obedience" (*Ethics*, 102), not only numbers him among the master's many disciples, but also reveals his disposition to accept as cogent and persuasive an account of fiction's ability to instantiate identity that I am arguing is formalist and mystified. Miller's explicit concern with developing a theory of ethics that will combat moral relativism leads him to locate James's ethical

come from rereading his work lies precisely in a *lack* of narrative continuity. Rereading is for James a process of disjunction whereby past and present artistic consciousnesses seem to encounter one another as independent and autonomous sensibilities. James compares the experience of this disassociation to retracing a path made from tracks left in a snowy field. His "present mode of motion," he discovers, "had quite unlearned the old pace and found itself naturally falling into another, which might sometimes indeed more or less agree with the original tracks, but might most often, or very nearly, break the surface in other places" (Prefaces, 336). The conceit is an odd one for representing artistic growth: James walks the same path again, though not exactly, while his past self remains as it were ahead of him, out of sight. In part the strangeness of these implications results from James's theory of revision: he must meet his old self "halfway, passive, receptive, appreciative, often even grateful": "Into his very footprints the responsive, the imaginative steps of the docile reader that I consentingly become for him all comfortably sink" (335–36). But this is to treat the past self as possessing the alterity of an interesting object, and the present self as the artist who strives in his responsiveness to represent the object on its own terms. So it is that James proves most "grateful" when the tracks of the two selves do not fully jibe, because such noncoincidence gives him a new perspective.[44] How, after all, could he study the tracks if his steps now filled them? And not only do "the deviations and differences" become his "very terms of cognition" (337); they also prove an essential source of interest. As the Preface to *Spoils* showed us, an object burdened with the vitality of the artist's consciousness has no interest for James. For "the buried, the latent life of a past composition [to] vibrate" (342), the artist must first treat that life *as* buried away from him—beneath the snow, or in a later figure, under the sea: "The prime consequence on one's own part of reperusal is a sense for ever so many more of the shining silver fish afloat in the deep sea of one's endeavour than the net of widest casting could pretend to gather in" (345). While James's confidence in the evolutionary march of his journey causes him to believe that the

---

contribution not in the concept of alterity that I have defined as the implicit source of ethical meaning in the Prefaces, but in the more vaguely defined "irresistible demand" (120) of the "good stuff" (James, Prefaces, 341) that, in Miller's estimation, serves a "categorical imperative" for self-improvement (*Ethics*, 120). See below for my own discussion of "the good stuff."

    [44] Hillis Miller argues by contrast that the footprints represent "the ground on which [they] are inscribed" (*Ethics*, 113).

story of his artistic development is narratable, and while it is this prog-ress that he wishes to chronicle in the "rich little history" (340) of his development, to recount that story would be to rewrite the past from the point of view of the present and thus sacrifice the authenticating double vision which is, for James, the only way that one's noncoinci-dence with one's past traces can be accurately measured. To replace double vision with retrospection is, for James, to express only who one is now. The startling encounter with a past self, the unpredictability of a relation that allows the present self an unremembered, necessary, and spontaneous view both of the artist he once was and the artist who he now is, can be described as a general phenomenon but cannot be spe-cifically narrated. Autobiography and self-knowledge are thus at odds for James. To tell a tale of one's artistic growth is to eliminate the expe-riential disjunction by which the past self remains, as James puts it, a "*living* affair" (342; James's emphasis).[45]

The Prefaces suggest that the self-knowledge that is falsified through retrospective autobiography *can* be consummated, however, in literary criticism; the power of the art work to objectify artistic consciousness through the terms of literary representation makes artistic self-knowledge something witnessed rather than narrated, a "watched renewal" rather than an "accepted repetition" (Prefaces, 345). James's encounter with his past self is made possible, after all, by his belief that an art work freezes artistic consciousness in a historical present: a novel counts as the "very record and mirror of the general adventure of one's intelligence" (342). Personal details are ultimately irrelevant to James's conception of artistic identity because it is the art work that tells us about the life and not the reverse. To judge the art work is to grasp the essence of the person: "The 'taste' of the poet is, at bottom and so far as the poet in him prevails over everything else, his active sense of life: in accordance with which truth to keep one's hand on it is to hold the silver clue to the whole labyrinth of his consciousness" (340). Indeed, the novel theory that James sketches in the Prefaces seems intended in part as a counterforce to the autobiograph-ical impulses aroused by the process of revision: James insists that the nov-els, and the past selves who wrote them, possess their own life so that he can shield them from autobiographical translation and collapse.[46]

---

[45] Eve Sedgwick has recently interpreted James's personification of the past as a past self to be indicative of a psychological tendency that she believes to be com-patible with contemporary theories of the "Inner Child" ("Queer," 8).

[46] As Jerome McGann puts it, "for James, the textual changes in the New York edition do not register a rewriting but a rereading. They are signs of an interpreta-

James's belief in a stable referent, the identity of the artistic subject that the artist attempts to represent, gives him a fixed standard by which to judge the artistic consciousness that is manifested in the "terms" of novelistic expression. Later in the Preface, the double "tracks" of his past and present consciousnesses metamorphose into an "immense array of terms, perceptional and expressional, that . . . in sentence, passage and page, simply looked over the heads of the standing terms—or perhaps rather, like alert winged creatures, perched on those diminished summits and aspired to clearer air" (Prefaces, 339). If James can measure his artistic growth by the distance between his past terms of expression and his present terms of perception, these terms are measurably distinct not because of some change in James but because of the terms' variable relation to the ideal artistic subject that is their referent.[47] It is this separation of terms and referent, moreover, and not some continuity between past and present authorial selves, that allows James to imagine that his works can be revised without being changed. Revision, James declares with deliberate unconventionality, does not create new "material"; it simply unearths "the buried, the latent life of a past composition." All that James needs to perform the resurrection of his subject to a life that he had not fully visualized before is a faith in the "good stuff" of the art work, which calls out to him, like Tinkerbell, with the plea, " 'Actively believe in us and then you'll see!' " (341).[48]

Yet however much James may insist that his revisions demonstrate the original as well as ongoing alterity of the objects whose interest generated his novels, the expressions of autobiographical desire at the beginning and end of the Prefaces do nevertheless threaten to foreclose some of the interest of James's novels as James defines that interest, insofar as the desire for autobiography suggests a more exclusive, projec-

---

tive move, a commentary ('close notes') which he is making upon his own text—the signs of what his further 'experience' has revealed to him about the meaning of his original writing. . . . James's texts change under the pressure of events, but the changes are not essential alterations; they are revelations—clarifications—of what was always and originally true" ("Revision," 95).

[47] As Hillis Miller notes, the process of coming to critical self-consciousness recorded here leads finally to the "terms" of literary criticism articulated in the Prefaces (*Ethics*, 120).

[48] For René Wellek, James's criticism is most about the achievement of sympathy: for James, Wellek believes, "the true method of criticism is always that of sympathy, of identification with the work of art" ("Henry James's Literary Theory," 298). This formulation allows us to see how what begins as self-dissociation ends up providing the opportunity of self-reidentification through "sympathy."

tive relation between James and his objects than he is elsewhere willing to entertain. The Prefaces were, after all, almost James's final bid to claim the title of Master, and they culminate in a paean to "the incomparable luxury of the artist," whose "literary deeds" always remain "traceable" in "attachment and reference" to the artist, even if they "stray" into "the desert." Throughout the Prefaces, as we have seen, James continually qualifies this personal "attachment and reference": the self he recaptures in his rereading is ideally only a window on the true object of interest; the artist's job is to make his consciousness available to the reader only so as to render his own sense of the prospect's depth and variety "contagious" (Preface, 345). Yet after the New York edition, James seems able to sustain this altruistic stance toward his novels only by abandoning fiction writing; in fact, he never completed another major work of fiction. In 1912, however, he did finish one volume of autobiography, *A Small Boy and Others*, and left a second volume, *Notes of a Son and Brother*, uncompleted at his death. Having discovered that the perfection of art lay in reading rather than writing, in self-apprehension rather than self-expression, in literary criticism rather than literary production, and having in the Prefaces fulfilled that critical vision, James had, as it were, theorized himself out of the art of writing novels.

Theory from the Reader's Point of View

While the whole thrust of James's point-of-view philosophy is, as we have seen, to deprivilege the novelist as a knower by representing the novel as a window from which the reader as well as the author could appreciate the interesting, ultimately unfathomable object before them, the emergence of novel theory from the Prefaces caused subsequent theorists to wonder how and if James's aesthetic principles could be detached from the context of authorial self-consciousness.[49] Could Jame-

---

[49] See Weinstein, *Henry James and the Requirements of the Imagination*, for an example of how a Jamesian criticism might be pragmatically rather than theoretically derived. Weinstein finds in James not a Lubbockian system but an authorization for an "eclectic" interpretive practice, one rooted in the subjective apprehension of the object, now the literary object of James's own novels: "If the reader senses a subjective and recurrent emphasis on a certain locale within the larger Jamesian domain, I can only answer that literary criticism is always in large part subjective and that to my mind this is the essential Henry James. Though the critic's honor depends upon the questioning and 'objectifying' process to which he submits his insights, to forgo those insights invites even deeper peril" (7).

sian theory be applied by someone other than James, and to works that James had not written? For R. P. Blackmur, James's description of the art work as an independent whole became the basis for claiming that a similarly autonomous work of literary criticism lay embedded in the Prefaces: as Blackmur argues in his 1934 Introduction to the Prefaces, James was right to think that the Prefaces "made an essay in general criticism which had an interest and a being aside from any connection with his own work" (Prefaces, viii). Yet the general applicability of the Prefaces as theory comes at a certain cost to the reader in Blackmur's account, who according to Blackmur must abjectly embrace James's self-sufficient wisdom without criticism: "All a commentator can do is to indicate by example and a little analysis, by a kind of provisional reasoned index, how the contents of his essay may be made more available" ("Introduction," viii).

Historians of Anglo-American novel theory have treated Percy Lubbock as the first and most faithful of James's "codifiers."[50] And indeed,

[50] Critics generally regard Lubbock's theoretical contribution as an extension of his avowed discipleship toward James. Millicent Bell describes the *Craft* as the "skilful drawing forth into theory James's technical principles" (*Edith Wharton*, 106). Schorer similarly praises Lubbock as having no idea of his own other than to do justice to James's ideas: "James was already dead for sixteen years before the flag was officially raised in Percy Lubbock's *The Craft of Fiction*, the first systematization in criticism of James's own methods and insights into method" ("Foreword," xii). Carroll refers to Lubbock as James's "most (too) faithful follower" (*Subject*, 51).

Some critics believe that what Lubbock brought to James—systematization—in fact made Lubbock's the superior contribution. John Aldridge (1952), for example, describes James's thoughts about fiction as "piecemeal" and "random" and credits Lubbock with "elevat[ing] the products of both James's critical and his creative sensibility to the status of a closely reasoned esthetic of literary form" (*Critiques*, 3). Aldridge goes on to quote Allen Tate, who declared Lubbock "successful in the same sense, and to no less degree than the famous lecture notes on the Greek drama taken down by an anonymous student at the Lyceum in the fourth century B.C." (3). Allen Tate also credits *Craft* as being "very nearly a model of critical procedure" ("Techniques," 32), an opinion voiced earlier by Pelham Edgar (1933), who credits Lubbock with setting out the "constituent elements of fiction—the bricks and mortar so to speak of the novelist's trade" (*Art*, 7). Phyllis Bentley (1947) credits Lubbock as being the only person before herself to attempt "an analysis of fictional narrative" (*Some Observations*, 3).

Booth praises Lubbock for being "clearer and more systematic than James" (*Rhetoric*, 24) but, like Carroll, believes that Lubbock's theory is ultimately inferior to James's. James E. Miller seeks to rescue James from Lubbock but ends up, in turn, producing his own Blackmurian type of systematization of the Prefaces: indexing rather than theorizing.

See Daniel Fogel, *Covert Relations*, for the biographical details of Lubbock's

so devoted is Lubbock's *Craft of Fiction* (1921) to the work of the Master that it constantly parrots not only James's ideas but his illustrative metaphors and idiosyncratic diction too.[51] This posture of abjection seems to hold even when Lubbock turns from James to other novelists—for instance, to Tolstoy:

> Tolstoy and his critic [stand] side by side, surveying the free and formless expanse of the world of life. The critic has nothing to say; he waits, looking to Tolstoy for guidance. And Tolstoy, with the help of some secret of his own, which is his genius, does not hesitate for an instant. His hand is plunged into the scene, he lifts out of it great fragments, right and left, ragged masses of life torn from their setting; he selects. And upon these trophies he sets to work with the full force of his imagination; he detects their significance, he disengages and throws aside whatever is accidental and meaningless; he re-makes them in conditions that are never known in life, conditions in which a thing is free to grow according to its own law, expressing itself unhindered; he liberates and completes. And then, upon all this new life—so like the old and yet so different, *more* like the old, as one may say, than the old ever had the chance of being—upon all this life that is now so much more intensely living than before, Tolstoy directs the skill of his art; he distributes it in a single, embracing design; he orders and disposes. And thus the critic receives his guidance, and *his* work begins. (*Craft*, 18; Lubbock's emphasis)

Unlike the "secret" of the interesting object that in James's paradigm the artist devoted himself to discovering, the "secret" of the author represents for Lubbock an unknowable motivation; authorial interest is something the reader takes for granted, believes in rather than tries to

---

friendship with James, especially the efforts of Lubbock during James's lifetime to gain for the "master" the critical appreciation that Lubbock felt he deserved. Fogel mentions that even Virginia Woolf called Lubbock "a devout Jacobean," and records her refusal to join the James fan club that he headed (83–84).

See Scholes and Kellogg, *Nature*, 272, and Michael Anesko, *"Friction,"* 4, for other references to Lubbock as James's "disciple." Leon Edel quotes from a letter that indicates James's own appreciation of the mutual benefit derived from Lubbock's devotion: commenting on an anonymous review that Lubbock published on James's work, James declared that the article "does that gentle and thoroughly literary and finely critical young man great honour, I think—but it does me no less" (*Henry James*, 420).

[51] Although James is everywhere invoked in *The Craft of Fiction* through Lubbock's paraphrasing of the Prefaces, he is not explicitly cited until page 110—and then he is named only so that Lubbock can distinguish his own contribution from the master's: "Picture and drama, therefore, I use because Henry James used them in discussing his own novels, when he reviewed them all in his later years; but I use them, I must add, in a rather more extended sense than he did" (110).

explain. The critic who stands "side by side" with the author, as if an equal partner in the task of novel writing, actually "has nothing to say." Instead, he looks "for guidance" to the author, who like a better God draws upon his own inscrutable "genius" to make life anew. If the sphere of labor for the critic in Lubbock's scheme seems profoundly limited by the author's power to shape life, it appears even more restricted when one considers the author's effect on the life he has shaped. The author, claims Lubbock, "liberates" and "completes," so that "a thing is free to grow according to its own law, expressing itself unhindered": with an almighty creator on the one hand and a self-expressive creation on the other, what "work" is left for the critic?

Ironically, however, Lubbock's deification of the novelist already constitutes an innovation to James's theory. In the description of Tolstoy, for instance, Lubbock's artist does not stop as James's had to wonder at the interesting object before him; rather, "his hand is plunged into the scene," he tears "ragged masses of life . . . from their setting," "and upon these trophies he sets to work with the full force of his imagination."[52] So vigorously does the artist intervene in "life," and so commandingly does he seem to master the reader along with life, that his subjective judgment cannot help but play a greater role in Lubbock's novel theory than it had in James's. Most literary historians have claimed the opposite about Lubbock: they tend to regard Lubbock's fa-

---

[52] Lubbock's description of Tolstoy seems an agglomeration of two different Prefaces. He combines the material metaphors from *Spoils* (quoted above) with the discussion of mastery in the Preface to *Daisy Miller*, from which I now quote:

> The simplest truth about a human entity, a situation, a relation, an aspect of life, however small, on behalf of which the claim to charmed attention is made, strains ever, under one's hand, more intensely, *most* intensely, to justify that claim; strains ever, as it were, toward the uttermost end or aim of one's meaning or of its own numerous connexions; struggles at each step, and in defiance of one's raised admonitory finger, fully and completely to express itself. Any art of representation is, I make out, a controlled and guarded acceptance, in fact a perfect economic mastery, of that conflict: the general sense of the expansive, the explosive principle in one's material thoroughly noted, adroitly allowed to flush and colour and animate the disputed value, but with its other appetites and treacheries, its characteristic space-hunger and space-cunning, kept down. (278; James's emphasis)

Significantly, James's artist does not seek trophies; it is not "life" he seeks to master, but the truthful representation of life through art. James's acute sense of the artistic subject as a subjectivity leads him to describe its representation as a negotiation between, on the one hand, the subject's irreducible and limitless identity and, on the other, the novel's generic identity as a limited and designed art form.

mous declaration that "the art of fiction does not begin until the novel-ist thinks of his story as a matter to be *shown*, to be so exhibited that it will tell itself" (*Craft*, 62; Lubbock's emphasis), as proof that Lubbock believes the novelist should strive above all to be objective about his subject matter. But when Lubbock insists that the novelist show rather than tell, he only means that the novelist should represent her judgments *indirectly* rather than expressly, like Flaubert:

> Flaubert does not announce his opinion in so many words, and thence it has been argued that the opinions of a really artistic writer ought not to appear in his story at all. But of course with every touch that he lays on his subject he must show what he thinks of it; his subject, indeed, the book which he finds in his selected fragment of life, is purely the representation of his view, his judgment, his opinion of it. The famous "impersonality" of Flaubert and his kind lies only in the greater tact with which they express their feelings— dramatizing them, embodying them in living form, instead of stating them directly. (67–68)

Rather than thinking through his subject, like the appreciative Jamesian artist, Lubbock's author writes a novel so he can show "what he thinks." In Lubbock's novel theory, "view" has become another word for "opinion" and "judgment."[53]

But Lubbock's stake in merely the illusion of objectivity makes him paradoxically more rigorous than James had been about excluding the novelist from the novel. James objects to Trollope's addresses to the reader on the contingent grounds of their content; it was what Trollope said and not *that* he said that disturbed James. For James, Trollope vio-lates the novelist's role as truth teller by insisting that his representative

---

[53] Lubbock's narrow understanding of indirection as having to do with authorial opinion contrasts with James's far more varied use of the term. For example, James frequently describes indirection as a technical resource that *as technique* contributes to the "value" of artistic representation. As he says in the Preface to *The Spoils of Poynton*:

> Circumventions of difficulty . . . are precisely the finest privilege of the crafts-man, who, to be worth his salt, and master of *any* contrived harmony, must take no tough technical problem for insoluble. These technical subterfuges and sub-tleties, these indirectly-expressed values, kept indirect in a higher interest, made subordinate to some general beauty, some artistic intention that can give an ac-count of itself, what are they after all but one of the nobler parts of our amuse-ment? (137; James's emphasis)

Compare the difference between James's emphasis on a "noble" artistic intention enhanced by technique with Lubbock's formulation of an authorial "judgment" of the subject that is surreptitiously veiled by technique.

practice is only "'make believe'" ("Art," 5). James comments,

> Such a betrayal of a sacred office seems to me, I confess, a terrible crime; it is what I mean by the attitude of apology, and it shocks me every whit as much in Trollope as it would have shocked me in Gibbon or Macaulay. It implies that the novelist is less occupied in looking for the truth (the truth, of course I mean, that he assumes, the premises that we must grant him, whatever they may be) than the historian, and in doing so it deprives him at a stroke of all his standing room. (6)

By contrast, Lubbock objects to Thackeray's first-person references absolutely, no matter what Thackeray says. Resisting James's belief that the artist "can never be responsible *enough*" for his work, Lubbock argues that the successful novelist

> pushes his responsibility further and further away from himself. The fiction that he devises is ultimately his; but it looks poor and thin if he openly claims it as his, or at any rate it becomes much more substantial as soon as he fathers it upon another. This is not *my* story, says the author; you know nothing of me; it is the story of this man or woman in whose words you have it, and he or she is a person whom you *can* know; and you may see for yourselves how the matter arose, the man and woman being such as they are; it all hangs together, and it makes a solid and significant piece of life. (*Craft*, 147; Lubbock's emphasis)

Claiming a novel as one's own makes it look "poor and thin," a partial and subjective fantasy rather than "a solid and significant piece of life." If anyone is to speak for himself in the Lubbockian novel, it must be a character, whose partiality is subordinated to the objective and coherent whole of the "piece" that paradoxically "hangs together."

For James, as we have seen, the operation of point of view within the novel served to personify the activity of wonder; James believed that, once objectified as a characterological point of view, the representation of wonder would in turn stimulate both authorial and readerly interest, turning the art work into a generator of value. For Lubbock, who associates point of view with subjective judgment, the operation of point of view in the novel hinges upon a relationship that is relatively incidental in James's theory: the relation of the narrator to the story. As Lubbock puts it, "the whole intricate question of method, in the craft of fiction, I take to be governed by the question of the point of view—the question of the relation in which the narrator stands to the story" (*Craft*, 251). James certainly distinguishes between the narrator and the author, but he does so in order to claim that he has *renounced* "the mere muffled majesty of irresponsible 'authorship'" (Prefaces, 328): telling the story through "somebody's impression of it" multiplies the sources of stimulation for the reader—"the terms of [the narrator's] access to [the story] and estimate of it contributing thus by some fine little law to intensification of interest" (327).[54] Lubbock, however, maintains that a narrator is the most convenient way for an author to hide his shaping consciousness, and Lubbock's fears about the partiality of point of view lead him to prefer a narrator-puppet who appears to step aside just as the author does: in a successful novel, writes Lubbock, a narrator "creates the picture,"

> but for us who look on, reading the book, there is nothing in the picture to make us perpetually turn from it and face towards the man in the foreground, watching for the effect it may produce in him. Attention is all concentrated in the life that he remembers and evokes. He himself, indeed, though the fact of his presence is very clear to us, tends to remain in shadow; it is as though he leant from a window, surveying the world, his figure outlined against the lighted square, his features not very distinctly discerned by the reader within. (*Craft*, 136)[55]

As in the Prefaces, a character frames a "window" for the reader, but now the character is a narrator who must seem to be absent from the window in order for the reader to see through it.[56]

Ideally, Lubbock thinks, this double insulation of the author from the reader will so disguise the author's judgments as to make the story seem "to tell itself": according to Lubbock, Maupassant is such an expert at impersonal narration that nothing in his stories "reminds us of his presence. He is behind us, out of sight, out of mind; the story occupies us, the moving scene, and nothing else" (*Craft*, 113). A novelist thus completely hidden, however, seems almost too wily for his own good. He

---

[54] Again, the difference between Lubbock and James is Lubbock's understanding of indirection as a means of authorial disguise versus James's understanding of indirection as an aesthetic good (see note 53).

[55] At times Lubbock states that there are two acceptable points of view for the reader: the reader either "faces towards the story-teller and listens to him" or "turns towards the story and watches it" (*Craft*, 111). But in fact Lubbock consistently prefers the second perspective to the first, as we can see when he invidiously compares Thackeray and Meredith to James: "Author and hero, Thackeray and Esmond, Meredith and Harry Richmond, have given their various accounts of emotional and intellectual adventure; but they might do more, they might bring the facts of the adventure upon the scene and leave them to make their impression" (156).

[56] While Lubbock would like in principle to differentiate a "narrator" from either an "author" or a "character," in practice he often blurs these distinctions.

may succeed in making his view "more substantial as soon as he fathers it upon another," but then it is the other now carrying his idea, and not the author, who attracts the reader's interest. According to Lubbock, Becky Sharpe in *Vanity Fair* lacks the "solidity" and "objectivity" of Beatrix in *Henry Esmond* because Becky has only the author to characterize her: "Thackeray's language about her does not carry the same weight as Esmond's about Beatrix, because nobody knows where Thackeray is, or what his relation may be to Becky" (*Craft*, 127). The author is no longer a voice of authority in the novel; he has become merely a distraction: "it is much more satisfactory to know who the story-teller is, and to see him as a part of the story, than to be deflected away from the book by the author, an arbitrary, unmeasurable, unappraisable factor" (140). Even a narrator such as Esmond, whom Lubbock describes as the thinnest of disguises for authorial opinion, amounts to more significant a presence in his novel than Thackeray does:

> It does not matter that Esmond's tone in his story is remarkably like Thackeray's in the stories that *he* tells; in Esmond's case the tone has a meaning in the story, is part of it, whereas in the other case it is related only to Thackeray, and Thackeray is in the void. (128; Lubbock's emphasis)[57]

The distance between one novelist lost in the void and another deifically surveying the free and formless expanse of life is less marked than one would think. In Lubbock's admiring eyes, Tolstoy treats masses of life as his trophies, but he also allows things to grow according to their own laws: even in the case of the successful novelist, Lubbock cannot decide whether the novel bespeaks the mastery of the novelist or the freedom of his characters, because the novelist proves his omnipotence by liberating his characters.[58] The *deus absconditus* of his fictional universe, the successful novelist thus seems to inhabit the same void as Thackeray does. Or rather, since Thackeray "flourishes the fact that the point of view" in his fiction "is his own, not to be confounded with that

---

[57] Lubbock's obsession with the issue of authorial disguise blinds him to the flagrant oddity of Thackeray's narrative management in *Henry Esmond*. His exclusive concern with the palpability of authorial intrusions into the fictional world leads him to ignore the strange shifts from third to first person within Esmond's narration that destabilize mimetic convention.

[58] The power relations between character and author are phrased starkly by Norman Friedman in his Lubbockian-influenced account of point of view: "When an author surrenders in fiction, he does so in order to conquer" ("Point of View," 142).

of anybody in the book," Tolstoy is actually more irrelevant to the reader than Thackeray is: "Over the whole of one side" of Thackeray's work, after all, Lubbock claims that "there is an inconclusive look, something that draws the eye away from the book itself, into space" (*Craft*, 115). Thackeray, it seems, is at once insecure about the viability of his characters and also jealous for our attention: "It is as though he never quite trusted his men and women when he had to place things entirely in their care, standing aside to let them act; he wanted to intervene continually" (103). Thanks to Lubbock's insistence that the author merely disguise his partial views and so centripetally focus attention on the characters instead of the author, Lubbock now praises the author who *refrains* from imposing his "arbitrary" will on his characters: with the storyteller "*in* the story," "nothing is now imported into the story from without; it is self-contained, it has no associations with anyone beyond its circle" (251–52; Lubbock's emphasis).

This reduction of the novelist to an antisocial presence in his own novel stands James's conception of authorial altruism on its head. Anxious to shake off "the muffled majesty of irresponsible 'authorship,'" James decided that he must participate in the oppressed society of his characters: "I get down into the arena and do my best to live and breathe and rub shoulders and converse with the persons engaged in the struggle that provides for the others in the circling tiers the entertainment of the great game" (Prefaces, 328). Only when James believed that he had subjected himself to the point of view of his characters did he feel that he had furthered "that most exquisite of all good causes[:] the appeal to variety, the appeal to incalculability, the appeal to a high refinement and a handsome wholeness of effect" (329). Lubbock, by contrast, thinks that the novelist must be walled off from the society of his characters in order for that society to achieve a wholeness of effect; but, significantly, this same restriction does not apply to the reader. On the contrary: Lubbock's relegation of the author to the void is what finally opens up employment for the passively admiring reader. The reader's job is to bring a novel's characters to the life that the novelist must not appear to give them—as with Clarissa:

> It is so easy to construct the idea of the exquisite creature, that she seems to step from the pages of her own accord; I, as I read, am aware of nothing but that a new acquaintance is gradually becoming better and better known to me. No conscious effort is needed to make a recognizable woman of her, though in fact I am fitting a multitude of small details together, as I proceed to give her the body and mind that she presently possesses. (8)

"The reader of a novel" is thus not only "himself a novelist" (17), but also a more sociable creator than the original author.[59]

Yet if the exiling of the author from the charmed "circle" of his novel gives the reader the elbow room for this creative task, what in Lubbock's theory gives him the right to undertake it? In other words, how will the reader's intervention in a story that properly "has no associations with anyone beyond its circle" not render the novel partial and subjective rather than objective and self-contained, just as an author's intervention would? Lubbock answers this question by tackling what he considers to be a more fundamental problem for the reader: how can one read a novel objectively, as a critic should, if its form is—like all literary forms—physically inaccessible?[60] Unlike sculpture or painting, whose plasticity, according to Lubbock, makes them immediately available to the senses as objects of study, the true form of the novel does not seem to be available for direct inspection. As Lubbock puts it, the critic "cannot lay his finger upon a single one of the effects to which he refers" (11). How then can *any* relation of the reader to the novel avoid subjective partiality? "For criticizing the craft of fiction," Lubbock complains, "we have no other language than that which has been devised for the material arts; and though we may feel that to talk of the colours and values and perspective of a novel is natural and legitimate, yet these are only metaphors, after all, that cannot be closely pressed" (11).[61] In short, Lubbock appears to admit that the objectivity of the novel is just as illusory in regard to the reader as it had first seemed in regard to the novelist.

Revealingly, the difference Lubbock sees between the plastic and lit-

---

[59] The responsibility that Lubbock deflects from the actual author becomes accredited to the reader: "The reader of a novel—by which I mean the critical reader—is himself a novelist; he is the maker of a book which may or may not please his taste when it is finished, but of a book for which he must take his own share of the responsibility" (*Craft*, 17).

[60] In discussing the general problem of literary form, Lubbock initially erases generic distinctions, designating all forms equally as "the book."

[61] See Abrams, *Mirror*, esp. 33–34 and 50–51, for the poetics tradition that informs Lubbock's grounding assumption that what is peculiar to the literary arts can be gleaned by comparing them to the plastic arts. Raymond Williams offers a sociohistorical explanation of why the theorization of literature in terms of craft labor enjoyed new popularity in particular cultural circumstances. Williams argues that, by imagining his labor as a craft, the artist living in a capitalist society made a "claim for a significant meaning of work—that of using human energy on material for an autonomous purpose—which was being radically displaced and denied, in most kinds of production" (*Marxism*, 161).

erary arts does not encourage him to question the premise that dictates his inquiry—he never doubts that it makes as much sense to talk about the form of "the book" as it does to talk about the form of a statue; and it certainly never occurs to him to turn the problem around and wonder if the "form" of a statue really is any more present to the viewer than the form of a book. Instead of abandoning the metaphors of plasticity that raise such phenomenological difficulties for him, which in Lubbock's mind would mean abandoning his quest for objectivity, Lubbock searches for a way in which the book could *literally* possess the "definite" materiality of a painting or a sculpture (*Craft*, 11). The literary object may, he concludes, be sighted after all—"perhaps it can be approached, perhaps the book can be seen, a little more closely in one way than in another" (12)—but the task requires us to complicate our commonsense notion of empirical sense impressions. For the book becomes visible and also concrete to the reader, Lubbock claims, only when it has first been internalized in the reader's brain:

> [The critic] must know how to handle the stuff which is continually forming in his mind while he reads; he must be able to recognize its fine variations and to take them all into account. Nobody can work in material of which the properties are unfamiliar, and a reader who tries to get possession of a book with nothing but his appreciation of the life and the ideas and the story in it is like a man who builds a wall without knowing the capacities of wood and clay and stone. Many different substances, as distinct to the practiced eye as stone and wood, go into the making of a novel, and it is necessary to see them for what they are. So only is it possible to use them aright, and to find, when the volume is closed, that a complete, coherent, appraisable book remains in the mind. (20)

The language of construction here is recognizably Jamesian: taking his interesting object as the foundation for his labors, James's artist, we recall, "only builds and piles high, lays together the blocks quarried in the deeps of his imagination and on his personal premises." But for Lubbock it is the act of reading, not writing, that concretizes; the physical "volume" and the actual words on its pages are no more than the ephemera from which the reader builds the solid mental "book itself, as the form of a statue is the statue itself" (24).[62] At times, Lubbock seems

[62] To emphasize the reader's active role, Lubbock follows Emerson in calling critical reading "creative reading." Yet, although explicitly derived from Emerson, Lubbock's social formalist version of "creative reading" could not be further from Emerson's transcendental philosophy. For Emerson, creative reading diminishes the distance between author and reader; when he claims that "one nature wrote and the

to long for some more direct and sufficient means of communicating the author's views to the reader than the written word: "The author does his part," Lubbock appears to lament, "but he cannot transfer his book like a bubble into the brain of the critic" (17). But even if the author could transfer his book like a bubble, this utopian mode of communication would hardly seem a match, in Lubbock's eyes, for the robustly material literary object constructed by the reader on his own "personal premises." In Lubbock's theory, then, what begins as readerly abjection, the reader's desire to make the author's point of view his own, results in readerly empowerment: the reader's mind, filled by the book he constructs, makes from the nothing that is his own point of view the something that is "his" book.

The further advantage for Lubbock of the novel's materializing only in the reader's brain—a constructivist theory of point of view that we might call noetic materialism—is that it gives the reader a more intimate and yet also less intrusive contact with the novel's characters than the author can achieve. The experience of reading *The Ambassadors*, for instance, leads Lubbock to maintain that it is "as though the reader himself were at the window, and as though the window opened straight into the depths of Strether's conscious existence" (*Craft*, 146). This direct access to the character's mind makes reading a novel a more powerful experience for Lubbock than watching a play: "Instead of a man upon the stage, concealing and betraying his thought, we watch the thought itself, the hidden thing, as it twists to and fro in his brain—watch it without any other aid to understanding but such as its own manner of bearing may supply" (157). But what sense does it make to claim that the reader can see "the thought itself" of a character, "without any other aid to understanding" besides the self-representation of the thought? Lubbock must mean that, once the reader internalizes the novel "in his brain," a character's thought becomes identical to the reader's thought. This immediacy of the character explains why Lubbock believes that, with "no conscious effort," he can discover in reading "that a new acquaintance is gradually becoming better and better known to me" (8); and it also explains why, unlike the author who "must break into the privacy of his characters and open their minds to us" (74), Lubbock be-

---

same reads" ("The American Scholar"), he is describing the reader's recognition of a common soul, a spiritual nature beyond particular individuals. For Lubbock, the identification of author and reader is in the service of the mutual construction of literary form, a project whose end—"to get in touch with the book as nearly as may be" (*Craft*, 13)—forgoes Emersonian spiritualism for Lubbockian materialism.

lieves that the reader does not have to violate the autonomy of characters in order to apprehend them fully. Treating the novel as an objective form peopled by independent characters whose society he can engage without the arbitrary intervention of his own subjectivity, Lubbock has elaborated James's philosophy of point of view—and the appreciation of alterity that undergirds it—into the novel theory that I call "social formalism." And behind the veil of his abject devotion to James, Lubbock has also quietly lifted the crown of altruism from the author's head and placed it on the reader's.

2

Vision as Voice

Wayne Booth, Gérard Genette, and Roland Barthes

In most books, the *I*, or first person, is omitted; in this it will be retained; that, in respect to egotism, is the main difference. We commonly do not remember that it is, after all, always the first person that is speaking.
—Henry David Thoreau, *Walden* (1854)

IN THE SIXTIES and seventies, a generation of theorists set out to advance the study of the novel by ridding it of Lubbockian objectivism. After fifty years of Anglo-American adulation, Lubbock was suddenly under attack not just by Anglo-American critics but also by European thinkers working out of a philosophical tradition grounded in the specialized disciplines of phenomenology, hermeneutics, linguistics, and aesthetics. It is a testament to the widespread acceptance of Lubbock's version of Jamesian novel theory that French thinkers who comfortably fit into a continental genealogy that would include Hegel and Jakobson would feel compelled to count Lubbock and James as ancestors in the field of novel theory, even if the Anglo-American forefathers are cited only to be overthrown. Within a twelve-year period, three major theoretical works—Wayne C. Booth's *The Rhetoric of Fiction* (1961), Roland Barthes' *S/Z* (1970), and Gérard Genette's *Narrative Discourse* (1972)—positioned themselves against the conception of novelistic realism that had derived from James and Lubbock, been employed by influential practical critics such as Warren Beck and R. P. Blackmur, and extended by Cleanth Brooks and Robert Penn Warren in their *Understanding Fiction* (1943).[1] The important philosophical differences among Booth, Genette, and Barthes helped inspire, as we know, theoretical schools as distinct as neo-

---

[1] See Chapter 1, note 5, for an account of the persistence of James's influence on Anglo-American literary theory and criticism.

Aristotelianism, narratology, and deconstruction; but thinkers who otherwise had so much to disagree about nonetheless agreed on one thing: that a theoretical description of the novel could not advance until the Lubbockian mantra—"show, don't tell"—was laid to rest.

The attack on the aesthetics of vision was first of all a challenge to what I have called Lubbock's noetic materialism. As we have seen, Lubbock understands reading to be an act of imaginative materialization. The words of a book convey to the reader the "form" of the novel. The reader's job is to label the parts and reconstruct the whole. Booth, Genette, and Barthes all begin their attack on Lubbockian "showing" by insisting that fiction should be understood not as a plastic object but as first and foremost a linguistic practice. The reader "sees" the form of the novel and "sees" the world of the novel only by *reading*; language, as they have helped us to learn, is not a vehicle or "bubble" transporting authorial vision, but a semiotic activity; the various terms devised by each theorist to describe literary representation—Booth's "rhetoric," Genette's "discourse," and Barthes' "writing"—indicate the different ways that each understands what the linguistic alternative to the Lubbockian aesthetic "object" might be.

Yet although the move from understanding the novel as a picture or an object to understanding it as a linguistic activity certainly is part of the more general theoretical turn from modernism to postmodernism, we have recently begun to appreciate how resolutely modern certain language philosophies can be.[2] As Julia Kristeva has said, classic semiotics shares the same "epistemological foundations" of the Cartesian subject.[3] More specifically in the realm of novel theory, David Carroll's pathbreaking study *The Subject in Question* (1987) has compellingly shown how, despite its critique of individualism, "structuralism perpetuates the premises of phenomenology" (26).[4] The difference between

---

[2] For example, Boyd Tonkin declares that "one of the commonest English-language responses to [Roland Barthes'] celebrity sees in it a belated replay of the professional reforms achieved by Richards, Empson and American New Criticism, but delayed for thirty years by the inflexibility of French academic life" ("Between Difference and Doctrine," 102).

[3] Kristeva declares of Saussurian structuralism and its offshoots in U.S. generative grammar and in French theories of discourse that its "speaking subject . . . is nothing other than the phenomenological subject which Husserl defined as a transcendental ego" ("Speaking Subject," 211–12).

[4] See Coward and Ellis for a Lacanian-Marxist critique of structural linguistics. They regard Saussure as the source of the problem, especially his belief that "thought . . . pre-exist[s] language" (*Language*, 23).

phenomenology and structuralism is, as Carroll astutely points out, less a matter of redefining what constitutes subjectivity and more a matter of relocating where the subject is to be found; Carroll's critique of Benveniste pertains to structuralist narrative theory generally: "The philosophical concept of being and the concept of the subject associated with it have been banished only to be reactivated within *discours*, as attributes of a present of *discours* which is dependent on a speech act" (23). For structuralism the subject remains a coherent and singular consciousness possessing a distinctive point of view; but rather than being conceptualized as the origin of language, the phenomenological subject is situated *within* language (25).[5] Carroll's critique of structuralism points the way to a larger philosophical understanding of the commonalities between what we might call the first wave of Anglo-American novel theory—represented by James and Lubbock—and the second wave—represented by Booth, Genette, and Barthes. As Carroll helps us see, and as I will attempt to explain, Booth's, Genette's, and Barthes' respective attacks on Lubbock's aesthetics of vision (that the novel should show rather than tell) reaffirm James's deeper philosophical assumptions about the novel's capacity to represent identity: first, the Jamesian definition of identity as point of view; and second, the Jamesian belief that the novel allows point of view to be authentically expressed, legibly represented, and thus rendered optimally interpretable for a discerning reader. The name the second wave of novel theorists give to the Jamesian novelistic subject is "voice."[6]

[5] Psychoanalysis has, of course, inspired a long and important countertradition. See Bersani, *Future*, esp. 286–315, for a critique of the unified phenomenological subject, especially as it pertains to narrative. See Butler, *Gender Trouble*, esp. 1–34, for a general social theory based upon the un-unified subject.

[6] See Chatman, *Coming to Terms*, for an important skeptical account of the anthropomorphism in Genette's model. Chatman asks, "How affective is the metaphor of a 'voice speaking' when applied to shown or even 'impersonally' told narratives?" (118).

In a review essay of 1983 that surveys the burgeoning field of narrative theory, Jonathan Culler challenges the dominant trend of narrative scholarship by questioning the passion for personification. Specifically he asks why we need to think of narrators as persons: "The more sophisticated we become in treating discursive details as reflections of the attitudes and assumptions of narrators, the more we encourage the notion that to interpret fiction is above all to identify in all detail the person who speaks it" ("Problems," 5). Culler goes on to call the "strategy of naturalization and anthropomorphism" a "continuation of fiction-making: dealing with details by imagining a narrator; telling a story about a narrator and his/her response so as to make sense of them" (6).

With "voice," the novel theorists of the second wave mean to demonstrate that the opposition between showing and telling is moot: showing cannot be better than telling, because showing is not an alternative to telling; in literature, it is simply an illusion produced by telling. There can be no objective representation, in other words, because language necessarily reflects—or, for Barthes, constitutes—the subjectivity of the agent who produces it. "Voice" thus designates for the second wave the authentic self-expression of identity that is integral to and inevitable in any act of novelistic communication.

But as I have demonstrated, James's understanding of point of view is completely compatible with this definition of voice. And we know as well that the problem of mediation is central to James's thinking about the novel: James's hermeneutics of point of view originates in his attempt to chart the operation of authorial interest; his account of what I am calling the novelistic subject is forged in and through his sense of point of view as nothing but mediated interpretation. Why does the second wave miss the importance of mediation in the origins of Anglo-American novel theory? To begin with, their critique of the aesthetics of

---

What Culler doesn't realize is that this fiction-making in the service of naturalization has come about precisely in attempting to delineate the categories that, in his earlier "Foreword" to *Narrative Discourse,* he had extolled as the neutral mechanics of fiction. As I will show, his praise of Genette for leading semiology beyond "the structure and codes which Barthes and Todorov studied" to the ways that these structures and codes "must be taken up and organized by a narrative" (8) results in Genette's naturalization of fictional agents. Culler himself in the "Foreword" authorizes the philosophical grounding for this tendency:

> Categories for the description of narrative discourse are in fact based on what we may for convenience call a model of the real world. According to this model, events necessarily take place both in a particular order and a definable number of times. A speaker has certain kinds of information about events and lacks other kinds. He either experienced them or he did not, and generally he stands in a definable relationship to the events he recounts. (12)

The question of the narrator's "experience" and "stance" is exactly what leads Genette not only to anthropomorphize the narrator but to collapse the difference between fiction and other forms of discourse.

See Banfield for a model of fiction that argues more rigorously for a nonnaturalized reading of fictional agents. "While there have been numerous attempts to submit narrative to the communication paradigm by positing a narrator addressing a reader for every text, once communication is defined nontautologically in rigorous linguistic terms, this position cannot be maintained" (*Unspeakable Sentences,* 10). She adds, "The linguistic division between subjectivity and objectivity becomes possible only when the hold of the communicative intent over language guaranteed by the dominance of speech over writing is broken" (17).

vision becomes increasingly detached from James's and Lubbock's actual arguments: as we will find, although Booth positions his theory explicitly in relation to James and Lubbock, Genette credits Lubbock as the Anglo-American father of novel theory but does not specifically engage his work, and Barthes fails to name either James or Lubbock as novel theorists. As James is more and more conflated with and known by his Lubbockian legacy, and as Lubbock's work is itself reduced to the slogan "show don't tell," it becomes easier both to ignore and to reproduce the philosophical assumptions that guide the Prefaces and *The Craft of Fiction.*

And one of the primary assumptions that is reproduced by the second wave is the Jamesian belief that the activity of novelistic representation authentically "shows" the true character of human identity. The localized debate about mimetic illusion—that novelist practices of "realism" can only pretend to "show" an objective world—obscures the second wave's larger agreement with James that novels do indeed make visible the objective character of their tellers.

The second wave's philosophical interest in textual linguisticality thus fails to escape the more profound belief in objectivism that grounds James's and Lubbock's theories; but it does have significant ramifications for the conception of the "social" in the social formalist paradigm. According to the second wave, the novel tells the truth of human identity through its linguisticality—and the truth that is told by language upsets the assumption of radical individualism upon which James and Lubbock base their theories. While the dyadic structure of interpersonal relation (especially that between representer and represented) that is so crucial to James and Lubbock remains in force for Booth, Genette, and Barthes, the second wave theorists seek to identify a transpersonal agent—language—that conditions the possibility of these personal relations. Simply put, where James and Lubbock describe a social world generated and circumscribed by the agents of the text—author, novelistic "subject," characters, and readers—Booth, Genette, and Barthes look at the way these agents are in turn conditioned by, respectively, "rhetoric," "discourse," and "writing."

While the move from vision to voice in the theory of fiction thus accomplishes an important critique of individualism, the theorization of the social provided by the second wave is still, as I hope to show, in fact based on the same formalist logic that informed the work of James and Lubbock. For the second wave, language is beyond the individual, but it is still *in* the text. What is common to the social formalist tradition is the attempt to enforce alterity through the staying of mediation—and to appeal to the materiality of novels (whether construed as art, books, fictions, narratives, or language) as the means of delimitation and instantiation. The second wave's more extensive conceptualization of mediation and its more varied notions of materiality allow them to think of the intrinsicality of the "other" as compatible with some sort of group or collective identity. For the second wave, the represented other takes on what we might call a public character. Although Genette and Booth will, like Lubbock, continue to conceptualize alterity as a characterological issue (and thus participate more straightforwardly in an ethics of altruism), for Booth the "other" that the fiction writer seeks to represent is ultimately nothing less than the shared values of a social community; and for Barthes the "others" that are represented in texts are semiotic "codes," the source of subjectivity per se. As I hope to show, however, despite their innovative theories of language, their more sophisticated engagement with sociality, and the anti-humanism of at least two of the theorists in this group, the second wave reproduces an old-fashioned moral universe grounded in the virtue of the representing agent. Even as the second wave theorizes subjectivity as produced by forces beyond an individual's control, they continue to define the novelist by her power to make the right moral choice: a writer's effort to represent the other as other remains not just a good deed, but a deed that is determinate of the novelistic endeavor. And despite their critique of the Lubbockian dream of a novelistic world free from the traces of "telling," the second wave, no different from the first, prefers a teller who expresses right values by absenting himself; the appreciation of alterity remains negative capability: the ability to constitute and express one's own identity best through the act of representing an other (or others) as intrinsically different from oneself.

In studying the Jamesian legacy of the second wave, it makes sense to start with James's most self-conscious inheritor: Wayne C. Booth explicitly frames his argument in *The Rhetoric of Fiction* as a return to James. Booth sets out to rescue James from his objectivist interpreters, among whom he counts Percy Lubbock. But as I will show, Booth's return to James proves to be a recapitulation of the Lubbockian interpretation of James. Like Lubbock, Booth understands fictional form as not just the necessary but the strategic instantiation of authorial point of view. Booth intends his key theoretical term—"voice"—to highlight complexities of subjective mediation neglected by Lubbock, but ultimately his description of the crafty techniques that authors use to affect their readers is more Lubbockian than Jamesian. By contrast, Gérard Genette seems to open up a wholly new path in novel theory, positioning himself against not only the Anglo-American tradition in general but Booth in particular. Committed to the project of narratological description, Genette believes this task is wholly distinct from interpretation, not to mention ethics. Indeed, so committed is he to a scientific description of narrative that his quest for objectivity leads him to produce a model that seems hardly to admit subjects of any sort to analytic consideration. In *Narrative Discourse* narrative subjects are, famously, never considered in themselves but only as effects of verbs.[7] Yet even in a project this far removed from the spirit of James's hermeneutics of point of view, the Jamesian novelistic subject resurfaces. Genette's structuralist conception of reference leads him to attribute to narrative the same power to materialize subjective identity that James attributed to "art." And his conception of the structures that define the specific practice of reference in fictional texts leads him, as I will show, to posit a Lubbockian version of the ethical challenge posed for the tellers of fiction by the representation of characterological "voice."

While Genette himself would no doubt claim that the linguistic selves he describes in *Narrative Discourse* apply only to the realm of narrative representation and are not intended to be descriptions of subjectivity per se, his narratological project rests upon a structuralist conception of language and personhood that cannot be easily severed from real human subjects—a point that is vividly evidenced by Roland Barthes' engagement with structuralism in *S/Z*. Barthes famously invokes structuralism in order to explode it. His deconstruction of the difference between subject and object, as well as between writer and reader, seems to leave no room for the centerpiece of Jamesian theory: the wonder that motivates the representation of alterity. Yet of all the theorists in the second wave, Barthes proves the most deeply committed to James's belief in the felt appreciation of alterity. The difference is that, in his model, the ap-

---

[7] Marc Blanchard describes the importance of the subject to Genette's theory as what we might call a return of the repressed. He labels Genette's chapter on voice

a last ditch attempt to synthesize the analysis of the various parts of the Proustian discourse in order to give it unity and meaning by referring it to the voice of the narrator articulating that discourse. In a few years since the heydays of structuralism, narratology has thus moved from a position of pseudo-scientific objectivity in reaction against the psychologisms of the old school of literary aesthetics, to a search for the subject making all narrative models operative. ("Sound of Songs," 122)

preciative viewer now dedicates himself to unveiling a plurality of interesting objects; Jamesian wonder finds its expansive analogue in Barthesian play. At the same time, Barthes unintentionally advances Lubbock's project in *The Craft of Fiction*: to rewrite James's theory from a reader's point of view. In *S/Z* readers become writers, interpreters become creators, and meaning itself is wholly novelized as it becomes never anything more than the activity of interested engagement.

The second wave of novel theorists do not, then, simply retain the phenomenological subject described by Carroll in his critique of narrative structuralism; instead, they invoke a more specific model of subjectivity in which the novelistic subject is distinguished more particularly by its formalism, its ability to instantiate the distinguishing feature of its own intrinsic identity while also making legible its relational identity to the author who seeks to represent this identity. While the second wave increasingly concerns itself with extraliterary issues—Booth defines rhetoric first and foremost as a social act of communication; Genette models literary study on scientific models of inquiry; Barthes conducts literary analysis as cultural critique—the social realities emphasized by the second wave are still primarily posited as interactions among what I have been calling novelistic subjects. The social in these theories thus remains detached from any significant cultural content and continues to be construed primarily in terms of the hermeneutics of point of view, of the relation between representer and represented. Booth, Genette, and Barthes all follow James in defining novelistic representation as a particular kind of ethical project: the working through the self to find the other, a self-projection that results in selflessness, an individualism that is paradoxically defined by its lack of particularity. It is their different conceptions of the novelistic subject's negative capability as well as their different conceptions of how to define the materiality of the art work that distinguish not just first- and second-wave novel theorists but the individual theorists within the second wave. The critique of Lubbockian objectivity mounted by the second wave is, in the final analysis, an attempt not to do away with the notion of novelistic "showing" but to better explain how fiction can "show" the objectively "subjective" social subject.

Booth

The opening pages of *The Rhetoric of Fiction* leave no uncertainty as to Booth's investment in the tradition I have been tracing. Booth explicitly sets about to attack what by 1962 he can accurately say has become the orthodoxy of novel theory: that novels should show, not tell. By deconstructing this opposition and thus exposing objectivism as a dominant aesthetic rather than a generic imperative, Booth famously helped Anglo-American novel theory reconsider not only the desirability but the possibility of impersonal fiction. That Booth should have based his own theory on a reappreciation of Henry James's Prefaces (the same documents that had been used to authorize the objectivism Booth deplores) suggests the complexities of influence within the tradition that I am analyzing—a complexity intensified by the fact that Booth's alternative to objectivism turns out to be another version of objectivism, and his philosophical "return" to James results in a model of the novelistic subject that is more akin to the theories of Lubbock than of James.[8]

Booth begins his critique of objectivism by taking a skeptical look at the objectivist demand that "overt signs of the author's presence" be eliminated from the novel. "What is it," he asks, "that we might expunge if we attempted to drive the author from the house of fiction?" (*Rhetoric*, 16). Booth then proceeds to show how shortsighted the Lubbockians had been when they claimed that a novelist's "obtrusive commentary" was the primary impediment to the "objective" presentation of an autonomous fictional world. Such overt commentary, Booth argues, is in fact only one of "the author's many voices" (16). The elimination of an author's narrative intrusions would still leave any number of formal expressions of authorial judgment intact:

> Even if we eliminate all such explicit judgments, the author's presence will be obvious on every occasion when he moves into or out of a character's mind—when he "shifts his point of view," as we have come to put it. Flaubert tells us that Emma's little attentions to Charles were "never, as he believed, for his sake ... but for her own, out of exasperated vanity" (p. 69). It is clearly Flaubert who constructs this juxtaposition of Emma's motive with Charles's belief about the motive, and the same obtrusive "voice" is evident whenever a new mind is introduced. (17)

Thanks to such formal devices as juxtaposition, the author need not speak *in propria persona* for his own "voice" to be heard. Thus, Booth argues, an author never merely "shows" us anything; "everything he *shows* will serve to *tell*" (20; Booth's emphasis). Rejecting Lubbock's

---

[8] Not all neo-Aristotelians, of course, reproduce Jamesian formalism. See, for example, Ralph Rader, especially "The Emergence of the Novel," "Defoe, Richardson, Joyce," and "From Richardson" for a theoretical model that positions itself outside the social formalist tradition that I am describing.

hope that the author could be exiled to the void, Booth correspondingly dismisses Lubbock's fear that the author would otherwise impose himself on his characters. The beauty of the novel, Booth claims, is that it can represent authorial views so indirectly, through an "implied" author, that the author can make his presence felt in the novel without his having to compromise the autonomy of his characters.[9] Indeed, it is the double vision accomplished by novelistic representation—the direct view of the characters, and the indirect view of the author—that for Booth constitutes the distinctiveness of the novel as a genre.[10]

In Booth's revision of Lubbock, the omnipresent author not only lets his characters speak for themselves but he retains his altruism toward the reader as well. Booth's logic regarding this crucial point is hard to follow throughout *The Rhetoric of Fiction* because he so often seems to claim the opposite, as for example in the final lines of his afterword to the second edition, when he asserts that "the author makes his readers":

> If he makes them badly—that is, if he simply waits, in all purity, for the occasional reader whose perceptions and norms happen to match his own, then his conception must be lofty indeed if we are to forgive him for his bad craftsmanship. But if he makes them well—that is, makes them see what they have never seen before, moves them into a new order of perception and experience altogether—he finds his reward in the peers he has created. (397–98)

According to this passage, the choice between readers who are the author's creatures and readers who are the author's peers is as false as the choice between a present and an absent or a domineering and a laissez-faire author. The good author helps readers help themselves; he makes readers only insofar as he "makes them see." And thanks to Booth's demonstrations that although "the author can to some extent choose his disguises, he can never choose to disappear" (20), what readers learn to see plainly is the author's designs on them.

Here again Booth's position often sounds contradictory. In a discus-

[9] Booth's concept of the implied author has become virtually a subdivision of narratology. See Chatman, *Terms*, esp. 74–89, for a salient narratological defense of the concept, and Juhl, *Interpretation*, esp. 163–85, for a nonnarratological critique.

[10] See Abrams for an important discussion of the historical roots of this generic account of fiction, especially his discussion of Schlegel, whom he quotes as describing the "magic" of Boccaccio's tales as lying in their indirect expression of authorial identity: "Everywhere the feeling of the author—even the innermost depths of his most intimate individuality—gleams through, visibly invisible" (Schlegel quoted by Abrams, *Mirror*, 241).

sion of Faulkner's representation of Jason Compson in *The Sound and the Fury*, for example, Booth appears to endorse the Lubbockian view that the reader's interest can thrive only in the author's seeming absence: "As we go through this catalogue of bigotry, crime, cruelty and ignorance, few of us would ask for commentary to clarify our judgment. It is not only that we need no guide. We would positively repudiate one if he offered himself to us" (*Rhetoric*, 307). But as always Booth proceeds to reduce Lubbock's absolutism about authorial absence to local and provisional effects. Although we as readers may begin by believing that we travel unaided through the moral wilderness of Jason's mind, we soon "discover" that we have been engaging all along in "a kind of collaboration" with the author not only to form judgments about Jason but also to improve ourselves:

> In dealing with Jason, we must help Faulkner write his work by rising to our best, most perceptive level. When we see the compound joke of Jason's not having anything against "jews as an individual" but just against "the race," we do so only by calling to bear on the passage our linguistic experience, our logical and moral sense, and our past experience with bigots. When we have seen all that Faulkner has packed into the sentence we feel almost as if we had written it ourselves, so effectively has he demanded of us our best creative effort. (307–8)

This "creative" reader is significantly different from the reader whom Lubbock believed "must take his own share of the responsibility" for a book (*Craft*, 17). Lubbock's reader works in the material of form, not moral judgment, and he helps construct an objective world that will protect the autonomy of the characters within it. But for Booth the "rights" of characters are generally beside the point of the reader's efforts to collaborate with the author in morally improving the reader: in the case of *The Sound and the Fury*, "we take delight in communion, and even in deep collusion, with the author behind Jason's back" (*Rhetoric*, 307).

But why does the reader need this authorial communion or collusion to improve himself? According to Booth, the author does more for the reader than lend her a helping hand; he also offers himself as a model. Or rather, he offers the model of himself as an implied author: just as the reader must make herself exemplary in order to collaborate with the author, so the author had to make himself exemplary in order to write the novel in the first place: "A great work establishes the 'sincerity' of its implied author, regardless of how grossly the man who created that author may belie in his *other* forms of conduct the values embodied in his work. For all we know, the only sincere moments of his life may have been lived as he wrote his novel" (*Rhetoric*, 75; Booth's emphasis). Like James, Booth singles out "sincerity" as the decisive trait of the successful author, and like James he turns the ordinary meaning of the term inside out. A sincere author, for Booth, does not reveal his true feelings but rather clears them away; raising himself to the level of an implied author means ridding himself not simply of vice or duplicity but of all partiality: "the weaker the novel, on the whole, the more likely we are to be able to make simple and accurate inferences about the real author's problems based on our experience of the implied author. There is this much truth to the demand for objectivity in the author: signs of the real author's untransformed loves and hates are almost always fatal" (86). With his animus against Jews as a race, not as particular persons, Jason Compson crystallizes the ethics of the novel for Booth, because he suggests that the "individual" is not the target of bigotry but rather its source.

"The great defenders of objectivity" were thus "working on an important matter" (*Rhetoric*, 75), Booth concedes, but they did not recognize the extent of the problem they were addressing:

> The author himself must achieve a kind of objectivity far more difficult and far more profound than the "objectivity" of surface hailed in many discussions of technique. He must first plumb to universal values about which his readers can really care. But it is not enough, I suspect, that he operate on some kind of eternal ground, as recommended by our religious critics. He must be sufficiently humble to seek for ways to help the reader to accept his view of that ground. The artist must in this sense be both a seer and revelator; . . . he must know how to transform his private vision, made up as it often is of ego-ridden private symbols, into something that is essentially public. (395)[11]

The self's best level is properly selfless: only when author and reader have shed their egos and stand on the common ground of "universal values" can they achieve any moral communion. And for Booth it is not so much the transcendent source of these values as, circularly, their sheer communality that makes them solid enough to constitute a ground. Only an "essentially public" vision can be objective, Booth ar-

[11] See Rader, "On the Literary Theoretical Contribution," esp. 184, for a discussion of the connection between Booth's formulation of the problem of authorial identity and neo-Aristotelianism generally.

gues, and only an author committed to objectivity can make his vision essentially public.

Communication is thus Booth's key to the novel: "Nothing the writer does can be finally understood in isolation from his effort to make it all accessible to someone else—his peers, himself as imagined reader, his audience" (*Rhetoric*, 397). This radically social conception of novel writing leads Booth to an extraordinary appropriation of James that extends the appreciation of alterity even further along social lines than Lubbock had:

> At the very moment of initial conception, at the instant when James exclaims to himself, "Here is my subject!" a rhetorical aspect is contained within the conception: the subject is thought of as *something that can be made public*, something that can be made into a communicated work. In so far as it turns out to be a true subject, its means of communication will spring from the essence and seem, when perfected, in harmony with it. (105; Booth's emphasis)

The otherness to which James felt he must always remain faithful is for Booth no longer an interesting object but a receptive public—or rather, if the object is to become a "true" artistic subject, its interest and its essence must be inseparable from its capacity to "be made public." Yet by insisting that a public vision transparently express universal values, Booth's account of the novel's ontogeny puts him in the odd position of deriving a theory from James that cannot accommodate the salient feature of his work: its linguistic and moral indeterminacy. In discussing the "moral complexity" of a story like "The Liar," Booth irritatedly asks, "Does James intend us merely to scoff, or to sympathize? Are the final lies of Mrs. Capadose contemptible, as Lyon thinks, or noble, or a little of both?" (353). Booth's dismay grows even greater when he turns to the moral "fog" generated by the ambiguities of later novelists: *Lolita*, for example, "throws us even more off balance" about life "than we were before" (372). As Booth complains about James's "Liar," "We are lost in wonder at the complexity of life" (353): thanks to Booth's expanded conception of the social—particularly his correlation of public vision with unanimity of interpretation—what for James had been the very goal of artistic production has now become not only an aesthetic weakness but an ethical flaw.[12]

---

[12] Booth does seem to qualify this distaste for James's ambiguities when he adds that "such perplexities" must simply be "kept within certain boundaries—wide as those boundaries may be." But the constraints on ambiguity that Booth envisages are actually so narrow as to admit only intricacy, not perplexity: "Our very recog-

Both Lubbock and Booth thus take from James the notion that the novel is the instantiation of authorial identity, the expression of an author's point of view. And, like Lubbock, Booth refashions James's theory so as to incorporate the reader more fully in the appreciation of alterity, shifting the artist's burden of sympathetic response, for the most part, to the reader. As in *The Craft of Fiction*, the author's job in *The Rhetoric of Fiction* is not so much to appreciate as to elicit appreciation; he is less a wondering than an interested agent who aims to persuade the reader to adopt his own vision of the world. Yet, for all Booth's insistence on the self-expressiveness of authorship, he ultimately denies individuality to the author as well as the reader: just as the reader's point of view should ideally dissolve into the author's, so the author's point of view should ideally dissolve into universal values. If for James all great artists share the same capacity for wonder, and if for Lubbock all great artists share the same capacity for invisibility, then for Booth all great artists share the same truths as well as the same capacity for transparently representing those truths. In each case, theoretical models that begin by explaining how works of fiction express individual authorial points of view end up subordinating the author to some other source of meaning and value: whether it is the interesting object, the self-expressive work of art, the reader, or, in Booth's case, universal truths.

Genette to Cohn

In *Narrative Discourse: An Essay in Method* (1972; trans. 1980), Gérard Genette, like Wayne Booth, makes a case for the advantages of his new theory by pointing out the deficiencies in the dominant understanding of the novel at midcentury. And like Booth, Genette identifies Anglo-American objectivists such as Percy Lubbock as the fountainhead of the theory he opposes. After establishing that the problem of narrative mediation was a topic of aesthetic interest long before the modern novel even existed, Genette jumps from the disagreement between Plato and Aristotle about the respective merits of mimesis and diegesis to a description of novel theory at the contemporary moment. The debate between mimesis and diegesis, he declares,

---

nition of complexity depends upon the clarity of our vision of the elements which go to make it up. The mixture of good and evil in the characters of this story will be overlooked or misapprehended unless we grasp clearly which elements are good and which bad" (*Rhetoric*, 353).

abruptly surged forth again in novel theory in the United States and England at the end of the nineteenth century and the beginning of the twentieth, with Henry James and his disciples [the footnote names Percy Lubbock], in the barely transposed terms of *showing* vs. *telling*, which speedily became the Ormazd and the Ahriman of novelistic aesthetics in the Anglo-American normative vulgate. (*Narrative Discourse*, 163)[13]

Unlike Booth, however, Genette claims he has no desire to save James from his followers; he even goes so far as to cite a quotation from Lubbock to characterize the Jamesian tradition as a whole: "The art of fiction does not begin until the novelist thinks of his story as matter to be *shown*, to be so exhibited that it will tell itself."[14] Genette is no more eager to align himself with Booth than with James, but he does admit that he and Booth are united in the "inspiration" to overthrow the dominant objectivist aesthetic (*Narrative Discourse Revisited*, 44). In fact, Genette introduces his own attack on the objectivists by reluctantly invoking Booth as a comrade in arms (*Narrative Discourse*, 163):

From our own strictly analytic point of view it must be added (as Booth's discussion, moreover, reveals in passing) that the very idea of *showing*, like that of imitation or narrative representation (and even more so, because of its naively visual character), is completely illusory: in contrast to dramatic representation, no narrative can "show" or "imitate" the story it tells. All it can do is tell it in a manner which is detailed, precise, "alive," and in that way give more or less the *illusion of mimesis*—which is the only narrative mimesis, for this unique and sufficient reason: that narration, oral or written, is a fact of language, and language signifies without imitating. (164)

The passage makes clear why Genette feels so doubtful about Booth. The object of their critiques may be the same, but the terms of their critiques are, in Genette's eyes, profoundly different: Booth looks to the subject of the show, Genette to the object; Booth thinks that all showing is really telling, the expression of authorial judgment, whereas Genette thinks that narrative discourse itself exemplifies the only thing that the narratologist needs to know: the nature of narrative discourse.[15] Genette

---

[13] In *Narrative Discourse Revisited* (1983; trans. 1988), his review and defense of *Narrative Discourse*, Genette regrets the totalizing leap from classical to modern theorists; but his sense of the importance of Anglo-American theories of the novel and of James in particular remains unrevised.

[14] Genette, *Narrative Discourse*, 163, quoting Lubbock, *Craft*, 62.

[15] In the larger history of twentieth-century literary theory, Genette's point has, of course, been made and remade. See, for example, Jakobson, who put the problem in 1921 in terms that are remarkably similar: "While in painting and in the other

is, however, not indifferent to the issue of the teller: on the contrary, he wants not only to rid novel theory of its bias for showing but fundamentally to reorient critical discourse by defining fiction as a value-free linguistic activity rather than the privileged instantiation of authorial point of view. In their eloquent debates, Booth and Genette trenchantly characterize the points of their theoretical disagreement. For Booth, "the important facts are simultaneously values, and to ignore the values is to turn the object studied into something less than itself" (*Rhetoric*, 419). For Genette, the facts of narratology pertain to logical structures that, like the laws of physics, are as inevitable as they are amoral.[16]

Genette's explicit attack on Booth in *Narrative Discourse Revisited* (1983, trans. 1988) thus in a very real sense articulates a theoretical alternative to the Jamesian formalist tradition that I have been tracing. Nowhere is this difference more evident than when Genette rejects a staple of Lubbockian and Boothian formalism, the ethics of point of view:

> But I do not believe that the techniques of narrative discourse are especially instrumental in producing these affective impulses. Sympathy or antipathy for a character depends essentially on the psychological or moral (or physical!) characteristics the author gives him, the behavior and speeches he attributes to him and very little on the techniques of the narrative in which he appears. (*Revisited*, 153)

Genette's wholesale rejection of what he calls Booth's functionalism— the notion that the forms of fiction have necessary moral effects—is grounded in his different sense of what it means to study the form of fiction. Booth defines form as any "telling"—from symbolism to point of view to title choice. To Genette, form is at once a more extensive and a more restricted concept. It is more extensive, because Genette clearly

---

visual arts the illusion of an objective and absolute faithfulness to reality is conceivable, 'natural' (in Plato's terminology), verisimilitude in a verbal expression or in a literary description obviously makes no sense whatever. Can the question be raised about a higher degree of verisimilitude of this or that poetic trope?" ("On Realism," 39).

[16] Booth declares that his book "could have profited from having Genette available at that time" (qtd. in Hopkins, "Interview," 47); in "Rhetorical Critics" he enthuses, "on almost every page of Genette I am learning how literature and criticism are *done*" (129). But in the latter essay he also takes Genette to task for ignoring what should be the center of rhetorical inquiry: how narrating can "heighten our sympathy" or "build our antipathy" and how "technique [is used] in the service of *vision*" (138–39; Booth's emphasis). For Genette's response, see *Narrative Discourse Revisited*, esp. 19–20.

demarcates his project as a study not just of the novel but of "narrative" itself. In his afterword to *The Rhetoric of Fiction*, Booth claims that he had once thought to call the book *The Rhetoric of Narration*; but for all its interest in narrative technique, *The Rhetoric of Fiction* resembles James's Prefaces in never attempting a general definition of narration, fiction, or the novel.[17] Form is also a more restricted concept for Genette than for Booth because Genette believes that the forms of narrative can be definitively categorized. Booth's rhetorical inquiry may lead him to classify narration by type, but the list he generates is meant to be exemplary rather than exhaustive. Genette, intent on distinguishing the "science" of narratology from the "empiricism and speculation" of interpretative criticism (*Narrative Discourse*, 263), eschews such open-endedness. Jonathan Culler begins his preface to *Narrative Discourse* by bemoaning the fact that, "while someone who wanted to learn about cars would have no trouble finding a manual, there is no comparable work for the student of literature"; yet with Genette, Culler continues, "the study of fiction" now has a "comprehensive survey" of its "basic concepts" and "technical vocabulary," not to mention a "systematic theory of narrative" (7).

Forster would certainly not have been surprised to see that claims for a science of fiction had come so far, but he might not have predicted that the theoretical endeavor aimed at securing the prestige of the novel had fulfilled its course by deprivileging not only the novel but art itself. For Genette, the novel is interesting as narrative—in this regard, Danielle Steele merits as much attention as Joyce. Of course one might argue that Genette, by extending the field of academic inquiry, has succeeded in elevating Steele along with Joyce; but one would still have to acknowledge the relative lowering of the field: if Lubbock appealed to theory as a way of raising the novel to a high literary art form, Genette, as Culler tells us, makes the study of Proust as mundane as car mechanics.

Nonetheless, the "rigorous mechanics" (*Revisited*, 8) of Genette's more prosaic search for an objective description of narrative would seem to have a better chance for success than Lubbock's. Lubbock's

---

[17] In Booth's clearest statement about genre, he says: "The rhetoric of *fiction* is thus only one of the larger branches of this huge topic. What we will say about any story, whether we call it fictional, historical, philosophical, or didactic, will in some respects resemble what we will say about all stories. . . . But the rhetoric of *fiction* that I chose to limit myself to presents quite special problems. Each kind of fiction presents more special problems still, and each particular story presents unique demands" (*Rhetoric*, 408–9; Booth's emphasis). What exactly are these special demands?

difficulty was, we remember, the paradox of deriving an account of the novel's objectivity from James's ostensibly subjectivist theory of point of view. Genette appears so dismissive of subjects that he defines narrative as "the expansion of a verb" (*Narrative Discourse*, 30) and categorizes narrative on the model of an extended verb form: by order, tense, mood, and voice. Genette never justifies this foundational association of narrative with the grammar of verbs;[18] but the greater difficulty for Genette's own attempt at an objective account of narrative appears to be that he refuses to eliminate subjectivity from his narrative system. Like the Jamesian tradition he critiques, Genette wants to have his author and absent him too. If narrative is, as Genette would have it, the extension of a verb—as in the sentence "Pierre has come"—even the most impersonal statement must, according to Genette, give us some information about its speaker and thus in some infinitesimal way "show" us his or her identity. As Genette puts it in *Narrative Discourse Revisited*, "in the most unobtrusive narrative someone is speaking to me":

> Whether fiction or history, narrative is a discourse; with language, one can produce only discourse; and even in a statement as "objective" as "Water boils at 100° C" [L'eau bout à 100 degrés], everyone can and must hear in the use [in French] of the "notorious" article a very direct appeal to his knowledge of the watery element. Narrative without a narrator, the utterance without an uttering, seem to me pure illusion and, as such, "unfalsifiable." (101)

Yet even though Genette sees narrators everywhere, he still wants to keep authors out of the narrative picture as much as possible. Limiting subjectivity to an attribute of or back-formation from the "verb" (rather than, say, making the verb an attribute of the subject), the very categories of Genette's grammatical model establish narratorial subjectivity as an intrinsic property of narrative discourse. Genette elaborates this notion as he explains the "three basic classes of determinations" of narrative that he has derived from the grammar of verbs:

---

[18] Genette maintains that "the *Odyssey* or the *Recherche* is only, in a certain way, an amplification (in the rhetorical sense) of statements such as *Ulysses comes home to Ithaca* or *Marcel becomes a writer*. This perhaps authorizes us to organize, or at any rate to formulate, the problems of analyzing narrative discourse according to categories borrowed from the grammar of verbs" (*Narrative Discourse*, 30). "To organize" would be to treat the relationship between narrative and grammar as an equation; "to formulate" would be to treat the relationship as an analogy. But leaving this equivocation aside, why should we treat the distillation of *The Odyssey* to a sentence about Ulysses as proving that verbs and not subjects, objects, or prepositions are the key to narrative?

Those dealing with temporal relations between narrative and story, which I will arrange under the heading of *tense*; those dealing with modalities (forms and degrees) of narrative "representation," and thus with the *mood* of the narrative; and finally, those dealing with the way in which the narration itself is implicated in the narrative, narrating in the sense in which I have defined it, that is, the narrative situation or its instance, and along with that its two protagonists: the narrator and his audience, real or implied. We might be tempted to set this third determination under the heading of "person," but for reasons that will be clear below, I prefer to adopt a term whose psychological connotations are less pronounced (very little less, alas), a term to which I will give a conceptual extension noticeably larger than "person"— an extension in which the "person" (referring to the traditional opposition between "first-person" and "third-person" narratives) will be merely one facet among others: this term is *voice*, whose grammatical meaning Vendryès, for example, defined thus: "Mode of action of the verb in its relations with the subject." Of course, what he is referring to is the subject of the statement, whereas for us *voice*, since it deals with the narrating, will refer to a relation with the subject (and more generally with the instance) of the enunciating. (*Narrative Discourse*, 31–32; Genette's emphasis)

David Carroll astutely underscores Genette's troubles in this passage:

Genette . . . attempts to eliminate all attributes of the "living," psychological subject from his categories, but as he himself must admit, with little success. . . . The "alas" should be underlined, for it shows that Genette is aware that he has not cut the "linguistic subject" off from the psychological and philosophical implications of the subject; but nowhere does Genette take account of this failure except to bemoan it. (*Subject*, 208 n. 23)

For Carroll, Genette is thus an example of a structuralist like Benveniste whose critique of the phenomenological subject simply hides the subject by relocating it in language.[19]

Yet what is surprising about Genette's doomed effort to treat persons as mere effects of language is how obsessed he proves, like Lubbock, with the self-sufficiency of subjectivity in narration. To understand this deep participation of Genette in the mimetic tradition he attacks, we first need a more detailed comprehension of the power to materialize that Genette accords to narrative discourse in general. Although Genette's linguistic description of narrative is predicated on the logic of

[19] See also J. M. Bernstein, who declares, "what Genette cannot imagine is a subjectivity that is not privative and exclusive, a 'we speak' which neither collapses into many exclusive subjectivities nor pretends to the elimination of all subjectivity from narrative" (*Philosophy*, 257).

semiology—each sign being composed of a signifier and a signified—his definition of narrative discourse as a "signifier" persistently ascribes to textuality per se its own signifying power. To begin with, although in describing subjectivity he uses interchangeably the terms "tellers," "speakers," and "narrators," his powerful sense of narrative discourse as something tangible leads him by contrast to describe it in one way only: as something written. More specifically, while Genette knows that the signifier itself is only an arbitrary symbol and that it derives its meaning through relationality, he nonetheless persistently ascribes value to the signifier's physicality. Even in his initial definition of "narrative" as "the signifier, statement, discourse, or narrative text itself," we can see the potential slippage in the equation of "signifier" and "text itself"; narrative in this context can only be "the text itself" insofar as the text is, in Lubbock's parlance, "the book"; but ink and paper are not really what Genette has in mind, as we can see when he adds that the signifier is "directly available to textual analysis, which is itself the only instrument of examination at our disposal in the field of literary narrative, and particularly fictional narrative" (*Narrative Discourse*, 27). Genette wants to privilege textual analysis on the basis of its empirical verifiability; textual analysis has a concreteness that he thinks contrasts with the fully ideal existence of fictional writing. But what can this "concrete text" be except the illusion of presentness produced by ink on a page? Clearly, Genette here is mistaking the identity of the signifier as form— an arbitrary sound or mark—with the "direct" apprehension of texts.

For Genette it is a short step from valorizing the signifier as material to according that material an agency of its own:

> It is thus the narrative, and that alone, that informs us here both of the events that it recounts and of the activity that supposedly gave birth to it. In other words, our knowledge of the two (the events and the action of writing) must be indirect, unavoidably mediated by the narrative discourse, inasmuch as the events are the very subject of that discourse and the activity of writing leaves in it traces, signs or indices that we can pick up and interpret—traces such as the presence of a first-person pronoun to mark the oneness of character and narrator, or a verb in the past tense to indicate that a recounted action occurred prior to the narrating action, not to mention more direct and more explicit indications. (*Narrative Discourse*, 28)

What is interesting about this account of mediation is its lack of parallelism: although Genette implies that the subject of narrative discourse (the "events") and the "activity of writing" (the narration) are equal to one another in the sense that they are both "indirectly" represented through the "directly" represented signifier, all indirection in this description is not the same. Whereas the representation of "events" has an abstract and constant relation to its signifier, the representation of the "activity of writing" seems to possess its own materiality, a visibility that exists as "traces," "signs" or "indices" within the larger materiality of narrative discourse. Like Booth, then, Genette may concede that authors are necessarily represented by their writing; but for Genette authorial self-representation is limited to the "traces" left by "the activity of writing" itself.

The limitation of the novelist's subjectivity first to "the activity of writing" and second to the traces left by that activity has particularly important consequences for Genette's discussion of fictional texts. As we have seen, Genette believes that fictional texts refer to nothing beyond themselves:

> If we wanted to study on their own account, let us say, the events recounted by Michelet in his *Histoire de France*, we could have recourse to all sorts of documents external to that work and concerned with the history of France; or, if we wanted to study on its own account the writing of that work, we could use other documents, just as external to Michelet's text, concerned with his life and his work during the years that he devoted to that text. Such a resource is not available to someone interested in either the events recounted by the narrative that the *Recherche du temps perdu* constitutes or the narrating act from which it arises. (*Narrative Discourse*, 27–28)

Although Genette goes on to say that he does not "mean to suggest that the narrative content of the *Recherche* has no connection with the life of its author, but simply that this connection is not such that the latter can be used for a rigorous analysis of the former (any more than the reverse)" (28), Genette's emphasis on "rigor" in this context has the same force as his emphasis on "direct" in his discussion of the representational power of the signifier: for Genette the ontological status of fiction by definition makes the act of reference self-contained and—in a reversal of the commonsense distinction—present in a way that "real" historical events, with their proliferating "documents," can never be. Fictional representation, unlike historical representation, thus may not allow us access to the "events recounted" or the "narrating act," but for Genette it has the advantage of epistemological certainty: the essential data concerning either the event or the author is already "in" the text.[20] For Genette, the author

[20] Genette's account of the authentic representation of fictional subjects derives from a theory of fictional reference that is explicitly at odds with theories of fiction that are grounded in the human rights of fictional characters. Indeed, he explicitly

of a fictional narrative is thus authentically represented in discourse—but only through the "traces" that he leaves behind as the implied "teller."

Describing narrative discourse as not just a signifier but a signified, Genette also defines language not as "imitation" but instantiation. Once we understand this, we can better see why Genette's initial and seemingly devastating critique of Lubbock in fact leads to a recuperation of the definition of novelistic realism as "showing." Genette's affinity with Lubbock is particularly apparent when he rephrases in "scientific" language Lubbock's central question about narrative technique: does the reader face toward the narrator or toward the story world?

> The strictly textual mimetic factors, it seems to me, come down to those two data already implicitly present in Plato's comments: the quantity of narrative information (a more developed or more *detailed* narrative) and the absence (or minimal presence) of the informer—in other words, of the narrator. . . . Finally, therefore, we will have to mark the contrast between mimetic and diegetic by a formula such as: *information + informer = C*, which implies that the quantity of information and the presence of the informer are in inverse ratio, mimesis being defined by a maximum of information and a minimum of the informer, diegesis by the opposite relationship. (*Narrative Discourse*, 166; Genette's emphasis)

Realism in general may be a convention of representation that varies from genre to genre and from one historical period to another; but in Genette's description of the calculus of narrative mediation, within these changing fashions the narrative sentence universally participates in a "textual" mimesis. In this mimetic economy, the narrator—the teller Genette allows to be available to inspection in fictional narratives—is first of all always conceived of as a *presence*, as a subjectivity, and second that subjectivity is—in contrast to the representational power of the signifier—an obscuring agent, something that blocks the reader's clear vision of the "events" that are the true reference, and thus the point, of narration.

---

disassociates himself from the latter position: "If it is true that fictional narrative alone can give us direct access to the subjectivity of the other, this is not due to some miraculous privilege, but because this other is a fictional being . . . whose thoughts the author imagines whenever he pretends to report them: one intuits with complete certainty only what one has invented oneself" ("Fictional Narrative," 762). But despite Genette's skepticism about theories that valorize characterological consciousness as the defining feature of characterological alterity, his own account of the interaction of narratorial agents is less removed from this psychological-humanist position than Genette would like it to be.

In sum, Genette, like Lubbock and Booth, describes narrative discourse as both referring to an autonomous fictional world and displaying the identity of the subjective agents who mediate that world through their attempt to "tell" about it. But whereas Booth argued that any and all narrative techniques had the potential to express the identity of the subjective agents who employed them, Genette is closer to Lubbock in emphasizing the revelatory power of one technique in particular—the use of point of view:

> Narrative "representation," or, more exactly, narrative information, has its degrees: the narrative can furnish the reader with more or fewer details, and in a more or less direct way, and can thus seem (to adopt a common and convenient spatial metaphor, which is not to be taken literally) to keep at a greater or lesser *distance* from what it tells. The narrative can also choose to regulate the information it delivers, not with a sort of even screening, but according to the capacities of knowledge of one or another participant in the story (a character or group of characters), with the narrative adopting or seeming to adopt what we ordinarily call the participant's "vision" or "point of view"; the narrative seems in that case (continuing the spatial metaphor) to take on, with regard to the story, one or another *perspective.* "Distance" and "perspective," thus provisionally designated and defined, are the two chief modalities of that *regulation of narrative information* that is mood—as the view I have of a picture depends for precision on the distance separating me from it, and for breadth on my position with respect to whatever partial obstruction is more or less blocking it. (*Narrative Discourse*, 162; Genette's emphasis)

Genette's paradigm, like Lubbock's, distinguishes between the potentially unmediated and unambiguous object of representation and the subjectivity that obscures the reader's full view of that object. As for Lubbock, the "screen" of the narrator's presence—the point of view that mediates the presentation of the fictional world—works to block the reader's full apprehension of the picture of reference. Remarkably, the substantiality that for Lubbock distinguished the plastic from the writerly arts is now for Genette a feature of narrative itself—even without a book first materializing in a reader's brain.

Genette, of course, tries to mark his conceptual difference from earlier theorists such as Lubbock by acknowledging—and thus disassociating himself from—the metaphorics of his terms, but even this gesture echoes Lubbock's own self-conscious discomfort about employing terms from the "material arts" that "are only metaphors, after all, that cannot be closely pressed" (Lubbock, 11). If Lubbock's metaphors reveal, moreover, his fundamental desire to think of novels themselves as objects and the worlds that they describe as objective, Genette's metaphors reveal an analogous desire to posit an objective and unambiguous referent for narrative discourse. As we have already seen, the impulse to place point of view under the grammatical category of "mood" emphasizes the primary importance Genette ascribes to his definition of narrative as a "verb"; subjectivity—the author's, the narrator's, and the characters'—is relegated in this model to the "traces" left on the narrative discourse. In his description of the mimetic nature of discourse, Genette further depersonalizes subjectivity by separating the issue of character from the structural function of point of view. In contrast to Booth, for whom the importance of narratorial "distance" was that it registered the moral judgment—sympathy or irony—of the narrator upon the narrated, in Genette's model, "distance" is first redefined as a morally neutral function of the amount of "information" a narrative supplies. In the calculus by which Genette computes the geometry of point of view, the "directness" or "indirectness" of representation is derived by the reader according to her sense of how much narrative "information" she sees. Like Lubbock, Genette never considers that the very perspectivism that he seeks to chart in his theoretical model might call into question the stability of reference and the quantification of mediation upon which that model is based.

Genette's theory of narrative thus not only finds a new way to understand novelistic representation as "showing," but does so by making the Lubbockian rivalry between teller and told a conflict that is a structural imperative of fictional narrative discourse. But what is most surprising about Genette's theory is that for all its attempt to detach mimesis from morality, his understanding of narrative discourse as mimetic leads him to reinscribe within his "manual" of narration a version of Jamesian altruism. Despite his explicit attempts to depsychologize the study of narrative, Genette ultimately makes a special case for the unmediated representation of fictional subjects based on his sense of the mimetic potential of language itself: "The truth is that mimesis in words can only be mimesis of words. Other than that, all we have and can have is degrees of diegesis. So we must distinguish here between narrative of events and 'narrative of words'" (*Narrative Discourse*, 164). This distinction leads Genette to create two categories of representation: the narrative of "words" and any other kind of narratives. While the narrative of words is still mediated by the logical category of a "teller," unlike narratives that are not of words, there is the possibility of a "zero degree" of mediation, what Genette calls the "documentary autonomy of a quotation" (171).[21]

By respecting the convention of fictional quotation as the "fidelity to the words really uttered" (*Narrative Discourse*, 171) by a character, Genette imagines a way for the reader to achieve a "direct view" of the referent of narrative discourse: quotation allows her to "see" a fictional character represented in the character's own terms. Given Genette's logic, the terms that represent identity are those that instantiate it: because language and language alone lends itself to "pure" imitation, then what a character says is, in narrative discourse, the only intrinsic indicator of who she is. Ethical consequences that are by now familiar to us thus follow from the possibility of representing characterological autonomy through quotation. First of all, Genette defines the authentic representation of subjectivity not in Lubbock's general terms (as "point of view") and not in Booth's terms (as universal values) but as citationality: language that can be quoted. The difference between characterological and narratorial identity is instantiated by what characters can be said to say. Genette's emphasis on linguisticality thus moves the debate in the Jamesian tradition about characterological autonomy from general discussions of point of view to specific discussions of the quantity of mediation to be discovered in every sentence of narrative discourse. The rivalry between representer and referent is now, in other words, something to be enacted, something to be *shown* through narrative discourse. If for Booth every decision about narrative technique represents the author's judgment and thus his identity, for Genette every narrative sentence becomes a choice about subjectivity: should the character's subjectivity be screened? Or should the character be allowed to speak in her own words? Finally, then, every narrative sentence becomes an ethical decision. What will the narrator choose to represent? His own subjectivity or the subjectivity of the character he depicts? Genette's weaker conception of the material of alterity—quotation—deprives him of the means used by Lubbock and Booth to mitigate the problem of the representational rivalry produced by subjective mediation; quotation, it

---

[21] For seminal critiques of Genette's theoretization of subjective mediation as spatial distancing, see Cohn, "Encirclement," esp. 175; and Bal, "Narrating," esp. 239, where she declares, "Every description is mimetic, every event is diegetic—that is what this theory comes down to." For Genette's responses to Cohn and Bal, see *Narrative Discourse Revisited*, 18, 51–62, 72–73, and 75–78.

seems, has enough plasticity to make individual identities legible but not enough to neutralize the power relation between representer and represented. Lubbock, we remember, appealed to noetic materialism as a way of grounding his dream of objective representation. Booth ascribed to the novel itself the special capacity for double vision, its generic ability to represent the identity of an "implied" author who might be everywhere present but whose identity would not interfere with the autonomy of his characters. For Genette the rivalry between novelistic subjects is structural, and therefore he feels it should be amoral; but ethical choice is insisted upon by his striking use of metaphors of inscription or colonization to describe the representation of characterological language. Genette calls "free indirect style," for example, the "beginning of [characterological] emancipation" (172). And in characterizing Flaubert's sustained and famous use of Free Indirect Discourse, he goes so far as to suggest a melodrama of alterity played out between narrator and character simply on the level of vocabulary: "his [Flaubert's] own language speak[s] this both loathsome and fascinating idiom of the 'other' without being wholly compromised or wholly innocent" (172).

Pascal and Cohn

Genette's sense of what we might call the alterity of vocabulary resonates, of course, with the dominant terms of a long-standing linguistic account of Free Indirect Discourse (FID) that implicitly informs his discussion of the ethics of quotation.[22] To understand the larger compatibility between the received narratological understanding of FID and the Jamesian tradition that I am tracing, I want to look briefly at the description of FID given by two Anglo-American theorists who published highly influential studies of FID about the same time as Genette's *Narrative Discourse*: Roy Pascal and Dorrit Cohn.[23] But before

[22] The most useful overview of theories about FID is McHale's. See Banfield, *Unspeakable Sentences*, esp. 23–63, for a thorough linguistic description of FID's grammatical familial relationships. Chatman gives us a succinct working definition. The difference between direct and indirect discourse is the difference between "'I have to go,' she said" and "She said that she had to go" (*Story*, 199); "free" discourse is when the "tag" and the quotation marks are omitted. See *Story*, 196–203, for Chatman's own theoretical formulation of the workings of FID.

[23] See McHale, "Islands," esp. 192, for an early comparison of Pascal and Cohn that stresses their methodological differences. Hernadi in the 1970's was also attempting to define FID. Shlomith Rimmon-Kenan offers an explanation of why FID came to mean so much to narrative theorists that is compatible with my own ac-

we plunge more deeply into the technicalities of narratological debate, it behooves us to remember exactly why Lubbock felt compelled to distinguish neither between "who speaks" and "who sees" nor between the voices of characters and narrators—why, that is, he was satisfied with a pictorial rather than a linguistic definition of point of view.

Lubbock's sense of the potency of point of view allows him to ascribe to it a more diffuse integrity; although he is certainly obsessed with the interplay between narratorial subjectivities and their objects, he thus feels no need to examine the micronegotiations between narrator and characterological subject that later narratologists will see played out in the novelistic sentence. For Lubbock, we remember, an author—or narrator (he frequently uses the terms interchangeably)—represents his own subjectivity primarily through the blatant act of self-reference. As long as a narrator does not explicitly talk about himself, he could in Lubbock's theory "speak" (for indeed for Lubbock that is necessarily what an author must do) without "telling," without, that is, interrupting the illusion of characterological point of view. When he describes the delights of James's narrative technique in his late novels, Lubbock regards the technique of what is now commonly called third-person narration, what Lubbock calls "oblique narration," as especially effective in promoting an altruistic representation of alterity:

> The seeing eye is with somebody in the book, but its vision is reinforced; the picture contains more, becomes richer and fuller, because it is the author's as well as his creature's, both at once. Nobody notices, but in fact there are now two brains behind that eye; and one of them is the author's, who adopts and shares the *position* of his creature, and at the same time supplements his wit. . . . The impression of the scene may be deepened as much as need be; it is not confined to the scope of one mind, and yet there is no blurring of the focus by a double point of view. And thus what I have called the sound of the narrator's voice (it is impossible to avoid this mixture of metaphors) is less insistent in oblique narration, even while it seems to be following the very same argument that it would in direct, because another voice is speedily mixed and blended with it. (*Craft,* 258–59; Lubbock's emphasis)

Lubbock reaches for "voice" to describe authorial presence, but in his example voice is also used to describe characterological identity at the

---

count: "The concept of FID evinced by contemporary narrative theory is due not only to its stylistic complexity but also to its constituting, in some sense, a miniature reflection of the nature of both mimesis (in the broad sense of representation) and literariness" (*Narrative Fiction,* 114).

moment it seems equal to and equally present with authorial identity. One might easily read the power dynamics the other way round and say that oblique narration draws attention to the character's limited "brain" by making palpable the author's supplementation.[24] But because Lubbock posits the relation between author and character as essentially a relation of patronage, the author's supplementation of the character through his own subordination—his condescension to restrict himself to the "position" of his "creature"—can be read by Lubbock only as sympathetic engagement that has altruistic results, like the inspiration of a Holy Spirit or a Muse.[25] The struggle to define precisely the narrative phenomenon of a mixture of minds that doesn't blur the focus causes Lubbock, as he admits, to mix metaphors too: vision and voice are as blended and yet distinct as "two brains" behind one "seeing eye."

Lubbock's attempt to define the "two in oneness" or "one in twoness" of narrative was mirrored in the work of continental linguists, and the two projects are vividly linked by the first extended analysis of Free Indirect Discourse written in English, *The Dual Voice: Free Indirect Speech and Its Function in the Nineteenth-Century European Novel* (1977) by Roy Pascal. Pascal asserts the importance of FID by introducing it as a missing link between European and Anglo-American studies of narrative mimesis; in Pascal's view, Anglo-American studies begin and end with James and Lubbock. According to Pascal, the development of the novel has been an evolutionary process. Using James to derive a theoretical definition of novelistic realism, Pascal charts a line of development from what he deems to be the awkward attempts of early novelists to master the novel's techniques to the full realization of the novel's formal potential by modern writers. While some authors—like Thackeray, George Eliot, and Zola—are in Pascal's account guilty of backsliding, these aberrations do not impede the novel's progress, which culminates, he believes, in the discovery and perfection of FID.

The mastery of FID is crucial to the novel's development because, for Pascal, it is the narrative technique that best accomplishes what he has defined—via James—as the genre's raison d'être: the novelist's represen-

[24] For example, Bal declares focalization to be "the most important, most penetrating, and most subtle means of manipulation" (*Narratology*, 116).

[25] Scholes and Kellogg's skeptical interpretation of this model of Lubbockian inspiration is phrased quite wonderfully: "The result of the disappearance of the narrator is not the refining away of the artist but a continual reminder of his presence—as if God were omnipresent and invisible, yet one could continually hear Him breathing" (*Nature*, 270).

tation of the "inner life, the mental and emotional activities and responses of their invented characters" (*Dual Voice*, 2). Pascal derives this
definition of the novel by paraphrasing James with a Lubbockian emphasis:

> What he [James] requires of a novel is that the "feel of life" of the fictional
> characters should be created, the feel of the choices open to them; a moral
> evaluation, if it is to be genuine and valid, can emerge only from the possi-
> bilities of *their* world, *their* personality, *their* mode of experience [Pascal's
> emphasis]. These objectives can be achieved only if the reader can get "with-
> in the skin" of the characters, can see and understand *in their terms*, from
> their perspective, without of course sacrificing his own objective position.
> . . . He does not lessen the responsibility of the author but embeds it within
> his creation. (5–6; my emphasis)

Pascal's interpretation of James might be best described as Lubbock
once-removed: Lubbock retains James's notion that the novel was first
and foremost an expression of the author's vision of life; for Pascal, the
only vision that the novel is obliged to represent is that of the characters. If James judges the success of the art work in terms of authorial
sincerity, Pascal's sole criterion for representational authenticity is the
"valid" representation of character, which is for him the integrity and
plausibility of characterological alterity to the degree that characters
seem responsible only to themselves for their moral choices. To convey
the characters' impression of life is to represent "their mode of experience," which can only be done if the representation is unmediated, presented in the characters' own "terms." Yet, if the achievement of alterity
is to be made perceptible as alterity—as subjective difference—then the
character's "terms" cannot according to Pascal be a matter simply of
first-person narration. Pascal believes that third-person narration makes
optimally visible the difference in identity between on the one hand narrator and character and on the other hand reader and character.

Pascal's brief overview of the discovery and early theorization of FID
shows how, from the outset, this syntactical form was associated with
an all-consuming appreciation of alterity. Pascal reminds us that the
German scholar Etienne Lorck believed that FID bespoke the deepest of
empathetic bonds between writer and character. The author, according
to Lorck, was able to "directly communicate the experience of the fictional character, in spite of its authorial, indirect form" because, as Pascal might say, the author had allowed the character to get within his
skin. In other words, the writer is able to depict the inward experience

of his character because he himself, in Lorck's words, "'inwardly expe-riences' the thought and the feeling of the character concerned" (*Dual Voice*, 14). In a move familiar from my account of James, the author's inward experience of character becomes not the projection of authorial identity onto a "creature" but the expression of authorial identity in and through its relation to a being who may not have a physical exis-tence but who is nonetheless fully "other" to the author. Because FID is moreover not an everyday usage but occurs primarily, if not exclusively, in narrative forms, Lorck further believes that fiction writing alone lends itself to this profound form of interpersonal communion. Para-doxically, the solitary act of creation turns out to be an intensely social experience: "an author, in the act of writing, can be alone with his imagined characters in the seclusion of his study, and only in this pri-vacy—which the presence of a second person shatters—can immerse himself into the psyche of his imaginary creatures" (14).

But if the understanding of FID was from the start linked with the appreciation of alterity, the theorization of the author's communion with his character ultimately gave way to the seemingly more concrete analysis of the interplay between author and character as mediated by the novel's narrator. Pascal's own account of "dual voice" is primarily interested in a single question: has an author been able to represent a character in his own terms? Like Lubbock he saves his worst criticism for novelists who do not trust characters to represent themselves. Lub-bock, following James, berates Thackeray; Pascal singles out George Eliot: "Often one feels like begging George Eliot, 'Please leave the char-acters alone, to themselves, please leave us alone, to make our own conclusions'" (*Dual Voice*, 89). For Pascal as for Lubbock, an author who does not trust his characters also does not trust his reader; Eliot's intrusions, he says, refuse the reader "more than a modicum of freedom of judgement" (89). But if Lubbock is content with the illusion of char-acterological freedom, Pascal is more strictly concerned that real charac-terological freedom be achieved—this means not just a character's free-dom from a chatty author, but also a character's freedom to express himself in his own terms.[26] In his close readings of major nineteenth-

---

[26] It may be instructive at this point to remember that although many novelists and novel theorists believe that characters should possess their own autonomy, it is the Jamesian tradition that attempts to theorize characterological freedom in terms of linguistic intrinsicality. Georg Lukács, for example, believes that the sign of char-acterological independence lies in action, not language:

century novelists, a group that includes Goethe, Balzac, Stendahl, and Austen, Pascal gauges the author's concern for characterological freedom based on the author's capacity to give his characters their own "personal, idiosyncratic style" (38). But as we can see in his judgment of Balzac and Stendahl, the representation of characterological individuality through stylistic individualism is not in itself a guarantee of alterity:

> Their rich, extravagant imaginations cannot, like Flaubert's, subject themselves to the characters they create. And one might say of Dickens, too, that his imagination cannot brook a rival; he, not a character, has to be the medium of description if all potentialities are to be uncovered. (67)

Even when an author represents within third-person narration a multitude of characterological points of view, Pascal argues, he has failed to realize true alterity as long as his point of view remains the dominating "medium of description." For Pascal, then, the development of a personal idiosyncratic style for each character is a good beginning, but the full representation of alterity requires that the author maintain the third person but surrender representational control and let the character be the medium of description in imagination, in consciousness, as well as in word.

Consequently, Pascal's close readings devote themselves to detecting the degree and kind of alterity that "oblique narration" allows. Pascal sees his project as supplemental to Lubbock's: *The Dual Voice* catalogues the subtle grammatical clues that create the "mixing and blending" of voices that Lubbock describes, and it attempts to chart more precisely the ethical implications of this mixing. In Pascal's grammatical analysis, a tense shift or a deictic is enough to indicate an author's adaptation of a character's point of view, a shift from one "voice" to another. Words like "here," "yesterday," "so," "thus," and "doubtless"— as well as more marked exclamations like "alas" or "my God"—signal to Pascal that the narrator "places himself, when reporting the words or thoughts of a character, directly into the experiential field of the character, and adopts the latter's perspective in regard to both time and place" (*Dual Voice*, 9).[27]

> The characters created by the great realists, once conceived in the vision of their creator, live an independent life of their own: their comings and goings, their development, their destiny is dictated by the inner dialectic of their social and individual existence. No writer is a true realist—or even a truly good writer, [sic] if he can direct the evolution of his own characters at will." (*European Realism*, 11)

[27] In the passage from which I quote, Pascal is technically only summarizing the early work on FID accomplished by Charles Bally. Pascal concludes this chapter by

But Pascal's microanalysis of the interplay between characterological and narratorial voices does not stop when it reaches the point where Pascal believes he can judge the fluctuation of subjective presence within a single sentence; for Pascal the duality allowed by FID need not consist

---

emphasizing what is controversial about Bally's work on FID (called *"le style indirect libre"* by Bally and "free indirect style" or FIS by Pascal); but Pascal himself everywhere relies upon the distinctions I have quoted. For example, here is a passage from Jane Austen's *Mansfield Park*, followed by Pascal's analysis.

> His sisters, to whom he [Edmund] had an opportunity of speaking the next morning were quite as impatient of his advice [...] as Tom.—Their mother had no objection to the plan [staging theatricals], and they were not in the least afraid of their father's disapprobation.—There could be no harm in what had been done in so many respectable families, and by so many women of the first consideration; and it must be scrupulousness run mad, that could see anything to censure in a plan like their's, comprehending only brothers and sisters, and intimate friends, and which would never be heard of beyond themselves. Julia *did* seem inclined to admit Maria's situation might require particular caution and delicacy—but that could not extend to *her*—*she* was at liberty; and Maria evidently considered her engagement as only raising her so much above restraint, and leaving her less occasion than Julia, to consult either father or mother. Edmund had little to hope, but he was still urging the subject, when Henry Crawford entered the room, fresh from the Parsonage, calling out, "No want of hands in our Theatre, Miss Bertram." (Austen, quoted by Pascal [54]; Austen's emphasis, Pascal's elision)

Now Pascal:

> In the framework of the narratorial description of Edmund's campaign of persuasion, the arguments of the sisters are given in FIS [FID], to which an abrupt end is put by Henry's intervention, given in direct speech. What is particularly interesting is not only the brilliant evocation of the manner in which the girls argue and speak, but the suggestions that what we are reading is Edmund's registration of what they say. The italicised "did" and "she" of Julia's argument, the "evidently" of Maria's, evoke not only the egoistic girls but also the listener, who is making his cautious and prudent conclusions. . . . The italicised words bear Julia's emphases in the first place, no doubt, but do they not bear a secondary accent, that of Edmund, just as the word "evidently" is an interposition by Edmund? . . . We find in Jane Austen's use of FIS many of the indicators and signals that Bally and Lips were to draw attention to . . . the exclamatory question, the characteristic intonation, and characteristic expressions. (Pascal, 54–55).

Pascal's analysis makes clear that he values FID for its power to enact subjective identification while retaining subjective difference. The multilayering of identification (the narrator to Edmund and Edmund to the girls) is conceivable because of the discursive clues that, for Pascal, preserve the differences between points of view (the third person, the invocation of Edmund's identity that Pascal hears in the "secondary accent" of the italicized words, and the double ownership he ascribes to the word "evidently"). That Pascal feels obliged to frame the more delicate nuances of his analysis as a question suggests how difficult it is to prove multilayering when the clues to subjectivity are limited to words *shared* by different subjects.

of a simple alternation between the narrator's voice and the character's voice—they can appear simultaneously. Pascal joins other scholars of FID in analyzing the "presence" of narrative judgment even within discourse that is indirectly quoted. His account of FID thus nuances Genette's calculus of alterity. For Pascal, even the imitation of characterological discourse can serve as a vehicle for narratorial self-representation: "The duality of narrator and character," as Pascal puts it, "may be heard as a tone of irony, or sympathy, of negation or approval, underlying the statement of the character" (*Dual Voice*, 17). When a character speaks, the narrator only seems silent; if one listens closely, one can hear his "voice" as an intonation within another's voice. And as with Booth, the narrator's voice/intonation is defined as one thing and one thing only: his *judgment* upon what he represents, "his tone of irony, or sympathy, of negation or approval." Yet, although the narrator now inhabits more of his narration than perhaps even Booth envisaged, his judgment and consequently his identity have been radically schematized: reduced to either identifying with or distancing himself from a character, the narrator seems thoroughly defined by the play of his sympathy.

Dorrit Cohn's *Transparent Minds* (1978), published only a year after *The Dual Voice*, in effect picks up Pascal's logic where it leaves off.[28] Cohn argues that the representation of another's consciousness is not simply an important feature of fiction but its distinguishing mark. Cohn quotes approvingly Kate Hamburger's assertion that "narrative fiction is the only literary genre, as well as the only kind of narrative, in which the unspoken thoughts, feelings, perceptions of a person other than the speaker can be portrayed" (*Transparent*, 7); as Cohn declares at the start of her study, "fictional consciousness is the special preserve of narrative fiction" (vi). Her substitution of the term "consciousness" for the more traditional "point of view" may seem merely a semantic difference between Cohn and the other theorists we have examined, but in fact the substitution reflects Cohn's more radical sense of how deeply an author can get "within the skin" of his characters. The advantage of fiction over other genres, according to Cohn, is that it can directly voice the "unspoken thoughts, feelings, perceptions," the private mind, of an "other" (7). Adopting a view of characterological alterity as strong as

[28] For a comparison of Genette and Cohn, see Nilli Diengott, "Mimetic Language," esp. 533. Diengott argues that Cohn's "mimetic bias" structures her terms, but that Genette's mimetic bias works in contradiction with his theory.

Pascal's, Cohn subordinates authorial sensibility to the novel's *generic* capacity for representing alterity.[29]

With Cohn, then, Jamesian theory seems to have done an about-face. For James, art was distinguished from life because it materialized the novelist's authentic identity through the terms of his artistic choices; those choices held the silver clue to authorial consciousness, representing the degree to which he sympathetically understood the interesting other. For Cohn, art is distinguished from life for a similar reason: it represents identity authentically. But whereas James regards the novel as an other-ing of his own consciousness, Cohn believes that the novel makes accessible the consciousness of another. Yet she does not dispense with author-ial agency altogether. Like Pascal, Cohn claims that the novel has developed in an evolutionary fashion, culminating with the "inward turn" of modernism, which she argues has fulfilled "the genre's most distinctive potential" (*Transparent*, 8). Fiction, she states, has progressed from "vo-cal to hushed authorial voices, from dissonant to consonant relations between narrators and protagonists, from maximal to minimal removes between the language of the text and the language of consciousness" (v). Without authors, this Whiggish history could not be sustained; it would lack the ethical motor propelling it forward: the choice of each author to either speak or else yield the floor to his characters. There is a "relation of inverse proportion between authorial and figural minds," Cohn explains: "the more conspicuous and idiosyncratic the narrator, the less apt he is to reveal the depth of his characters' psyches or, for that matter, to create psyches that have depth to reveal" (25). Or again, adopting more Lubbockian terms, Cohn characterizes the author as a jealous god frightened by the prospect of his incarnation in characters:

---

[29] Elsewhere, Cohn argues for the nonnaturalizability of the narratorial agent:

It is precisely because this "somebody" assumes optical and cognitive powers un-available to a real person that we feel the need to dissociate the statements of a fictional text from its authorial source, even if we imagine them (on Searle's model) as merely "pretended" statements. Ultimately, we are compelled to ac-cept that the language transmitted to us in heterodiegetic fiction cannot be imagined by analogy to *any* plausible real-world discourse situation, no matter whether we personalize or depersonalize its origin. ("Signposts," 796)

Yet, as I seek to prove, in Cohn's theory the failure of one kind of mimetic analogy does not preclude the construction of another: if fictional discourse does not resem-ble any "real-world discourse situation," it nonetheless produces narratorial agents who possess social and ethical relations derived from a model of "real" persons.

It almost seems as though the authorial narrator jealously guards his pre-
rogative as the sole thinking agent within his novel, sensing that his equi-
poise would be endangered by approaching another mind too closely and
staying with it too long; for this other mind, contrary to his own disincar-
nated mental existence, belongs to an incarnated and therefore distinctly
limited being. (25)

Clearly, Cohn agrees with Booth that the successful author (who is also
the morally upstanding author) must keep his own ego out of the novel;
but once the ego is gone, Cohn hears characters talking, not universal
values. For James, "getting within the skin of the character" meant the
author's vampirish possession of the character, but for Cohn it means
the character's vampirish draining of the author: "a fully developed figural consciousness siphons away the emotional and intellectual energy
formerly lodged in the expansive narrator" (25).[30]

Both Pascal and Cohn, then, perceive a melodramatic subplot in
every novel: who will end up as the dominant "thinking agent," the
character or the narrator? Like Genette, they habitually resort to metaphors of purity and corruption when characterizing moments of indeterminacy in this struggle. Cohn, for instance, describes some stream of
consciousness in *Portrait of the Artist* as "unpolluted by authorial interference" (*Transparent*, 72). Of Mrs. Ramsay she wonders if it is "the
narrator whose language becomes contaminated by the figural idiom"
(136). But, as Cohn makes clear in her discussion of the narrated
monologue, the novel cannot constitute a field of ethics if this rivalry
between character and author is ever resolved:

The narrated monologue itself, however, is not *vision avec*, but what we
might call *pensée avec*: here the coincidence of perspectives is compounded
by a consonance of voices, with the language of the text momentarily reso-
nating with the language of the figural mind. In this sense one can regard the
narrated monologue as the quintessence of figural narration, if not of narration itself: as the moment when the thought-thread of a character is most
tightly woven into the texture of third-person narration. (111)

A narrator's "*identification*" with a "character's mentality" is not,
Cohn emphasizes, an "*identity*" (112); even a good author can never
unite with his characters once and for all. The sympathetic "coincidence

[30] Cohn quotes James on getting into the skin of his characters (*Transparent
Minds*, 115).

of perspectives" is at best a "momentary" achievement, accomplished word by word.[31]

Barthes

Genette's explicit mention of Lubbock and his extended engagement with Booth would be enough in themselves to establish the relevance of this French thinker to the Anglo-American tradition of novel theory; when we turn to his contemporary, Roland Barthes, however, the link to Anglo-American novel theory may seem less obvious, not just because Barthes fails to name Anglo-American novel theorists, either fore-fathers or contemporaries, but because his most extended meditation on novelistic conventions of representation, *S/Z*, is so devoted to debunking novelistic aesthetics that it might even be characterized as an anti-novel theory.[32] But Barthes' wholesale critique of phenomenologist philoso-phy—and the aesthetics of vision it privileges—is exactly what makes his work crucial to the Anglo-American tradition that I am tracing. Af-ter Barthes, it became less and less possible for theorists of the novel to conceptualize the novelistic subject as an individual consciousness, dis-crete, coherent, and substantive; after Barthes it also became difficult to think of mediation as simply an epistemological problem for the artist rather than an ontological attribute of all subjectivity. Barthes is thus crucial to the tradition that I am tracing because by critiquing the phe-nomenological assumptions that lie behind what he calls the classic novel's realism, he also suggests a new direction for novel studies, a path that would encourage the study of the novel as a study of dis-

---

[31] Cohn's interest in the interplay of narrative voices thus does not protect her from Lentricchia's general indictment of all structuralists: "Structuralists, by defini-tion, cannot attend to nonrepeatable textures of voice; structuralists by definition, are tone-deaf" (Lentricchia, *Ariel*, 11).

[32] Michael Moriarty argues that Barthes "never shows the slightest interest in, or even acquaintance with, Anglo-American criticism" ("Longest Cultural Journey," 104). I would maintain that in the case of novel theory, the Anglo-American tradi-tion had such general influence that Barthes would be aware of it without having to have actually read either James or Lubbock. Moriarty, I would point out, wants to have it both ways: when actual reference to the Anglo-American tradition is made by French theorists, he offhandedly dismisses these citations as insignificant; Mori-arty cites Genette's and Todorov's respective invocation of Lubbock and Booth but claims that "it is hard to assert deep influence here" (104). The example of Genette and Todorov is, obviously, absolutely significant for my argument, since it suggests that novel theory is the one topic that breaks the general French silence about An-glo-American theory.

courses mobilized by a text rather than the enumeration of the genre's essential formal or structural elements.

If the first wave of novel theory attempted to gain aesthetic prestige for the novel by championing the qualities that were peculiar to it, Barthes might be said to advance the prestige of the novel through a negative argument: he challenges the possibility and value of literary exceptionalism of all kinds. Barthes tells us that he has chosen Balzac's novel virtually at random; any other classic novel might have allowed him to mount his critique of novelistic realism and any other text at all would have enabled him to make many of his largest philosophical points. Genette's theory leveled the aesthetic playing field by making any novel—and even any narrative—the object of serious theoretical analysis; by defining any text at all as an object of literary study, Barthes explodes the very notion of a field: what remains of the literary, in other words, is located in the activity of interpretation rather than the intrinsic character of the object.

But although *S/Z* would thus be a crux text for any account of the development of novel theory, as a social formalist text it also has a much more specific importance to my study of the Jamesian tradition. That *S/Z* participates in social formalism without referencing the Anglo-American roots of this tradition suggests first of all that the development of social formalism is only partly a result of intertextual self-reference: while certain theoretical assumptions are perpetuated because theorists are reading each other and revising each other, these explicit and self-conscious interconnections gain their deeper significance from the repetition of a larger, implicit philosophical commonality; as I have been arguing, studying the relationship between the explicit claims and the implicit assumptions of individual theories is what allows us to define the full logic of social formalism. I am not, however, suggesting that Barthes is only and forever a social formalist.[33] Rather, I want to stress that it is only in his most extended meditation on the novel that this famously eclectic thinker is moved to reproduce the social formalism of novel theory. From the perspective of social formalism, it is not at all random that Barthes would choose to elucidate his theory by way of the novel: his commitment to values that I have been identifying as novelis-

[33] For a reading of Barthes' work as a reaction to the "euphoria and disillusion-ment, liberation and dissipation, carnival and catastrophe, which was 1968," see Eagleton, *Literary Theory*, 142–50. For a biographical contextualization of Barthes' work, see Louis-Jean Calvet, *Roland Barthes*.

tic—specifically the appreciation of alterity and the concomitant search for a stabilizing materiality—informs his philosophical engagement with the aesthetics of vision. Barthes' contribution to the social formalist tradition lies in his expansion of its purview: *S/Z* debunks localized aesthetic debates about realism to describe the underlying novelistic reality of any and all discourse.

Barthes' critique of phenomenological point of view in *S/Z* is, of course, part of a more general theoretical shift that has enabled the defamiliarization of the Jamesian tradition. His specific critique of the aesthetics of vision helps us to identify the distinctive tenuousness of the novelistic subject within the work of James, Lubbock, Booth, and Genette. As we have seen, each theorist posits the subject as a point of view, and then radically destabilizes it by evacuating from point of view any distinguishing feature other than the capacity for alterity. Thus while Barthes' deconstructed subject may seem far removed from these theorists' explicit definition of subjectivity, it is nonetheless quite powerfully connected to the implicit operation of point of view in the social formalist tradition. But if it is important to see how the Jamesian tradition contains within it a type of deconstructed subject, it is equally important to see how Barthes' critique of phenomenology retains an allegiance to key Jamesian concepts. While Barthes' theorization of subjects as "texts" certainly opens up the possibility for an entirely new paradigm of identity, in practice Barthes does not do away with the phenomenological subject/object distinction; he instead maintains it as a shadow category: as I will show, in *S/Z* subject and object are contingent and temporary unities that, by allowing distinctions to cohere, enable as well as limit the otherwise endless "play" of meaning.

Thus while Barthes famously attacks the notion of a unified or single point of view, his own ethical commitment to alterity leads him to establish a subject whose own multiplicity is (re)unified by the act of appreciating the multiplicity of the interesting other(s) that are the object of representation. The multiplicity of the appreciated other is, in turn, stayed and limited by the subject's act of appreciation. We find in *S/Z* that although Barthes questions almost all of the humanistic values that James, Lubbock, Booth, and Genette subscribe to, he shares with these social formalists the belief that alterity can be instantiated on the one hand through the interpreter's capacity for alterity and on the other through a special materiality that Barthes calls writing. Barthes' deconstructed phenomenological subject does, however, bring the second wave of social formalism to an extreme conclusion: in Barthes' theory both subject and object are dehumanized to the point where personal identity is defined almost exclusively by the will to alterity and the pliability of materiality. While Barthes is the theorist of the second wave most concerned with developing a literary theory that is also a cultural theory, his deconstructed understanding of the social and his valorization of writing both encourage him to produce the least recognizably human version of social formalism that we have yet to see: Barthes' interpreting agents possess so few human attributes that subjects and objects seem virtually interchangeable. The "voices" that Barthes holds out as an alternative to "classic" theories of point of view thus, as I will show, ultimately bespeak their full compatibility with the hybrid identity of the Jamesian interesting object: that half-human, half-thing that inaugurated the imbrication of alterity and materiality in the social formalist tradition.

ACCORDING TO the "classic" aesthetics of nineteenth-century fiction, writes Roland Barthes in *S/Z*, "every literary description is a *view*." But, he argues, the "speaker" of this fiction

> stands at the window, not so much to see, but to establish what he sees by its very frame: the window frame creates the scene. To describe is thus to place the empty frame which the realistic author always carries with him (more important than his easel) before a collection or continuum of objects which cannot be put into words without this obsessive operation (which could be as laughable as a "gag"); in order to speak about it, the writer, through this initial rite, first transforms the "real" into a depicted (framed) object; having done this, he can take down this object, *remove* it from his picture: in short: de-depict it (to depict is to unroll the carpet of the codes, to refer not from a language to a referent but from one code to another). (*S/Z*, 54–55; Barthes' emphasis)

At first reading we might think that we are back in James's house of fiction, but though many of the terms are the same, Barthes' edifice is all window and no house: the author's point of view has become not relative but arbitrary. And, rather than provide the reader a particular unmediated access to a coherent object, the window of point of view imposes coherence on "a collection or continuum of objects"; the Barthesian novelist mistakes his framed view for an unmediated vision of a coherent object. He does not, in other words, know that his window frame is in effect a picture frame: that the view has been created. So unaware is he of his frame's mediating power that he "de-depicts" the object by treating it as found. The de-depicted object then becomes the writer's stable referent for verbal description; he can now put the object "into words." As Barthes states in another conceit reminiscent of James:

> A classic narrative always gives this impression: the author first conceives the signified (or the generality) and then finds for it, according to the chance of his imagination, "good" signifiers, probative examples; the classic author is like an artisan bent over the workbench of meaning and selecting the best *expressions* for the concept he has already formed. (173; Barthes' emphasis)

Barthes thus portrays the objectivism of classic aesthetics as a delusion: although the realist writer may think that he is only describing what he sees, he is in fact both inventing his "object" and repressing the true multiplicity of his "view."[34] For Barthes, the classic literary theorist labors under the same delusion as the writer, insofar as he imagines that his object of study is discrete enough and coherent enough to form the basis of an equally discrete and coherent theory. The truth is, however, that

> literature itself is never anything but a single text: the one text is not an (inductive) access to a Model, but entrance into a network with a thousand entrances; to take this entrance is to aim, ultimately, not at a legal structure of norms and departures, a narrative or poetic Law, but at a perspective (of fragments, of voices from other texts, other codes), whose vanishing point is nonetheless ceaselessly pushed back, mysteriously opened: each (single) text is the very theory (and not the mere example) of this vanishing, of this difference which indefinitely returns, insubmissive. (*S/Z*, 12)

Whether in theory or in practice, Barthes argues, the aesthetics of point of view always has the same motivation: to justify faith in the coherent self of possessive individualism. That is why "in the classic text the majority of the utterances are assigned an origin, we can identify their parentage, who is speaking" (41). For Barthes, actual subjectivity is really as textual, which is to say as multiple and indeterminate, as the continuum one views or the network one critiques: the "deceptive plenitude" of subjectivity, Barthes declares, "is merely the wake of all the codes which constitute me" (10).

Yet if Barthes believes that classic aesthetics was so wrong to privilege the novel (not to mention its authors and readers) as objectively

---

[34] For a critique of Barthes' definition of classic realism, see Cedric Watts: "The doctrine underestimates the intelligence of readers, who can distinguish between a novel and a window; and it underestimates the intelligence of authors, the better of whom are concerned to alert readers critically to reality rather than to deceive them" ("Bottom's Children," 32).

autonomous, why does Barthes devote *S/Z* to a reading of a classic novella, Balzac's *Sarrasine*? Barthes' answer is that he wants to expose the
"natural" ideology that *Sarrasine*, like all classic fiction, champions. *S/Z*
is, by this account, a careful balancing act between skepticism about
theory and the truth-claims (or theory) supporting that skepticism. To
assert without dogmatizing, and to expose without revealing, require
the *"slow-motion"* reading (*S/Z*, 12; Barthes' emphasis) that Genette,
Pascal, and Cohn also employ in their critiques of objectivity: "The
step-by-step commentary is of necessity a renewal of the entrances to
the text, it avoids structuring the text *excessively*, avoids giving it that
additional structure which would come from a dissertation and would
close it: it stars the text, instead of assembling it" (13; Barthes' emphasis).[35]

This critical "dispersion" of the text should not, Barthes cautions, be
mistaken for a pluralist toleration of different truth-claims:

> The interpretation demanded by a specific text, in its plurality, is in no way
> liberal: it is not a question of conceding some meanings, of magnanimously
> acknowledging that each one has its share of truth; it is a question, against
> all in-difference, of asserting the very existence of plurality, which is not that
> of the true, the probable, or even the possible. (*S/Z*, 6)

But even if we were to grant that Barthes' criticism in *S/Z* presents the
text as more mercurial than a "magnanimous" pluralism would, we
would still have to admit that Barthes continues to regard criticism as
an ethical, indeed an altruistic activity: he believes that the interpreter
should honor the plurality of the text. Yet since he has also maintained
that text and interpreter are part of the same semiological network, how
does his interpreter ever wander far enough from the plurality of the
text in order to deny its "existence"? In other words, although Barthes
claims to free himself from the point-of-view philosophy of the objectivists, he actually retains a belief in the phenomenological positionality
that structures this philosophy; and for Barthes as for all the theorists

---

[35] See D. A. Miller for a discussion of the gay cultural codes that Barthes leaves
unstarred (*Bringing Out Roland Barthes*, esp. 13). See Michael Moriarty, *Roland
Barthes*; Rick Rylance, *Roland Barthes*; and Culler, *Barthes*, for overviews of
Barthes' work and fuller discussions of the importance of *Sarrasine* to Barthes' theo-
retical project. Moriarty, for example, points out that Sarrasine, a drawer and a
modeler of clay, is a figure for both the "realist author and . . . the asymbolic critic"
(*Roland Barthes*, 129). See John Holloway, "Language," for a critical discussion of
Barthes' interpretation of Saussure.

we have examined, that positionality is the site of the ideally ethical operation of interpretative desire. Barthes' "perspective," in other words, is the legacy of Jamesian point of view.[36]

To understand why Barthes preserves the phenomenological distinction between subject and object even when he has radically redefined subjectivity as textuality, we need first to appreciate the distinction Barthes wants to draw between the edenic world of pure production—what he calls the "writerly"—and the fallen world of representation—what he calls the "readerly."[37] The concept of the "writerly" is for Barthes an ideal that stands outside representation because any manifestation would compromise its value as pure force, pure energy: one would be tempted to say pure spirit, if the notion were not in such flagrant contradiction to the premises of Barthes' investigation.[38] The writerly cannot be represented and thus (like Yahweh) can barely even be discussed:

> There may be nothing to say about writerly texts. First of all, where can we find them? Certainly not in reading (or at least very rarely: by accident, fleetingly, obliquely in certain limit-works): the writerly text is not a thing, we would have a hard time finding it in a bookstore. Further, its model being a productive (and no longer a representative) one, it demolishes any criticism which, once produced, would mix with it: to rewrite the writerly text would consist only in disseminating it, in dispersing it within the field of infinite difference. (*S/Z*, 4–5)

As pure productivity, the writerly is unreproducible. Barthes is explicit about the paradoxical nature of his ideal: "The writerly is the novelistic without the novel, poetry without the poem, the essay without the dissertation, writing without style, production without product, structuration without structure" (5). In contrast to the Barthesian ideal of the writerly, readerly texts fall short of pure paradox; they do manifest

[36] Culler likewise argues for the importance of understanding Barthes as a moralist, although he singles out *Le plaisir du texte* (1973) as making clear "the ethical cast" of Barthes' thought (*Barthes*, 20). See Ronald Bush for a related critique of the "ethical sense" in the work of Paul de Man. Bush intriguingly argues that deconstruction partakes of the "modernist desire to save us from ourselves" ("Paul de Man," 53–54).

[37] See Frank Lentricchia for a comparison of the writerly with Hegel's Spirit (*After the New Criticism*, 143).

[38] As Geoffrey Strickland notes, "one seems bound to come back to religious language to account for the appeal of Barthes and the direction of his later writing" (*Structuralism*, 141).

themselves, they can be found in bookstores. But, Barthes insists, although all readerly texts are the same in that they stay the "infinite play of the world" (5), some readerly texts deny such plurality more than others. The writerly thus counts for Barthes as both an ideal limit and a term of relative evaluation; he believes that one can ask of any literary work, how writerly is this readerly text?

In asking this question Barthes introduces a familiar ethical component into the otherwise estranging world of deconstructive semiology. If the writerly is a good to be achieved, and this good can be achieved in better and worse ways, then agency itself is defined ethically as the success or failure of this achievement. Subject and object may be the wake of codes that constitute them, but the agency of text, authors, and readers is reasserted in the ethical condition of knowing and enacting the writerly. The good text reveals its writerly nature by resisting the temptations of the readerly. The good reader reveals a text's writerliness and also resists her own readerliness.[39]

In his discussion of how to distinguish degrees of writerliness within the general class of the readerly, Barthes makes clear how both subject and object are reconstituted through the interplay of interpretation: readerly texts, he argues,

> are products (and not productions), they make up the enormous mass of our literature. How differentiate this mass once again? Here, we require a second operation, consequent upon the evaluation which has separated the texts, more delicate than that evaluation, based upon the appreciation [*l'appréciation*] of a certain quantity—of the *more or less* each text can mobilize. This new operation is *interpretation* (in the Nietzschean sense of the word). To interpret a text is not to give it a (more or less justified, more or less free) meaning, but on the contrary to appreciate what *plural* constitutes it. (*S/Z*, 5; Barthes' emphasis)

Jamesian "wonder" resurfaces as Barthesian "appreciation." According to James, we recall, the artist's capacity for wonder enables him to distinguish between the chaotic mass of life and the intrinsically interesting objects within it. The readerly activity that Barthes commends (the readerly activity, that is, that approximates the ideal of the writerly) seems almost the obverse of James's paradigm—the appreciative inter-

---

[39] See Barbara Johnson for a powerful formulation of how Barthes' reading of the thematics of castration in *Sarrasine* contradicts his theoretical definition of "castration as the desirable essence of the writerly" (*Critical*, 11–12). Johnson argues that insofar as he makes "identity narrative," he also makes it "literary" (12).

preter appears to favor indeterminacy over "meaning"—but Barthes has simply redefined the object of James's ethics as something plural rather than singular.

The deep continuity between James and Barthes comes clearer in a manifesto from *S/Z* that uncannily echoes James's account of the rereading he undertook to begin revising his works:

> We are, in fact, concerned not to manifest a structure but to produce a structuration. The blanks and looseness of the analysis will be like footprints marking the escape of the text; for if the text is subject to some form, this form is not unitary, architectonic, finite; it is the fragment, the shard, the broken or obliterated network. (20)

Where James claimed that the difference between his past and present "footprints" helped him see both his own identity and that of his artistic subject more clearly, Barthes suggests that we piece out the "vanishing" network from the "form" of its shard. James's appeal to personal experience—specifically to the unique circumstance of the authorial rereading experience—is thus reformulated by Barthes as the universal condition of "analysis." But significantly in Barthes' description as well as James's, it is the noncoincidence of subject and object, of interpreter and interpreted, that preserves alterity: for James, the spontaneous view of both the artist he once was and the artist he now is insured a freedom and authenticity for that past self; for Barthes the noncoincidence of interpreter and interpreted insures the freedom of the text. In both cases, form is the means of detecting the interpreted other (past self, text); but this incarnation, to represent authentically the alterity of the interpreted other and to stimulate the interest of the interpreter, must be partial and suggestive rather than complete.

Dedicated as he is to the "ludic advantage" of multiplicity itself, Barthes may still seem far from either James's search for the stable referent that is the identity of the artistic subject or Booth's earnestly positivist quest for "some ultimate signified" (*S/Z*, 165), but however diffuse Barthes' object—the fragment, the shard, the broken or obliterated network—he still insists that the reader not project her own "voice" (151) onto it, defining a discourse that "is speaking according to the reader's interests" as illustrative not of the writerly ideal, but of the classic realist narrative. In fact, Barthes often extols the moral virtue of authentic interpretation just as earnestly as Booth does: "Only writing, by assuming the largest possible plural in its own task, can oppose without appeal to force the imperialism of each language" (*S/Z*, 206).

The difference between Booth's moralism and Barthes' is that Barthes, like Lubbock, values freedom in the text above all else, as he demonstrates in his praise for Flaubert, one of the novelists that Lubbock, too, admires:

> Working with an irony impregnated with uncertainty, [Flaubert] achieves a salutary discomfort of writing: he does not stop the play of codes (or stops it only partially), so that (and this is indubitably the *proof* of writing) *one never knows if he is responsible for what he writes* (if there is a subject *behind* his language); for the very being of writing (the meaning of the labor that constitutes it) is to keep the question *Who is speaking?* from ever being answered. (140; Barthes' emphasis)

Admirably refusing to answer the question "Who is speaking?" Flaubert willingly consigns himself to the void. The result is, as Lubbock maintained, a fictional space not flattened out by the weight of the author's presence but opened up by his absence; the postclassic text, Barthes maintains, has become "a multiple space no longer based on painting (the 'picture') but rather on [that locus classicus for "showing"] the theater (the stage)" (56).

In Barthes' account, it is true, the inhabitants of this newly vacated stage are "utterances," not characters; but for Barthes the codes, which give meaning to these utterances, have the qualities of subjectivity.[40] He calls them "voices":

> Each code is one of the forces that can take over the text (of which the text is the network), one of the voices out of which the text is woven. Alongside each utterance, one might say that off-stage voices can be heard: they are the codes: in their interweaving, these voices (whose origin is "lost" in the vast perspective of the *already-written*) de-originate the utterance: the convergence of the voices (of the codes) becomes *writing*. (*S/Z*, 21; Barthes' emphasis)

The vocal codes are more efficient doubletalkers than Lubbock's characters, speaking for themselves without restricting the significance of their utterances to self-expression, because unlike Lubbock's characters Barthes' voices are imagined as "off-stage," disembodied, hence neither

---

[40] Insisting elsewhere that one should not overlook characters, Barthes attributes the same quasi-independence to them that he ascribes to codes: "The discourse creates in the character its own accomplice: a form of theurgical detachment by which, mythically, God has given himself a subject, man a helpmate, etc., whose relative independence, once they have been created, allows for *playing*" (*S/Z*, 178; Barthes' emphasis).

confinable nor traceable. But the figurative language of materiality that Barthes uses to describe the voices (especially the metaphor of interweaving) also suggests that they are in a more abstract sense embodied, not as people but as the very substance of writing itself.

Despite, then, his explicit and repeated championship of the writerly as transcendent and unrepresentable spirit, in *S/Z* as a whole, Barthes' definition of the codes as voices is indicative not only of his Jamesian desire to conceptualize the (plural) other as knowable but also his Jamesian solution to the problem of mediation: the postulation of a novelistic subject who is both person and thing, agent and material. What distinguishes Barthes from James is that Barthes attributes to the vocal codes a collective and cultural identity (so absolute as to seem free, i.e. without origin), possessing an authority and agency far greater than any particular speaking subject. If the vocal codes therefore seem more inhuman than James's artistic subject, for Barthes they possess more of what he considers to be human meaning. For example, when he introduces his own methodological procedure in *S/Z*, the self-described arbitrariness of his own interests is limited by the enabling "substance" he creates, a life-giving materialization that gives voice to alterity and prevents appreciation from becoming self-projection:

> We shall not set forth the criticism of a text, or a criticism of *this* text; we shall propose the semantic substance (divided but not distributed) of several kinds of criticism (psychological, psychoanalytical, thematic, historical, structural); it will then be up to each kind of criticism (if it should so desire) to come into play, to make its voice heard, which is the hearing of one of the voices in the text. What we seek is to sketch the stereographic space of writing (which will here be a classic, readerly writing). (14–15; Barthes' emphasis)

Whereas James thought it was his duty to become the "quarter in which his subject most completely expresses itself," Barthes believes that the voices he has mobilized should take their own active role in self-expression. Unlike the better self-expression that James attempts to provide altruistically for his interesting object, the voices that Barthes seeks to appreciate are prior to and beyond any individual human perception; they give meaning to the text—and to subjects as texts—as much as the interpreter's interest gives life to them, and thus possess an agency and consequence beyond that of the alterity of self-expression.[41]

---

[41] Barthes' most provocative formulation of this symbiosis comes in his famous figure of the braid (*S/Z*, 160). His attempt to find a metaphoric language that will

But although Barthes insists on the transpersonal meaning of the codes, his hybrid characterization of them as both person and thing, as vocal material, shows that he—like James—in some deep way imagines his confrontation with the interesting object as a subjective encounter that is enabled by textual materialization, however fleeting and contingent that manifestation may be. Trying to capture the blending in "voices" of definiteness and indistinctness, of singularity and multiplicity, Barthes produces an unembarrassed version of Lubbockian synesthesia:

> The best way to conceive the classical plural is then to listen to the text as an iridescent exchange carried on by multiple voices, on different wavelengths and subject from time to time to a sudden *dissolve*, leaving a gap which enables the utterance to shift from one point of view to another, without warning: the writing is set up across this tonal instability (which in the modern text becomes atonality), which makes it a glistening texture of ephemeral origins. (41–42; Barthes' emphasis)

Although Barthes means this description to pertain to the "readerly" classical text, the dilemma he describes is his own: the text as a view is solid and objective, the text as a voice is subjective and unstable; if Barthes cannot accept objectivist aesthetics, neither does he believe that he can entirely reject it without also losing the alterity on which his own ethics of reading is based.[42] To break the deadlock, Barthes represents the text as, ideally, something to be both seen and heard: a "stereographic space" (21).

The difference between Barthes and Lubbock is that the Barthesian

---

suitably express the hybrid quality of the codes (as vocal subjectivity and as material thing) is reflected by the kaleidoscopic variety of figures he invokes, the height of which is reached as he seeks to describe the difference between the self-expressive alterity of the codes as they exist outside appreciation and the identity of the codes when engaged by the "hand" (rather than the Jamesian eye) of the interpreter:

> The grouping of codes, as they enter into the work, into the movement of the reading, constitute a braid (*text, fabric, braid*: the same thing); each thread, each code, is a voice; these braided—or braiding—voices form the writing: when it is alone, the voice does no labor, transforms nothing: it *expresses*: but as soon as the hand intervenes to gather and intertwine the inert threads, there is labor, there is transformation. (160; Barthes' emphasis)

[42] Diana Knight reads Barthes' commitment to alterity as a reinscription of the absented author: "Despite banishing the author as civil figure and owner of his discourse, Barthes also, and perhaps more than anyone, taught us to desire the author as the Other dispersed in that discourse" ("Roland Barthes," 831).

reader appreciates the stereography of the text with the eyes and ears of an anarchist:

> A multivalent text can carry out its basic duplicity only if it subverts the opposition between true and false, if it fails to attribute quotations (even when seeking to discredit them) to explicit authorities, if it flouts all respect for origin, paternity, propriety, if it destroys the voice which could give the text its ("organic") unity, in short, if it coldly and fraudulently abolishes quotation marks which must, as we say, in all *honesty*, enclose a quotation and juridically distribute the ownership of the sentences to their respective proprietors, like subdivisions of a field. (*S/Z*, 44–45; Barthes' emphasis)[43]

To coordinate this textual anarchism with the appreciation of alterity, Barthes must discard as a goal what every other theorist we have discussed assumes is fundamental to that ethics—communication. Drawing the logical conclusion from a radical position such as Booth's, in which author and reader can communicate only when they realize that universal values are all one *can* communicate, Barthes declares that "idyllic communication . . . suppresses everything *other*, every subject [*tout autre, tout sujet*]" (*S/Z*, 132; Barthes' emphasis). The free society of the Barthesian text is instead "like a telephone network gone haywire":

> The lines are simultaneously twisted and routed according to a whole new system of splicings, of which the reader is the ultimate beneficiary: over-all reception is never jammed, yet it is broken, refracted, caught up in a system of interferences; the various listeners (here we ought to be able to say *écouteur* as we say *voyeur*) seem to be located at every corner of the utterance, each waiting for an origin he reverses with a second gesture into the flux of the reading. Thus, in contrast to idyllic communication, to pure

---

[43] For Blanchot, the indeterminacy of narrative voice in the novel produces not anarchy but mimetic complexity. However, although his analysis of vocal fluctuation is in this respect compatible with that of Cohn and Pascal, for Blanchot as for Barthes, the vocal fluctuation points to the textuality of subjectivity. For Blanchot, the melodrama of social formalism is disrupted by metafictional desire. Blanchot asks of an ambiguous passage:

> But who is telling the story here? Not the reporter, the one who formally—and also a little shamefacedly—does the speaking, and actually takes over, so much so that he seems to us to be an intruder, but rather that which cannot tell a story because it bears—this is its wisdom, this is its madness—the torment of impossible narration, knowing (with a closed knowledge anterior to the reason-unreason split) that it is the measure of this outside, where, as we reach it, we are in danger of falling under the attraction of a completely exterior speech: pure extravagance. (*Gaze*, 143)

communication (which would be, for example, that of the formalized sciences), readerly writing stages a certain "noise," it is the writing of noise, of impure communication. (132)

And yet, Barthes continues, "this noise is not confused, massive, unnameable; it is a clear noise made up of connections, not superpositions" (132). Singular and plural, definite and indistinct: in Barthes' most elaborate conception of the text that has cast off the "imperialist" shackles of possessive individualism while continuing to welcome the society of the reader, the fullness of communication has become "cacography" (132).[44]

---

[44] Terence Hawkes's more optimistic reading of Barthes' critique of the "bourgeois social order" is perhaps a result of his explicatory project, which tends to treat sympathetically the theories it surveys.

Kristeva locates her own theoretical agreement with Barthes in relation to this model of communication that I have critiqued. She approves of Barthes' definition of communication as a conversation between a subject and language: Barthes "doesn't speak *about* literature, he speaks *to* literature as to his other as instigator" ("How Does," 120; Kristeva's emphasis). She believes that Barthes' definition of language as an ontological "struggle" poses an important alternative to the objectivism of scientific discourse.

3

The Visible Vocality of Ideology

The Social Formalism of
the Bakhtin Circle

[A]ny Marxist criticism worth the name must thus adopt a well-
nigh impossible double optic; seeking on the one hand to take the
full pressure of a cultural artefact while striving at the same time to
displace it into its enabling material conditions and set it within a
complex field of social power. What this means in effect is that one
will find oneself bending the stick too far towards formalism and
then too far towards contextualism, in search of that ever-receding
discourse which would in allegorical manner speak simultaneously
of an artistic device and a whole material history, of a turn of
narrative and a style of social consciousness.
     —Terry Eagleton, "Introduction" to *Marxist Literary Theory* (1996)

IN THE WAKE of the second wave of novel theory, the aesthetic debate between showing and telling was now felt to be decisively won;
but the project of formulating an explicitly social theory of the novel
had just begun. The linguistic and public subject respectively conceptualized by Booth, Genette, and Barthes helped to redefine the goal of
the theory of the novel: while the second wave contributed implicitly to
novel theory's foundational desire—the demonstration that the novel's
technical intricacies easily matched those of drama or poetry (the valorization of the unique "technical troubles" deplored by Forster)—this
was, importantly, an aim that rested uneasily alongside the second
wave's more general investigation of literature as a linguistic practice.
As we have seen, the project of reconceptualizing not just the novel but
literature generally as an effect of social interests beyond the author's
control worked to discredit the poetics that had authorized novel theory
as a discipline even as it incited new enthusiasm for, in Ruth Bernard
Yeazell's words, the study of the novel's relation "to the language and
systems of representation that it shared with the wider culture, and to

the more or less open ways in which it participated in that culture."[1] The immediate and widespread influence of M. M. Bakhtin's *The Dialogic Imagination* upon its 1981 U.S. publication suggests that for an overwhelming number of Anglo-American scholars Bakhtin's writings from the 1920s and 1930s pointed a way back to the future of novel theory.[2] Bakhtin's critique of the formalisms of his time and period (especially Russian formalism and Saussurean linguistics) seemed to open up a path from which Anglo-American novel theory might bid goodbye to New Critical, neo-Aristotelian, and narratological formalisms once and for all.[3] Yet as my own analysis of Bakhtin's work will try to show,

---

[1] Yeazell, "Introduction," *Sex*, vii.

[2] Alan Singer describes the turn to Bakhtinian post-structuralist literary theory as part of the turn away from the "univocal or monologic subject" posited by literary formalism ("Ventriloquism," 73). Don Bialostosky argues more specifically that Bakhtin "challenges [Seymour] Chatman's basic distinction between story and discourse and subsumes Chatman's view of the only possible relation among narrator, hero, and listener into a scheme of wider and more interesting possibilities" ("Bakhtin," 110). A. C. Goodson believes that "without the structuralism of the seventies, there would have been no Bakhtin reception of the scope we are witness to" ("Structuralism," 30). Prabhakara Jha sees Bakhtin as the solution to the search for "abstract formal and social characteristics" of the subject ("Lukács," 64).

Ken Hirschkop's work stands as an important counterbalance to the generally messianic reading of Bakhtin. In a series of brilliant essays, Hirschkop has provided us with a critical overview as well as a cultural and philosophical contextualization of Bakhtin's thought ("Introduction"). He has challenged the conventional notion of Bakhtinian dialogism as conversation, finding in Bakhtin a more political formulation of the concept that in fact reveals the limits of dialogue ("Is Dialogism for Real?" and "The Author"). He has also attacked the related mimetic valorization of the concrete that critics have deduced from Bakhtin by understanding the notion in Kantian terms ("On Value"). And finally he has astutely characterized the major trends in Anglo-American Bakhtin criticism ("The Author"). Hirschkop's work has influenced some of the best critical interpretations of Bakhtin; see, for example, Hitchcock (*Dialogics*, 3).

[3] Denis Donoghue has skeptically asserted that Bakhtin "has been turned into a hero for our time for reasons mostly sentimental" ("Reading Bakhtin," 115). Ann Jefferson puts Bakhtin specifically in the tradition of novel theory, but she, like Bialostosky, takes Bakhtin to be the answer to the conflicts that have preceded him ("Realism Reconsidered," 173). Wallace Martin is not so apocalyptic, but he does praise Bakhtin for adding "content" to the technical analyses that interested narratology for so long (*Recent Theories*, 150). Marianna Torgovnick also offers an overview of novel theory's evolution from James through Bakhtin ("Still," esp. 202); while I agree with her that point of view is a central issue for these theorists, I would add that it is intimately connected with their notions of literary realism.

See McKeon (*Origins*, esp. 1–22) for a particularly striking example of Bakhtin's importance to the new social study of the novel as a genre. McKeon believes that Bakhtin provides a "solution" to the inadequacies he finds in Ian Watt's and North-

rather than providing a real alternative to formalism, Bakhtin's language philosophy in fact extends the logic of James's aesthetic theory into a full-blown social theory.

Bakhtin's Anglo-American popularity derived from a double appeal, or, more precisely, his appeal to a double desire: the acknowledged Anglo-American need to move beyond aesthetic formalism and the unacknowledged need to retain the essential tenets of social formalism as I have been describing them. While a survey of Bakhtin's ardent proponents might lead us to believe that his thinking was so diffuse as to mean all things to all people—he attracted admirers as diverse as Terry Eagleton, Paul de Man, David Lodge, Michael Holquist, Tzvetan Todorov, and Julia Kristeva—in fact the reception of his work was dominated by two rival literary theoretical camps: deconstruction and poststructuralist humanism. In arguing for the deep continuities between Bakhtin and the social formalist tradition, I want also to suggest that the Bakhtinian deconstructionists and the Bakhtinian humanists are not as deeply at odds as they take themselves to be and that it is Bakhtin's social formalism that attracts both camps to his work.

By defining art not just as a form of writing but as social discourse and by analyzing it for the ideological value that it expresses, Bakhtin's language theory attracts deconstructionists who want to preserve what they take to be the truth of semiotic play but who also want to imagine the linguistic power relations that Barthes describes as having political consequences—and salutary ones, at that; in Bakhtin they find a way to reconceive Barthes' semiotic anarchism as Bakhtinian carnival. Barthes' call for the resistance to the "imperialism" of linguistic ownership is reformulated by Bakhtinian deconstructionists as an assertion of lan-

---

rop Frye's respective genre theories. Yet the passages that McKeon quotes from Bakhtin to ground his own genre theory, since they are statements Bakhtin makes about the nature of all language, give no strong sense of the novel's particular identity as a genre, other than its capacity to be and represent social discourse (see 12). In "solving" the problem of how genre can have both formal and social identities, McKeon simply asserts (through Bakhtin) that social ideology is inherent in all *language*—and thus, since the novel is a linguistic form, its form must be constituted by social languages. His attempt to offer a strong definition of genre thus instead makes the concept of genre no different from the representational activity of any and all social language.

For a more extended critique of McKeon's conception of ideology, see Warner, "Realist Literary History" (McKeon responds to Warner in his "Defense"); for a critique of McKeon's notion of genre, see Rader, "Emergence." Rader powerfully argues that the "understanding of genres in history is a very different thing from the history of genres" (69). See also McKeon's "Reply" to Rader.

guage's inherent potential for the subversion of any type of social authority. For humanists, Bakhtin's description of the novel as a type of social discourse seems to provide a way of discussing the ethical meaning of "real" human agents and not just their "implied" artistic shadowings.

The Anglo-American deconstructive interest in Bakhtin can be quickly deduced from an early review essay of his work written by David Carroll (1983).[4] Carroll finds in Bakhtin's concept of "dialogism" a way of defining interpretation not as the pursuit of knowledge but rather as an act of alterity—he even implies that knowledge, construed as a "meta" activity, is itself a hegemonic activity that inhibits alterity:

> A critical, dialogic approach to form and history would have as its goal neither the return to history as the ground of all grounds nor the return to any formal or textual system as the context of history. It would not be oriented towards saving history or "saving the text" from alien, intruding languages and strategies, but rather towards saving each from itself, from succumbing to the metanarratological, metahistorical ends each has so often been made to serve. ("Alterity," 83)

Barthes' belief that language should be displayed rather than used finds its echo in Carroll's understanding of Bakhtinian dialogue as the articu-

---

[4] For an interpretation of Bakhtin's compatibility with deconstruction, see Mac-Cannell, "Temporality," esp. 974. For an astute formulation of the ethical problematic within a Bakhtinian version of deconstruction, see Emerson, "Problems," 513. Lahcen Haddad claims that Bakhtin's work represents a "serious" challenge to deconstruction, arguing that Bakhtin, rather than Fredric Jameson, provides Anglo-American critics with a social theory that avoids "the articulation of imaginary and utopian relations in symbolic categories that impede and cancel their historical significance" ("Bakhtin's Imaginary Utopia," 146). Tzvetan Todorov espouses both a deconstructive version of Bakhtin and a humanist version. He puts a Barthesian spin on dialogism when he defines "dialogic criticism" as speaking "not *of* works but *to* works, or rather, *with* works" ("Dialogic Criticism," 72; Todorov's emphasis). But in another essay he stresses what we might call the "dialogism within" that constitutes the human condition: "It is the human being itself that is irreducibly heterogeneous; it is human 'being' that exists only in dialogue: within being one finds the other" (*Mikhail Bakhtin*, x–xi). Ironically, Todorov is criticized by David Danow for hegemonically limiting Bakhtin to any theoretical position ("M. M. Bakhtin," 141). Gary Saul Morson avoids the threat of domination by eschewing argumentation altogether and conducting his response to Bakhtin through a dialogue ("Who Speaks"). Bialostosky follows this extreme interpretation of dialogism in his argument that "Bakhtin's dialogics is founded in the inseparability of thesis and person" ("Dialogics as an Art," 789); and he goes so far as to recommend that the reader, in practicing dialogics, "try to re-create the image of specific persons who voice their ideas in specific texts and contexts" ("Dialogics as an Art," 790).

lation rather than the resolution of difference. But Carroll's sense of what it means for language to resist service—the "metanarratological, metahistorical ends"—marks a significant departure from Barthes. For Barthes the plurality of the codes evidences the larger "writerly" identity of language itself: the tonal instability of the codes both denotes and subverts reference. While Carroll would agree that language should be, not mean, he does not describe plurality as generated from an activity, in Barthes' words an "iridescent exchange," but as a collection of discursive identities that each are defined by a positive content: in resisting service, history and text "save each from itself" and thus save each for itself. The resistance to service is for Carroll the assertion of individuality—in this case discursive individuality—as long as that individuality is contextualized as part of a larger heterogeneity. Carroll credits Bakhtin with not only understanding the value of discursive heterogeneity but also relying on it as a critical strategy. Just as Barthes deliberately deployed ambiguity, paradox, and multivalence to qualify his will to theory, so, according to Carroll, should Bakhtin's work be read performatively: "The fundamental heterogeneity of Bakhtin's critical strategy undermines the ends it projects for itself, and in this way heterogeneity is affirmed and retained as a critical principle that cannot be negated or transcended, even through the carnivalization of society or the dialogization of discourse" ("Alterity," 82–83).[5] Bakhtin's arguments, in other words, resist their own "meta" potential by failing to cohere as a logical theory; the failure of logic is, for Carroll, the triumph of alterity over

---

[5] As early as 1983 we have Paul de Man hedging—almost playfully it seems, since the rest of his analysis is so insightful—about the significance of Bakhtin's inscrutability. Although he acknowledges that "it is not a foregone conclusion whether Bakhtin's discourse is itself dialogical or simply contradictory," he also asserts that the "richest" passages in Bakhtin are "also among the most contradictory and, for that reason, monologically aberrant. More than any other, they reveal the metaphysical *impensé* of Bakhtin's thought, the dogmatic foundations that make the dialogical ideology so attractive and so diverse" ("Dialogue," 104–5). De Man suggests here that the difference between the dialogic and the contradictory may be negligible, that the dialogic may in effect be another name for the contradictory. He uses this understanding of Bakhtin to usher in a reading of Rousseau's prefatory post-face to *La nouvelle Héloise*, a reading that is indistinguishable from his other deconstructive performances, the end of which is to expose the "utterly inconclusive" "hermeneutic quest" (106). Based on this example of critical practice, we can see why Bakhtin might be appealing to de Man: Bakhtin's contradictoriness—or dialogism—changes nothing because it *is* nothing; it simply gives de Man another occasion to do what he likes to do, since for him Bakhtin's work is only a new articulation of the same old interpretative strategy, one that permits the quest for finalizable meaning even as/because it thwarts comprehension.

domination: Bakhtin uses language for the democratic expression of the identities that define different discourses and thus defeats the temptation to make language serve only his own meaning.

The deconstructive interpretation of Bakhtin, then, finds in his work an ethical imperative to honor the impersonal diversity that is language; the humanists, on the other hand, find in Bakhtin a new reason to honor the plurality of subjects that are instantiated through language. Since a leader of the humanist appropriation of Bakhtin is none other than Wayne Booth, and since Booth has written extensively on why Anglo-American novel theory cannot do without Bakhtin, we can best understand the important and explicit link between Jamesian and Bakhtinian formalism by looking closely at Booth's introduction to the 1984 edition, the first U.S. edition, of Bakhtin's *Problems of Dostoevsky's Poetics*, an essay in which Booth makes explicit how Bakhtin has changed his mind about novel theory: "If I had not been ignorant, like almost everyone else, of the work of Bakhtin and his circle, I might have grappled with a much more sophisticated attack on the 'author's voice' in fiction, one that would have forced me to reformulate, if not fundamentally to modify, my [position]" (xix).[6]

As Booth identifies it, Bakhtin's value lies in his "challenge" to his earlier neo-Aristotelian overevaluation of narrative technique and the concomitant conceptualization of the aesthetic object as a unified work of art. According to Booth, Bakhtin has taught him that aesthetic unity is a misguided standard of evaluation; subjective plurality is the true end of art.[7] Good fiction, Booth, now believes

> has little to do with whether or not the author claims privileges of omniscience or exercises inside views. Indeed it has nothing at all to do with the author's effort to produce a single unified effect. Its subject is not the ordering of technical means toward certain effects so much as the quality of the author's imaginative gift—the ability or willingness to allow voices into the work that are not fundamentally under the "monological" control of the novelist's own ideology. ("Introduction," xix–xx)

But if Bakhtin's "challenge" for Booth is the demand that theory and criticism turn their attention to the "quality of the author's imaginative

---

[6] Bialostosky rightly notes that "Booth's current inquiries into the ethics of fiction make him less interested in Bakhtin's bearings on the technical issues of the rhetoric of fiction than on the evaluative issues that now concern him" ("Booth's Rhetoric," 215). See Booth's *Critical Understanding* (1979) and *The Company We Keep* (1988).

[7] Booth tellingly critiques his former neo-Aristotelian position by arguing for a Bakhtinian reading of Aristotle. See "Introduction," xviii.

gift," we might wonder what exactly Booth finds new in this lesson; as we have seen, *The Rhetoric of Fiction* has insisted all along that the implied author's moral vision is what makes great fiction. The Bakhtinian contribution to the Boothian project, then, seems to lie exclusively in the definition of the author's "best self," now better because, by containing other voices, it is *more* than the limited subjectivity of an actual author:

> The artist's essential tasks [sic] is not simply to make the most effective work possible, as viewed *in* its kind. It is rather to achieve a view of the world superior to all other views; fiction of the right kind, pursuing the right tasks, is the best instrument of understanding that has ever been devised. It is indeed the only conceptual device we have that can do justice, by achieving a kind of objectivity quite different from that hailed by most western critics, to the essential, irreducible multi-centeredness, or "polyphony," of human life. In freeing us from narrowly subjective views, the best novels achieve a universally desirable quality, regardless of the particular effects that in an Aristotelian view might be considered their ends. Like the universally desirable "sublime" pursued by Longinus, the quality pursued by Bakhtin is a kind of "sublimity of freed perspectives" that will always, on all fictional occasions, be superior to every other. (xx; Booth's emphasis)

Booth has found in Bakhtin a new way of conceptualizing the implied author's objectivity. A specific moral position—right values—has given way to polyphony, a plurality of subjective points of view. If in fact we can't agree about which values are universal, then we can, it seems, turn instead to the representation of moral difference as perspectival relativism. But whether he is discussing right value or "irreducible multi-centeredness," the moral imperative for Booth is the same: the artist's job is "to achieve a view of the world superior to all other views." Now, however, instead of transcending subjective partiality, Booth recommends that the "narrowness" of individual point of view be overcome through the "sublimity of freed perspectives"; an author gains this view not by egotistical self-projection but by supplementation. This subjective multiplicity is, Booth believes, objective because it transcends the author's partiality by supplementing it with other voices, other subjective attitudes that, combined, constitute a total, and therefore ideal, vision of life.

While Booth would have Bakhtin's theory provide the next step forward for novel theory, when we realize how much the new-fashioned Bakhtinian/Booth still sounds like the same old Percy Lubbock, we may want to conclude instead that the Jamesian tradition has in fact found a

way of staying where it always had been.[8] By declaring that Bakhtin has
taught him to reconsider "the author's voice in fiction," Booth ultimately erodes what had been the primary distinction between himself
and Lubbock: Booth's belief that showing was always telling, that the
author's "voice" in fiction, the moral judgment that constituted his
point of view, is always there if one knows how to look for it, no matter
how cleverly it might be veiled. In claiming to have learned from Bakhtin that good fiction allows "voices into the work that are not fundamentally under the 'monological' control of the novelist's own ideology" ("Introduction," xx), Booth ends up significantly redefining his
notion of the author's voice: where it had been the necessary and dominant expression of the moral value that defined individual identity, en-
compassing every aesthetic effect in a novel, now it is the expression of
authorial identity as simply one identity among many. Booth's "Bakhtinian" reformulation of the power and terms of authorial self-
expression reinstitutes the rivalry between character and narrator for
self-representation that defined the Lubbockian version of Jamesian altruism. Booth goes so far as to upbraid himself for having in *The
Rhetoric of Fiction* contributed to the theorization of characterological
oppression:

> Again and again I have sought, like most of my Western colleagues, to put
> into propositional form my summaries of what an *author* is up to, and of
> how a given character's role *contributes* to the author's overall plan. At
> times I have even allowed myself to talk as if characters could be reduced to
> pawns in a huge game of chess of which the author alone knows all the
> rules. (xxiv; Booth's emphasis)

As Booth understands Bakhtin, the novel as a genre should be first and
foremost dedicated to the representation of characterological alterity;
the novelistic technique of polyphony insures, according to Booth, that
characters will appear not as created beings that voice the author's intention, not, to use Lubbock's term, "trophies" of authorial self-
expression, but as truly and wholly autonomous subjects (xxii).[9] Booth,

[8] Ross Posnock describes the politics resulting from Jamesian wonder in much the
same terms: "In political terms, James's heterogeneity translates into something re-
sembling an expressivist pluralism that disperses power and rigid identification with
one role or place and replaces them with a dynamic of shifting involvements that
resists finitude and definition while breeding possibility and spontaneity" (*Trial*,
76).

[9] Lennard J. Davis raises this same question when he notes in regard to Bakhtin,
"everything that comes from the author is autocratically determined. . . . The fact

then, like Genette, Pascal, and Cohn imagines characterological self-expression to possess its own a priori and inviolable intrinsicality: polyphony insures that characters will speak for themselves, or, as the Bakhtinian Booth now puts it, exercise their "freedom to say what they will, in their own way" (xxii).[10]

Although Booth has said that Bakhtin's importance lies in his insistence that we look at the quality of the author's imaginative gift, which means the author's ability to allow his characters free expression, despite his expressed renunciation of anything that might look like formalism, Booth does not abandon his old interest in narrative technique, but, on the contrary, finds in Bakhtin a reason to believe that fictional resources are instrumental in the practice of authorial altruism: "Is it not true, as Bakhtin claims, that the techniques for freeing characters from the author's direct control are inherently superior to those that make it easy for the author to dominate?" ("Introduction," xxiv). This is a question that was at the heart of *The Craft of Fiction*, and Booth's deep agreement with Lubbock is reflected by their shared estimate of which nineteenth-century Russian novelists successfully achieve characterological alterity, an agreement that is ultimately more important than the "new" theory of voice that Booth says he has discovered in Bakhtin. Dostoevsky was, for Lubbock, one of the few authors who gave us a direct view of his characters, and he is for Booth one of the few authors who allows his characters' voices to be heard. For both Lubbock and Booth, Turgenev and Tolstoy fail to achieve full alterity:

> Turgenev, Tolstoy, indeed most who are called novelists, never release their characters from a dominating monologue conducted by the author; in their works, characters seldom escape to become full *subjects*, telling their own tales. Instead they generally remain as objects *used* by the author to fulfill preordained demands. (xxii; Booth's emphasis)

But Booth, unlike Lubbock, makes clear the ethical foundation for these aesthetic judgments. The appreciation of alterity is, in this humanist world, an approximation of divinity: as Booth puts it, "[Bakhtin's]

---

that the novel substitutes a simulacrum of conversation does not mean that the truly dialogic is being represented". (*Resisting*, 178).

[10] Although Booth has said that he was becoming "increasingly uneasy" about the distinction between the biographical and implied authors, and although he also has said that "these days I want to worry about the flesh and blood author, too" (qtd. in Hopkins, "Interview," 49), he finds in Bakhtin a way of eliminating the distinction between fictional and corporeal manifestations of subjectivity.

'God-term'—though he [Bakhtin] does not rely on religious language—
is something like 'sympathetic understanding' or 'comprehensive vision,'
and his way of talking about it is always in terms of the 'multi-voicedness' or 'multi-centeredness' of the world as we experience it" (xxi).[11]

The primary difference between on the one hand the Bakhtinian
Booth and on the other hand Lubbock and his second-wave inheritors,
Genette, Pascal and Cohn, has to do more with Booth's willingness to
present his position as ethical and less with the actual differences in
their understanding of the novel's ethical stakes. And if Booth is willing
to come out and declare the ideal novelist to be godlike, he is also willing to make explicit a claim that the Jamesians assume at every moment
but refrain from articulating: that the novel is distinguished as a literary
genre, as a discursive form, by its special capacity for fostering the appreciation of alterity:

> Only "the novel," with its supreme realization of the potentialities inherent
> in prose, offers the possibility of doing justice to voices other than the
> author's own, and only the novel invites us to do so. This is not a matter
> only of length; epics have all the space in the world but they still tend to be
> monologic. It is more a matter of the technical resources of narrative in
> prose—the inherent capacity of narrative to incorporate languages other
> than the author's (or reader's) own. In various kinds of indirect discourse,
> novelists can maintain a kind of choral vitality, the very same words convey-
> ing two or more speaking voices. ("Introduction," xxii)

Booth has discovered Free Indirect Discourse and thereby a way to
claim, with Lubbock, Genette, Pascal, and Cohn, that the novel's generic particularity—the appreciation of alterity—lies in its capacity to represent two subjects in "the very same words." Booth thus joins Genette,
Pascal, and Cohn in correlating characterological autonomy with the alterity of vocabulary; but what seems different here, the "Bakhtinian"
twist, is that the rivalry between subject and object, between representer

---

[11] Booth has elsewhere defined his religious faith in words very similar to what he
calls Bakhtin's "God-term." He says,

> To improve our capacity to share understandings is a value that is built into our
> condition as human beings. We don't need to say anything about God or religion
> to make the point, but I should add what may be obvious: I have ultimately a
> kind of religious faith in that value, a faith based on notions about what kind of
> creatures we are, how we are made, and how we are related to the Great I Am,
> the Supreme and highly Critical Understander. We were made in understanding;
> we become human only *in* understanding. (qtd. in Hopkins, "Interview," 62–63;
> Booth's emphasis.)

and represented, seems to have left no palpable traces: the novelist can absent himself so completely from the representation of other voices as to eliminate even the play of sympathy or irony that characterized the second wave's theorization of FID. But it is important to note that this extreme form of negative capability is made possible by Booth's explicitly exalted and optimistic sense of the novel's own capacity for representation; the objectivity obtained by the god-like author goes hand-in-hand with the objectifying capacities that Booth attributes to the novel itself. Booth's understanding of Bakhtinian polyphony thus significantly modifies the conjunction of altruism and negative capability that has been a distinguishing feature of the social formalist tradition: thanks to Booth's belief in the novel's inherent ability to represent subjects objectively, the social formalist goal of representing the other in her own terms is accomplished through no self-sacrifice from—and therefore no self-erasure of—the altruistic author. It is now not just the author but "the novel" as representing agent who "offers the possibility of doing justice to voices other than the author's own"; and it is now the novel that allows the author's identity to be expressed both by his negative capability and by his positive vocal manifestation.

We should note that even this appeal to the novel's generic capacity for objectivity has its roots in *The Rhetoric of Fiction*. In that work, Booth attributed to the novel what I have called the capacity for double vision: thanks to the novel's ability to partition the representation of the author from the representation of his characters, it could, according to Booth, represent the identity of an omnipresent "implied" author without compromising the illusion of characterological autonomy. The important difference between this earlier conception of the novel's objectifying capacity and Booth's later conversion to polyphony is that Booth's "Bakhtinian" sense of the novel's ability to represent multiplicitous and heterogeneous "others" enables the author to think of himself as not simply self-represented, but represented by his own powers in conjunction with those representational powers possessed by the novel itself. This shared responsibility for representation makes it possible for a novelist to express his own voice—as actualized and not simply implied—without fear of violating either the alterity of his characters or the aesthetic success of his novel. The "choral vitality" that the novel makes possible thus allows the author himself to be both conductor and participant; he can display his capacity for alterity by the number of different voices that he has represented and, in making his own voice heard, he can also represent in positive terms (i.e. not simply relational terms) the intrinsicality of his own identity. The power relations that undergird novelistic representation always have, in other words, the potential to resolve themselves as a harmony of voices—that are equal because they are equally representable and represented.[12]

A full reading of Bakhtin's theory thus needs to make sense of the Carrollian understanding of Bakhtinian heterogeneity as the politically consequential liberation of language and the Boothian understanding of the novel as the supreme egalitarian expression of human diversity. Key to the connection between these interpretations of Bakhtin is a term that is untheorized by both: ideology. Ideology is, I want to argue, the concept that underwrites Bakhtin's theory of social identity, which in turn is the basis of his theory of the novel. Defined by Bakhtin as the social value created by the modes of production, ideology is presented as an explicit marxist alternative to subjectivist theories that describe identity as originating in an individual consciousness. Consciousness, Bakhtin insists, is not simply influenced by social relations, but is constituted as social relation. His primary, indeed virtually exclusive, way of proving this claim is first to define consciousness as fundamentally linguistic and then to define language as ideological.

But although he begins from a philosophical position that is in direct opposition to that which informs James's Prefaces, Bakhtin's theory of ideology leads him to reproduce the social formalist terms that define novelistic alterity. Like James, he believes that the self can be represented in terms of the other thanks to two things: the imagination of the representer—her inherent capacity for alterity—and the instantiating power of the material of representation—in Bakhtin's case, social discourse generally and novelistic discourse in particular. As I will show, Bakhtin's desire to attribute to language—and to the novel—an inherent

---

[12] One of Booth's most confusing modifications of the wholesale enthusiasm he has expressed for Bakhtin comes in "Freedom of Interpretation." In admitting the "feminist challenge" to Bakhtin, Booth seems to acknowledge social constraints that might limit subjective freedom. He nonetheless concludes by reaffirming the dialogic principle—and his description vividly reveals how dialogics paradoxically allows for individual autonomy and complete social mediation:

> [Bakhtin] shows us that we are not freed merely by learning how to cast off the powers that made us; we are freed by taking in the many voices we have inherited and discovering, in our inescapably choral permanence, which voices must be cast out of our choir. Each of the voices within is already itself such a chorus, and thus each voice was always at least partially free even as we took it in. ("Freedom," 76)

and material capacity for objective representation, a capacity that works through but ultimately transcends subjective mediation, is the legacy of his particular attempt to fashion a marxist materialist understanding of ideology. Bakhtin tries to argue that the "terms" of representation are expressions not of the private relations between the author and the object of his interest (as they were for James) but of the author's relation to the social "voices" that exist in language itself. Bakhtin conceptualizes the interesting other not simply as the referent of novelistic representation but as an inhabitant of the material of that representation: language is on his view populated with exotopic identities and thus becomes the ideally legible body of social diversity.

Given his sincere determination to formulate a rigorous social theory, why does Bakhtin end up reproducing the phenomenologist/materialist logic of social formalism? Bakhtin is led away from marxism and into social formalism primarily due to his almost circular definition of ideological value as linguistic social relation. As I want to show, sociality is for Bakhtin a subject's relation with the languages that constitute her identity. As worked out in Bakhtin's writings, an individual consciousness is defined vaguely and abstractly by values derived from particular social experiences such as class position, historical moment, or national culture; the achievement of self-conscious discursive self-representation becomes for Bakhtin an ethical value more important than any of the "ideological" values residing in the speaker's language. In Bakhtin's theory, then, an individual's language expresses her ideology only in the most general political sense: like the play of sympathy and irony that characterized the second wave's theorization of FID, an individual's beliefs, as Bakhtin describes them, are either subversive or hegemonic depending upon the degree and type of interrelation she establishes with the identities that inhabit her language. The multiplicity that seemingly distinguishes the Bakhtinian subject from the more conventional phenomenological subject posited by Genette, Pascal, and Cohn is diminished, as I hope to show, by the consolidating capacity for empathy that Bakhtin ascribes to his speaking subject. Her self-consciousness about the ideological positions that reside in the language she speaks makes Bakhtinian politics primarily a *performative* gesture of an individual: no matter what her history, nationality, gender, or economic class, a speaker always has the freedom to choose her position in relation to the identities that inhere in the words that she uses. As such, language is for Bakhtin what art is for James: an intensely "living" affair. The weight of past experience (in James's case artistic, in Bakhtin's ideological) has value insofar as it is perceptible, and deployable, in the present moment of communication. For Bakhtin, every sentence, every word, becomes an opportunity for social intercourse, which he defines as personal relation: at any particular moment of expression, the speaker communicates not just with an interlocutor, not just a projected reader, but also with the social identities that reside within the language she deploys.

For Bakhtin, as for all the social formalists I have been analyzing, the appreciation of alterity is thus the single most important task of novelistic representation. But because Bakhtin—like Barthes—believes alterity itself to be a condition of reality, not something generated strictly by the artist's capacity for wonder, the author's ethical position is less a matter of altruism and more the enlightened fulfillment of a universal moral duty. The Bakhtinian novelist, like the Jamesian novelist, cannot help but express his "vision of life" in the act of representation and, like the Jamesian novelist, he can be more or less capable of constituting that vision in relation to an other. But whereas for James the artist positioned himself in relation to an interesting object upon whom he then conferred subjectivity—an accomplishment that bestowed upon the Jamesian artist a special genius for empathetic appreciation—for Bakhtin the artist's goal is no different from that of any language user: since language embodies a multitude of heterogeneous subjects, and since any particular speaker is thereby constituted by a social plurality, the ethical project for any language user is to become self-conscious of this truth: that words, the apparent verbal objects that we use to communicate, in fact embody heterogeneous social subjects that have a human and social identity prior to any particular individual's engagement with them.

By defining the novelist as a self-representing linguistic agent rather than a Jamesian viewer and picture maker, the second wave of social formalists began a reexamination of the power relations that were implicit in Jamesian and Lubbockian accounts of novelistic representation; because James and Lubbock take for granted the author's representational privilege, their theories seem naive to thinkers like Bakhtin who believe that mediation cannot be discussed apart from the operation of social power. Social formalism thus develops from an ethics of altruism—the notion that the novelist spontaneously desires to represent the wonderful other as an interesting subject—to an ethics of linguistic intrinsicality—the notion that the novelist should strive to represent the other in her "own terms" as a speaking subject—to a politics of linguistic diversity—the notion that the novelist can subvert social hegemony by representing the heterogeneousness of individual and social identity, defined as a mediated plurality of ideological "speaking" subjects whose definitive alterity is understood exclusively in linguistic terms.

Because Bakhtin's social formalism is so theoretically complicated, and because it is developed over a number of key texts, my analysis will require some detail. The essays that deal most explicitly with novel theory, *Problems of Dostoevsky's Poetics* and "Discourse in the Novel," are frequently read in isolation from essays, such as "Discourse in Life and Discourse in Art" and *Marxism and the Philosophy of Language*, that attempt a broader philosophical account of literature as social discourse. This partitioning allows interpreters of Bakhtin to deny or ignore the contradictions that in my view have persistently characterized Bakhtinian thought. By tracing the development of Bakhtin's thinking about the relationship between literature and society, I hope to contribute in a general way to our emerging understanding of this important theorist and to show more specifically that social formalism is neither accidental nor incidental to his work but in fact lies at the heart of his project.

But I also want to read Bakhtin in detail because his theory of the novel culminates in important ways the tradition that I have been tracing. If the social formalist tradition begins with James's cultural legitimatization of the novel, after Bakhtin the novelistic becomes the value to which not just language but culture itself is held. In Bakhtin's work social discourse is frankly lauded for its ability to embody and to foster the empathetic human spirit that Bakhtin takes to be an ultimate ethical good—and thus the novelistic in its social formalist definition comes to extend beyond genre, beyond art, and into any and all representational activity. The Bakhtinian novelist, like the Barthesian reader, need only remove the veil from "natural" discourse to display its novelized identity. The embracement of Bakhtin's theory of the novel in our contemporary moment is thus the culmination of a tradition in which the specification of the novel's generic characteristics has always been secondary to the study of its ethical work, formally manifested. The relativization and personification that novelization comes to represent—the understanding of meaning as always only social empathy—not only puts an end to aesthetics but in effect puts an end to any project that imagines itself to be beyond or outside of subjective and political self-interest, including that of literary theory. If in his Preface to *The Golden Bowl* James imagined theory to be the end of art, then after Bakhtin novelization has become the end of theory.

"Discourse in Life and Discourse in Art" and 'Marxism and the Philosophy of Language'

To move from the Anglo-American interest in Bakhtin to a study of Bakhtinian theory itself is first of all to exchange the problem of appropriation for the problem of authorship. Which texts are Bakhtin's? Answering this question has, as one critic puts it, become a "topos of current Bakhtinian scholarship" (Godzich, Foreword, viii). The issue has become a topos because, as long as the evidence remains inconclusive, each critic must forge her own working solution. Four major essays are in dispute: "Discourse in Life and Discourse in Art" (1926), *Freudianism: A Critical Sketch* (1927), and *Marxism and the Philosophy of Language* (1929), all originally published under the name V. N. Vološinov; and *The Formal Method in Literary Scholarship*, originally published in 1928 under the name P. M. Medvedev. Some critics like Michael Holquist and Katerina Clark have a stake in establishing Bakhtin as the conceptual, if not actual, author of these four works; other critics like I. R. Titunik insist that, until new evidence is uncovered to prove otherwise, we should continue to regard Vološinov and Medvedev as the rightful authors of the disputed texts.[13] In their biography of Bakhtin, Clark and Holquist detail how the social context of the time—the collective endeavors of the "Bakhtin Circle" and the political persecution that made authorship a life-threatening occupation (Medvedev was arrested and then shot by the secret police in 1938)—worked to subvert traditional publication procedures.[14] Because the authorship of these texts remains truly undecidable, and because we need to be reminded of this real indeterminacy, I will follow those who, however awkwardly, resort to the compromise virgule (Medvedev/Bakhtin; Vološinov/Bakhtin) in order to denote both the possibility of coauthorship or considerable influence and the fact of our current uncertainty.[15] Since the confusion surrounding these texts is so great, it might be tempting to dismiss them altogether and deal only with the works we know to be Ba-

[13] See Clark and Holquist, *Mikhail Bakhtin*, 170, for their attempt to extend the concept of authorship through an application of Bakhtinian concepts. See Titunik, "Translator's Introduction," xviii–xix, for a capsulized overview of the various leading positions on the subject. See Shevtsova, "Dialogism," for the importance of understanding Bakhtin's concept of ideology through the disputed texts.

[14] See Clark and Holquist, *Mikhail Bakhtin*, 95–119.

[15] In using the virgule, however, I do not mean to follow Albert J. Wehrle's suggestion that "the slash separating the names . . . be taken as the conventional signifier/signified bar" ("Introduction," xvii).

khtin's. But these early texts discuss a set of problems that provide valuable background for understanding some of the contradictions that surface again and again in the work signed by Bakhtin. Specifically, they share his interest in a new science called "sociopoetics," a system of analysis that would bring, according to its founders, objectivity to the study of literature. More importantly, however, they constitute a sustained attempt to find this objective method by way of marxist theory.[16]

All four of these essays take as their starting point the marxist premise that objective material conditions form the base of social life. Yet although the members of the Bakhtin Circle accept Marx's general notion of economic materialism, they anticipate (and in some cases have been praised by) post-structuralist theorists such as Althusser, Macheray, Williams, and Jameson in demanding a more nuanced account of the rela-

---

[16] See Hirschkop, "Introduction," and Bernard-Donals for critiques of Bakhtin's materialism that are compatible with mine. One of the earliest readings of Bakhtin as a marxist can be found in Tony Bennett's *Formalism* (see esp. 95). For other insightful readings of Bakhtin's relation to marxism, see Forgacs, "Marxist," esp. 190–99; LaCapra, *Rethinking*, esp. 320–22; Selden, "Russian Formalism," esp. 101; Young, "Back to Bakhtin"; and especially Gardiner's recent full-length study of Bakhtin and ideology, *Dialogics of Critique*. The attempt of these critics to gauge Bakhtin's connection to marxism stands in striking contrast to the influential work of Clark and Holquist, who argue that Bakhtin simply used marxist discourse as a mask for theology (*Mikhail Bakhtin*, 80). Morson and Emerson have recently admitted that marxism should be taken seriously as one of Bakhtin's influences, but they ultimately conclude that his "theories of language and literature . . . were sociological without being Marxist; he answered the challenge of his friends with his sociology without theoretism" ("Introduction," 49, repeated in their *Mikhail Bakhtin*, 119). This statement reveals how much Morson and Emerson equate marxism, not with economic materialism, but with systematization per se. Morson and Emerson ultimately want not to resolve Bakhtin's theoretical contradictions but to understand them instead as a liberating pluralism. Free from systematic logic, Bakhtin, according to Morson and Emerson, can thus enact through his own writing the "dialogics" that they take to be his primary contribution (see esp. "Introduction," 48). As they put it, "a fundamental tenet of Bakhtin's thought is that knowledge, to be genuine and valuable, does not have to be a system; neither does it have to describe its object as a system" (47). I would argue that Bakhtin's social formalism is indeed a system of thought that, however vexed, characterizes not only the work signed by Bakhtin but also the "disputed texts" ascribed to members of the Bakhtin Circle and that it defines their joint effort to find in literary formalism a stable ground for marxist ideology.

See Gossman for a critique of Bakhtinian marxism as "hopelessly idealist and metaphysical" ("Review," 341). Gossman also astutely points out that Bakhtin's "social classes seem to be no more than agents of enduring principles or forces locked in conflict with each other in what, in the end, resembles a gigantic psychomachy more than a history of a system" ("Review," 345).

tionship between base and superstructure, between material conditions and ideology.[17] In *The Formal Method* this need is explicitly articulated:

> Between the general theory of superstructures and their relationship to the base and the concrete study of each specific ideological phenomenon there seems to be a certain gap, a shifting and hazy area that the scholar picks his way through at his own risk, or often simply skips over, shutting his eyes to all difficulties and ambiguities. (Medvedev/Bakhtin, *Formal Method*, 3)

As the Bakhtin Circle sees it, sociological analysis needs, on the one hand, to close the gap between base and superstructure and, on the other, to expand its conception of ideology in order to account for "the distinctive features of material, forms, and purposes of each area of ideological creation" (3).[18] In particular, the Bakhtin Circle proposes to examine one of those features, "the essential plurality of the languages of ideology" (3).[19]

The Circle participates in a long and long-contested tradition in marxist theory by focusing almost exclusively on the complexities of ideology. Rarely do these authors mention the forces of production, and never do they specify how economic conditions determine ideology.[20]

---

[17] As Althusser famously puts it, the economic base is "determinant in the last instance," but this does not preclude the "reciprocal action of the superstructure on the base" ("Ideology," 130).

[18] See Erlich, *Russian Formalism*, esp. 77–78 and 114–15, for a discussion of the relation of the Bakhtin Circle to the Russian Formalists.

[19] David Musselwhite makes an emphatic case for Vološinov's importance to marxism: "It is not until we turn to the work of Voloshinov that we find Marx's, albeit fragmentary, comments on language and consciousness . . . directly engaged with" ("Towards a Political Aesthetics," 11).

[20] Perry Anderson has noted that the interest in the study of ideology to the exclusion of the study of the modes of production is characteristic of Western marxism generally. He believes that the study of ideology, moreover, has been dominated by the study of aesthetics. As he puts it, "The great wealth and variety of the corpus of writing produced in this domain, far richer and subtler than anything within the classical heritage of historical materialism, may in the end prove to be the most permanent collective gain of this tradition [Western marxism]" (*Considerations*, 78).

Peter Dews holds the Althusserian concept of "relative autonomy" responsible for the partitioning of ideology and economy. Because it "was no longer necessary to trace the form and function of each superstructural instance back to its determination by the economy," Dews argues, "art, politics, science, ideology [could each have] its own particular immanent structure and temporal rhythm which merited an independent and untrammelled investigation" ("Althusser," 114).

Terry Lovell is right to remind us, as I want to show in my analysis of the social formalism of the Bakhtin Circle, that "the problem which Althusser and his followers are attempting to solve in their development of the theory of ideology is one

When they do offer social history, it reads like marxist *Cliff's Notes*. Freud's work, for example, is historicized only to the point of being declared a symptom of late European capitalism (Bakhtin/Vološinov, *Freudianism*, 11). In *Marxism*, a chapter is devoted to the "history of forms of utterances in language constructions," but the "history" is so generalized that Bakhtin/Vološinov are able to conclude by recapitulating their argument in list form, charting the history of western civilization in four stages: from "authoritarian dogmatism" (the Middle Ages) to "rationalistic dogmatism" (the seventeenth and eighteenth centuries) to "realistic and critical individualism" (end of the eighteenth century and early nineteenth century) and finally to "relativistic individualism" (the present period). Although they end the chapter reminding us that "the conditions of verbal communication, its forms, and its methods of differentiation are dictated by the social and economic prerequisites of a given period" (Vološinov/Bakhtin, *Marxism*, 123), they clearly have interest neither in specifying how the economic base establishes those conditions nor in nuancing the commonplaces they use to characterize each period. What they are concerned with is not base, but ideology; not the specific economic conditions, but the specific languages used by each period ostensibly reflecting those conditions.

Given the fact that economic materialism in and of itself is undeveloped in these texts, some critics have concluded that the use of marxist terminology is a rhetorical strategy and not an integral part of the analyses. Clark and Holquist trace the complexities of the issue: while scrupulously noting the times when Bakhtin produced politically correct marxist analyses, these biographers finally conclude that marxism is an alien discourse for Bakhtin, one that social exigencies force him to use but to which he was uncommitted.[21] Perhaps with the deliberate choice of metaphor, Clark and Holquist claim that

> Bakhtin was frequently able to capitalize on the common ground between Marxist terminology and his own thought. Much of the supposedly Marxist terminology he uses can readily be translated into his own characteristic terminology without conceptual violence. For instance, the "base/superstructure" distinction can stand for the "given/conceived" distinction that Bakhtin took from Neo-Kantianism.[22]

which has plagued marxism since its inception. It has oscillated between allowing the realm of ideology too much and too little autonomy" ("Social Relations," 248).

[21] Clark and Holquist, *Mikhail Bakhtin*, 146–70.

[22] Clark and Holquist, *Mikhail Bakhtin*, 156. Anyone interested in Bakhtin of course owes a tremendous debt to Clark and Holquist. Both scholars are largely re-

Wlad Godzich, while not advocating that we read Bakhtin as a Kantian, otherwise extends this argument to include the work of the Bakhtin Circle as a whole, for whom he thinks marxist discourse was simply a savvy political strategy: "Given the intellectual intinerary [sic] of the Circle, it is not mandatory that his labor take place under the banner of Marxism, although it would be desirable to have such a powerful ally" ("Foreword," xiv).

Yet to read the marxist terminology of the Bakhtin Circle as simply rhetorical is to render inexplicable the primary goal of these texts, what in fact constitutes their communality: the objective analysis of ideological forms.[23] As I will show, far from being inessential and "translatable," the repeatedly employed marxist terms suggest the Circle's extreme interpretation of a marxist tenet: the materialist definition of consciousness as ideology.[24] So committed are they to materialism that they understand ideology not only as material by virtue of its representative relation to the forms of production but also as material in and of itself. It is this faith in the materiality of ideology per se that leads them to separate ideology from economy and therefore to partition on the one hand the study of ideological forms from the study of the economic base and on the other the study of human consciousness from substantive social conditions.

But in arguing that the authors of these disputed texts were committed to the marxist concepts that they rely on, I will not be saying that marxist beliefs are the only ones held by the Circle. On the contrary, I will show that, although these writers explicitly reject subjectivism in favor of materialism, every description they give of material reality rein-

---

sponsible for the dissemination of Bakhtin's work to an English-speaking audience. Their editions, translations, and analyses of Bakhtin are so prolific that it would be a project in itself to characterize their collective and individual interpretations of Bakhtin. To speak in the most general of terms, then, the picture of Bakhtin that emerges from Clark and Holquist's description is that of a socially concerned religious humanist: "Ultimately, Bakhtin's thought is a philosophy of creation, a meditation on the mysteries inherent in God's making people and people's making selves, with the activity of people creating other people in literary authorship as a paradigm for thinking at all levels of creating" (80). While I think that Clark and Holquist at every moment reveal the paradoxes in Bakhtin's work, they rarely acknowledge them as problematic, nor do they seem to think Bakhtin's genius compromised in any way.

[23] Titunik finds marxism so essential to these early texts that he uses this fact to argue against Bakhtin's authorship of them ("Translator's Introduction," xvii).

[24] Terry Eagleton praises the Bakhtin Circle for offering a pathbreaking materialist description of consciousness (*Literary Theory*, 117).

scribes the conflict between idealism and materialism, between subjectivity and objectivity, the very conflict that marxist monism was to have resolved for them. By focusing on two of the disputed essays signed by Vološinov—"Discourse in Life and Discourse in Art," and *Marxism and the Philosophy of Language*—we can see how Vološinov/Bakhtin's application of marxism is continually thwarted by their attachment to the notion of a personal subject whose identity is more self-derived than ideologically determined. The struggle to eliminate this contradiction results in a pattern of argumentation that provides the conceptual background for understanding Bakhtin's *Problems of Dostoevsky's Poetics* and "Discourse and the Novel." Over the course of these works, Vološinov/Bakhtin move from an acceptance of naive marxism, to the deconstruction of this overly simple view of social determinism, to the postmarxist construct of a social self that, without grounding in a material base and with no other social theory to account for its value, is devoid not just of substantive ideological meaning, but of any identity other than the will to social relation.

In "Discourse in Life and Discourse in Art," Vološinov/Bakhtin begin by arguing against the view that "form in and of itself . . . possesses its own special, not sociological, but specifically artistic nature and system of governance" (93). In the service of demonstrating that aesthetic meaning is no different from social meaning, Vološinov/Bakhtin criticize the kind of objectivism, advocated by the Russian Formalists, that pretends it can derive aesthetic significance from the art work in and of itself:

> "The artistic" in its total integrity is not located in the artifact and not located in the separately considered psyches of creator and contemplator; it encompasses all three of these factors. It is a *special form of interrelationship between creator and contemplator fixed in a work of art*. (97; their emphasis)

Yet even in this thesis statement we can already see the blurry distinction being made between the formal and the material. The artistic may not be *located* in the artifact, but it is *fixed* there. The art work may be expressive of a social dynamic rather than an aesthetic absolute, but it still remains the locus of meaning, the place that gives material embodiment to a dynamic, that makes the social concrete. We see here an underlying tension between two different senses of the "material." On the one hand, the material as mere form has no meaning; it is simply an arbitrary vehicle for expression. Yet, on the other hand, when form seems to bespeak the social, Vološinov/Bakhtin read form as the material of ideology, and thus claim an objective meaning for it. Importantly, this objective meaning does not, like the aesthetic absolutism it replaces, have any readily specifiable content other than the value of the social "interrelationships" it expresses. Or, put another way, the value of objective meaning as it is defined here is only the instantiation of social interrelation.

Because in "Discourse in Life and Discourse in Art" Vološinov/Bakhtin predicate the special character of artistic communication on the general character of all social discourse, we need to look at their analysis of "discourse in life" before we can fully understand their concept of "discourse in art." Although they argue that discourse in art is a special case of the social communication that characterizes "discourse in life," we will find that life discourse is, like art discourse, a variety of social formalism.

Vološinov/Bakhtin's paradigm for discourse in life is predicated on the marxist assumption that the material conditions of life determine a common understanding that is prior to any specific act of communication. Because they want to show that even the most minimal verbal statement can only be understood within the common understanding produced by social forces, Vološinov/Bakhtin offer the following scenario as their exemplum: "Two people are sitting in a room. They are both silent. Then one of them says, 'Well!' The other does not respond" ("Discourse," 99). Vološinov/Bakhtin go on to argue that although "to outsiders" this exchange is incomprehensible, it can be completely meaningful for the two interlocutors. They use this example to show that "phonetic, morphological, and semantic factors," i.e. the linguistic features of the words themselves, will do little to reduce the ambiguity of the exchange. In choosing to analyze a one-word utterance, Vološinov/Bakhtin seem to minimize what in *Freudianism* they called the "constraints" inherent in the material of language (i.e. its grammatical forms). Now meaning becomes specifiable only when an "outsider" becomes an "insider," only when we, like the participants, understand the full, *extraverbal* context within which the exchange has taken place. This extraverbal context, although outside of language's materiality, is derived from other material conditions. Vološinov/Bakhtin identify two kinds of objective material conditions that work together to produce two kinds of "common understanding": the material forces of production determine the shared ideology informing the dialogue; and the locale of the dialogue, the material conditions of the speakers' setting, enables their immediate understanding. The meaning produced by this ex-tra-verbal context, by these two kinds of objective material conditions, is, so Vološinov/Bakhtin argue, somehow "assumed in the word well" (99):

> Only those points on which we are all united can become the assumed part of an utterance. Furthermore, this fundamentally social phenomenon is completely objective; it consists, above all, of *the material unity of world that enters the speakers' purview* (in our example, the room, the snow out-side the window, and so on) and of *the unity of the real conditions of life* that generate a *community of value judgments*—the speakers' belonging to the same family, profession, class, or other social group, and their belonging to the same time period. (100; their emphasis)

Their paradigmatic example reveals Vološinov/Bakhtin's paradig-matic confusion.[25] Again, the logic is based in marxist premises: the ma-terial unity that forms the real conditions of life results in a community of value judgments (or ideology). But the material reality that Marx means, the modes of production that result in the social divisions of "family, profession, class, or other social group," are assumed rather than examined while physical conditions (the room, the snow) are fore-grounded as the immediate source of unity. This elision and substitution make it seem as if Vološinov/Bakhtin are merely extending Marx's con-cepts but what begins as a marxist analysis has inadvertently turned into a subjectivist account: the reduction of external material conditions from the forms of production to a room suggests that because material conditions are external, they hold objective meaning; but in fact the speaker must be conscious of these external conditions if they are to in-form his meaning. Unlike ideology, which would exist even apart from an individual's self-consciousness about it, the meaning of the word "well" depends upon the speakers' shared understanding of their "pur-view," the communality of their location. In other words, Vološinov/Ba-khtin want literal point of view to equal semantic point of view; they want what is accidental and dependent upon subjective perception to be an objective force that creates unified understanding.

This argument not only confuses marxist and nonmarxist notions of materiality, but also posits a simplistic correlation between base and su-

---

[25] A host of critics would disagree with my position. For different reasons, Martin (*Recent Theories*, 150), Jefferson ("Realism," 173), and MacCannell ("Temporali-ty," 979) find Vološinov/Bakhtin's insertion of the extraverbal into the utterance a strategic success rather than a logical mistake.

perstructure. In their later work, they do try to refine this model, but even if we for the time being grant this one-to-one correspondence, we may balk when they extrapolate from the necessary connection between base and ideology to a necessary connection between ideology and language use. This is a connection that they make again in *Freudianism*. But, in a way that indicates the purely speculative character of their theoretical project, their analysis in "Discourse" now comes to completely opposite conclusions. Whereas in *Freudianism* minority values are those that, because they had to be hidden, were internalized and thus had the potential to become nonverbal, now the values that "have entered the flesh and blood of all representatives of the group" and are in "no need of special verbal formulation" ("Discourse," 101) are majority values. And whereas in the Freud book the sign of a healthy society is the congruence between internal and external speech, now the evidence for social health is found in what is unexpressed, whether the discourse be internal or external: "healthy social value judgment remains within life and from that position organizes the very form of an utterance and its intonation, but it does not at all aim to find suitable expression in the content side of discourse" (101–2). The equation of belief and inexpressibility leads Vološinov/Bakhtin to conclude that a "viable value judgment exists wholly without incorporation into the content of discourse and is not derivable therefrom; instead, it determines the *very selection of the verbal material and the form of the verbal whole*" (101–2; their emphasis). The lack of direct expression is, in other words, the negative proof of secure ideology. Form is the objective expression of the speaker's assumed values because it expresses more than a speaker can say. If she were to "say" her values, they would become "content"—and thereby signify a social instability that promises a "reevaluation is in the offing" (101). The implication is that subjective self-consciousness contaminates the objectivity of ideology; when form is turned into content, what was objective because it was beyond individual control now becomes partial and so suspicious.

Because the meaning of form is still generated by forces outside of form, i.e. by "the healthy social value judgment [that] remains within life," Vološinov/Bakhtin seem so far to avoid ascribing semantic power to form itself. But ultimately the extraverbal is incorporated into the utterance:

> The extraverbal situation is far from being merely the external cause of an utterance—it does not operate on the utterance from outside, as if it were a

mechanical force. Rather, *the situation enters into the utterance as an essential constitutive part of the structure of its import.* ("Discourse," 100; their emphasis)

The utterance thus is defined as a two-part entity composed of the "assumed value" and the expressed words. This division allows Vološinov/Bakhtin ostensibly to distinguish themselves from the formalists that they are devoted to criticizing. Unlike them, the material, in this case verbal expression, is not sufficient for understanding. Yet, in including the material within a larger form called the "utterance," Vološinov/Bakhtin have simply found a larger container for meaning. Moreover, in defining the utterance as containing assumed value—the extraverbal context—the material conditions, be they economic or simply environmental, that were said to have generated the assumed value of the utterance are effectively bracketed. Value, although ultimately connected to objective material conditions, need not be discussed in relation to them since the value produced by those conditions is contained within the form of the utterance. The study of discourse may not be theoretically separable from economic materialism, but one need not study the forces of production to discuss the value contained in discourse. Similarly one need only study the forms of discourse to specify the social value each expresses—which is what Vološinov/Bakhtin go on to do, not just in this essay but in the rest of their work.

Once ideology has been located within the forms of language, it seems a small step to locate an individual's meaning there as well. Yet it is this move in "Discourse" that changes the whole course of Vološinov/Bakhtin's argument. We have seen that form contains more meaning than an individual can say. But now Vološinov/Bakhtin allow that an individual can also express more than she says. Given the kinds of determinacy Vološinov/Bakhtin have thus far insisted on, we may not be surprised to learn that, in their account, an individual does not create meaning but personalizes it. And personalization itself comes about in one way: through a social positioning made possible by language. Through "intonation," say Vološinov/Bakhtin, a speaker expresses her sense of the values that she assumes her interlocutor to have. If she assumes that his values are sympathetic to hers, her intonation will be of one sort; if she imagines him to be hostile, she will adopt a different tone. They leave vague exactly what sorts of tones these might be.

Because intonation is deliberately produced by an individual speaker, Vološinov/Bakhtin seem reluctant to call it a formal property of the ut-

terance itself. This would imply that, like ideological meaning, it is beyond the speaker's control, when in fact intonation is important precisely because it allows individual control. Although Vološinov/Bakhtin
realize that intonation, like any other social value, must ultimately be
connected to the material forces of production and thus remind us that
the "active social position" expressed in intonation is "conditioned by
the very bases of [the speaker's] social being" (104), the changeability,
nuance, and spontancity of intonation cause it to be highly unpredictable, making it the "verbal factor of greatest sensitivity, elasticity, and
freedom" ("Discourse," 105). This crescendo of nouns shows the irresistible move Vološinov/Bakhtin make from what I have called personalization to out-and-out subjectivism. Intonation is not simply responsive, not simply supple, but ultimately without constraint, let alone social determination.

Vološinov/Bakhtin try to make intonation the bridge between internal and external, between individual subjectivity and social ideology.
Whereas form simply expressed "assumed values," "intonation always
lies on the border of the verbal and the nonverbal, the said and the un-
said" ("Discourse," 102). This border state makes it part of discourse,
but also part of something called "life": "In intonation, discourse comes
directly into contact with life." In giving intonation this hybrid status, in
making it both formal and semantic, both verbal and extraverbal, Volo-
šinov/Bakhtin move from discussing language in terms of material objectivity to describing it as a living organism. Intonation suddenly becomes a conduit of animation: it "pumps energy from a life situation
into the verbal discourse" (106). If intonation conducts the "life force,"
and if it is the speaker who intones, then the individual and not larger
social values is the ultimate source of discursive animation. While ideology may provide language with objective meaning, marxism in Vološi-
nov/Bakhtin's hands requires a humanistic infusion to connect the social
and the personal.

Of course in using the metaphor of intonation as a way of accounting
for personal attitudes, Vološinov/Bakhtin reveal how much their thinking depends on an oral and logocentric paradigm. In this paradigm,
words are the material available for expression; they are filled with
meaning that the speaker uses but does not determine. But when words
are spoken, they are produced by a body and thus seem to belong to
that body. In many ways, both body and voice become a third type of
materiality, an even smaller "room" for the social. Although we know
that certain tones communicate certain values only because of the same

social conventions that give meaning to language, tone seems personal because it is expressed by a voice particular to a given individual.[26] Thus what is social and physical is read metaphorically as personal, possessive, and attitudinal. Interestingly, in using intonation as a synecdoche for the personal, Vološinov/Bakhtin suppress the human body—and all the nonverbal, nonintellectual functions that might contribute to human identity—in order to equate individual identity with individual language use. While for Vološinov/Bakhtin there can be many types of materiality—indeed, as we will see, too many types—there seems to be a limit to animation; only in eliding the human subject's agency can language itself gain life of its own.

Although Vološinov/Bakhtin are not troubled by the difficulties created for their social theory by the metaphoric term "intonation," they seem to displace the problem as they consider instead the *speaker's* use of metaphor, specifically his tendency toward personification. To make matters even more complicated, there turn out to be two kinds of intonation: the first, as we have seen, expresses the speaker's sense of her interlocutor's attitude toward her speech; the second expresses the speaker's attitude toward the topic of her discourse: "Intonation has established an active attitude toward the referent, toward the object of the utterance, an attitude of a kind verging on *apostrophe* to that object as the incarnate, living culprit, while the listener—the second participant—is, as it were, called in *as witness and ally*" ("Discourse," 103; their emphasis). Vološinov/Bakhtin now imagine speech as social even aside from the context that informs it. Yet they give little explanation as to why the speaker addresses the object of her discourse; they seem to take it as a psychological fact of "active," "living," "engaged" communication: "Almost any example of live intonation in emotionally charged behavioral speech proceeds as if it addressed, behind inanimate objects and phenomena, animate participants and agents in life; in other words, it has an inherent *tendency toward personification*" (103; their emphasis). Vološinov/Bakhtin go so far as to call this personified object the "hero" of the "verbal production" (103). However, although they begin by describing the hero as the speaker's psychological projection, by the

---

[26] Holquist makes a similar point in order to draw conclusions opposite from mine: "Implicit in all this is the notion that all transcription systems—including the speaking voice in a living utterance—are inadequate to the multiplicity of the meanings they seek to convey. My voice gives the illusion of unity to what I say; I am, in fact, constantly expressing a plenitude of meanings, some intended, others of which I am unaware" ("Introduction," xx).

time they summarize their concepts, Vološinov/Bakhtin are ascribing real and not projected agency to the topic of discourse: "Thus, as we now have a right to claim, *any locution actually said aloud or written down for intelligible communication* (i.e. anything but words merely reposing in a dictionary) *is the expression and product of the social interaction of three participants: the speaker* (author), *the listener* (reader), and *the topic* (the who or what) *of speech* (the hero)" (105; their emphasis). By metaphoric metamorphosis, Vološinov/Bakhtin thus give first ideology, then personhood to language.

We see, then, how far the concept of intonation has taken us. What began as a model of language that stressed the power of form in relation to objective forces of production now has shifted to psychological generalizations about the speaker's attitude toward her interlocutor and her topic of discourse. The ideological meaning, the "assumed value" produced by material conditions, is now virtually absent as Vološinov/Bakhtin focus on the "three participants" who create the meaning of a specific utterance.

The move away from the importance of assumed value to the importance of actively created value is—at long last—the way that Vološinov/Bakhtin move from discourse in life to discourse in art. Given what Vološinov/Bakhtin have said about the importance of the extraverbal context in understanding the word "well," we might think that an art work is destined to be unintelligible, removed as it is from the material conditions of its production. But Vološinov/Bakhtin argue just the opposite. Because the art work cannot rely on a common immediate context, it—in a pattern that may seem familiar to us by now—must incorporate the extraverbal into the verbal:

> A poetic work cannot rely on objects and events in the immediate milieu as things "understood" without making even the slightest allusion to them in the verbal part of the utterance. In this regard, a great deal more is demanded of discourse in literature: Much that could remain outside the utterance in life must find verbal representation. Nothing must be left unsaid in a poetic work from the pragmatic-referential point of view. ("Discourse," 106)

Because the artist cannot rely on assumed values for her communication, she must, it would seem, have an insight into her assumed values that allows her to express them on the level of form and content. Whereas in ordinary speech acts the explicit articulation of value was a sign of that value's ideological dubiety, in art form and content work together for maximal representational effect: "The form expresses some specific evaluation of the object depicted" (108). The special demands of the art work—that it reproduce within itself the material conditions external to all other speech acts—demands that result from the special unsocialness of written discourse, require in turn a special subjectivity, one that can successfully control the relationship between form and content.

But, again, Vološinov/Bakhtin elide this implied human agency as they stress the *art work's power* to contain subjectivity, even that of that personified topic, "the hero":

> The author, hero, and listener that we have been talking about all this time are to be understood not as entities outside the artistic event but only as entities of the very perception of an artistic work, entities that are essential constitutive factors of the work. They are the living forces that determine form and style and are distinctly detectable by any competent contemplator. This means that all those definitions that a historian of literature and society mighty [sic] apply to the author and his heroes—the author's biography, the precise qualification of heroes in chronological and sociological terms and so on—are excluded here: They do not enter directly into the structure of the work but remain outside it. ("Discourse," 109–10)

Vološinov/Bakhtin's marxist argument has virtually reversed itself. What began as an attack on the Russian Formalists' attempt to deny the social nature of meaning ends by excluding any information that might situate the art work in a social context. "The living forces that determine form and style" are now reduced, not just to subjective agents (author, hero, and listener), but to intrinsic, "distinctly detectable" properties of the work itself. Vološinov/Bakhtin go so far as to say that art criticism should ultimately eschew any consideration of the forces of production:

> For a historian of the literature of the capitalist era, the market is a very important factor, but for theoretical poetics, which studies the basic ideological structure of art, that external factor is irrelevant. However, even in the historical study of literature the history of the book market must not be confused with the history of literature. (115)

If the book market counts as an "external factor" irrelevant to theoretical poetics, then all forces of production must be.[27] Yet if art criticism

[27] As Susan Stewart remarks, "Yet we never find in his work a discussion of the effects of industrial practice or mechanical reproduction on ideological thought. If we look for a pattern of absences in these texts, we may gradually limn the image of

finds such things irrelevant, then it loses its marxist argument—at least
as this argument has been construed by Vološinov/Bakhtin—for social
objectivity. Author, hero, and listener have no necessary social relation
to one another—indeed they have no meaningful ideological relation at
all; they stand as constructs that allow Vološinov/Bakhtin to define social selves by their purely hypothetical relation within the forms of language, a relation that they may find "distinctly detectable by any com-
petent contemplator," but which is no longer necessary and, given the
fraught theoretical context in which it appears, may be discernible only
to the authors themselves.

IF ANY WORK were to resolve the conflict between materialism and
idealism in favor of a coherent materialist position, one would imagine
that text would be *Marxism and the Philosophy of Language* (1929).
Marxism quickly signals its difference from "Discourse" by its familiar-
ity with semiotic theory.[28] Whereas Saussurean linguistics stresses the
arbitrary connection between the signifier and the signified, marxist linguistics, so Vološinov/Bakhtin proclaim, stresses the necessary ideological content inherent in the sign's materiality. But Vološinov/Bakhtin
fetishize plasticity—the sensuous properties of form—as they make a
correlation between externality and objectivity:

> Every phenomenon functioning as an ideological sign has some kind of ma-
> terial embodiment, whether in sound, physical mass, color, movements of
> the body, or the like. In this sense, the reality of the sign is fully objective
> and lends itself to a unitary, monistic, objective method of study. (*Marxism*,
> 11)

Yet the materiality of the sign is not the only type of objectivity that it
possesses. Since the economic base determines the sign's ideological value, the ideological sign possesses a necessary *socioeconomic* objectivity:

> The reality of ideological phenomena is the objective reality of social signs.
> The laws of this reality are the laws of semiotic communication and are di-
> rectly determined by the total aggregate of social and economic laws. (13)

Vološinov/Bakhtin collapse these two properties of the ideological
sign—its physical materiality and the materiality it derives from the

---

the futurist machine and its totalitarian capacity for the negation of dialogue"
("Shouts," 279).

  [28] See Mocnik for a "reactivation" of Bakhtin's "criticism of classical linguistic
structuralism" ("Toward a Materialist Concept," 171).

economic conditions it reflects—when they claim that "the existence of the sign is nothing but the materialization of [social] communication" (13). Now it seems that the sign's materiality is less important for its plasticity and more important as the concretization of ideology.

Vološinov/Bakhtin do not see that their proliferation of materialities ultimately undermines the power Marx ascribes to the forces of production. Instead they simply try to reclaim that power by invoking the forces of production when they need to establish a necessary connection between economic determinism and verbal communication. While their desire to locate a source of objectivity causes them to proliferate materialities, their desire to make meaning objective causes them to restrict semiotic signification in order to make it ideological, to equate it with the objective representation of social value:

> Production relations and the sociopolitical order shaped by those relations determine the full range of verbal contacts between people, all the forms and means of their verbal communication—at work, in political life, in ideological creativity. In turn, from the *conditions, forms, and types of verbal communication* derive not only the forms but also the themes [the content] of speech performances. (*Marxism*, 19; my emphasis)

According to these theorists, if production relations determine social contact, they also give that contact an inherent ideological value. Verbal communication thus, Vološinov/Bakhtin argue, takes necessary, economically determined forms. Language forms are, remember, the materialization of social laws. Therefore, *what* gets said is as determined as how it is said.

In fact this dual determination is what will lead them to collapse the difference between signifier and signified. Following Marx, they assert that, because a society represents only that which it is interested in, the very fact of representation, the very existence of a sign, implies necessary production—and thus social—value:

> In order for any item, from whatever domain of reality it may come, to enter the social purview of the group and elicit ideological semiotic reaction, it must be associated with the vital socioeconomic prerequisites of the particular group's existence; it must somehow, even if only obliquely, make contact with the bases of the group's material life. (*Marxism*, 22)

In attributing inherent ideological meaning to the sign, Vološinov/Bakhtin create a new term that will signal the particular kind of content, the necessary social attitudes expressed toward a referent, that they want to ascribe to language. They call this content the "theme" of the sign (22). Thus the modes of production condition the referent of the sign, i.e. material reality, while necessary social attitudes that arise from the modes of production condition the form and the theme of the sign. Yet because form and theme are both ideological and both express the same objective meaning, they are for all practical purposes indistinguishable:

> The theme of an ideological sign and the form of an ideological sign are inextricably bound together and are separable only in the abstract. Ultimately, the same set of forces and the same material prerequisites bring both the one and the other to life. (22)

This of course does not mean that the forces of production are constant; only their general power to create ideology is. As the economic base changes and its social relations change, signs will also change. Certain forms of social interaction and even certain referents will become obsolete, ceasing to be part of social reality. Conversely, the expansion of the economic base will create not only new objects of social interest—and thus of representation—but also, more complexly, a social valuation that is dynamic and interactive. Because this is one of the few places where Vološinov/Bakhtin attend to the specifics of economic development, it is worth quoting at length.

> As the economic basis expands, it promotes an actual expansion in the scope of existence which is accessible, comprehensible, and vital to man. The prehistoric herdsman was virtually interested in nothing, and virtually nothing had any bearing on him. Man at the end of the epoch of capitalism is directly concerned about everything, his interests reaching the remotest corners of the earth and even the most distant stars. This expansion of evaluative purview comes about dialectically. New aspects of existence, once they are drawn into the sphere of social interest, once they make contact with the human word and human emotion, do not coexist peacefully with other elements of existence previously drawn in, but engage them in struggle, reevaluate them, and bring about a change in their position within the unity of the evaluative purview. This dialectical generative process is reflected in the generation of semantic properties in language. A new significance emanates from an old one, and does so with its help, but this happens so that the new significance can enter into contradiction with the old one and restructure it. (*Marxism*, 106)

As the forms of production change, as the herdsman is replaced by the capitalist, so too does social value or "interest" expand. Because this expansion is a historical process, the "sphere of social interest" is not static. On the contrary, the old contends with the new; before a new unity can be created, a new "evaluative purview," old and new values must actively "struggle" with one another.

The objective content inherent in language is thus not only ideological, is not just simply objective, but also complexly and dynamically historical and political. Vološinov/Bakhtin may have restricted semiotic meaning to "thematic" meaning, to social value, but even within this restriction, the sign's objective representation of social value is not predicated on a simple one-to-one correspondence between the forces of production and ideology. In their insistence that meaning is created through social conflict, Vološinov/Bakhtin distinguish themselves as early proponents of what is now an influential position in marxist studies. Anticipating Althusser, Jameson, and Williams, they argue that the ideological sign does not simply *reflect* the conditions of objective reality: this "dialectical generative process" is not simply a chronological clash between old and new; insofar as capitalism itself promotes an unstable possession of meaning where different groups competitively strive to own meaning, to project their self-interested meaning as the right meaning

> existence reflected in the sign is not merely reflected but *refracted*. How is this refraction of existence in the ideological sign determined? By an intersecting of differently oriented social interests within one and the same sign community, i.e. *by the class struggle.*[29] (*Marxism*, 23; their emphasis)

These competing social values cannot be said to equal the form of the sign because different classes use the same signs. If the sign itself does not "reflect" this difference, if the dynamic nature of the class struggle makes it impossible to attribute a singular ideology to any one sign, then how does a single sign express this multiplicity of meaning? To describe these competing values, to describe "thematic" fluctuation within determined form, Vološinov/Bakhtin return to the vocal metaphor that we have seen in "Discourse"; importantly, however, what before suggested the individual's power to personalize meaning now is described in terms that emphasize the collective character of this voice; "intona-

---

[29] Peter Steiner argues that "metasemiotic definition led the Bachtinians to a thorough revision of formalist theories of language, the medium of literature. From a linguistic point of view, a verbal sign that reflects or refracts another verbal sign is exactly like an utterance commenting on or replying to another utterance" (*Russian Formalism*, 263). Susan Stewart points out that ideology now becomes an "ongoing product and producer of social practices. The semantic transition from reflection to refraction marks a movement from repetition to production" ("Shouts," 277).

tion" is replaced by the "social multiaccentuality of the ideological sign."

Yet when Vološinov/Bakhtin elaborate on the political manifestations of this struggle over the ownership of ideological meaning, they get no further than the description of a repressive ideology fostered by the dominant social class. Although in *Marxism* we are reminded that the dominant class "is always somewhat reactionary and tries, as it were, to stabilize the preceding factor in the dialectic flux of social generative process" (24), their description of the relation of dominant ideology to the individual loses its political edge as Vološinov/Bakhtin go on to reformulate the relationship between the individual and social consciousness. Given their dialectical definition of the ideological sign, there can never be stability; class struggle is fought out even within the sign itself.[30] Nor are majority values those that, as they said in "Discourse," "have entered the flesh and blood of all representatives of the group" and are therefore in "no need of special verbal formulation" ("Discourse," 101). Vološinov/Bakhtin now imagine that within the limits of class and other kinds of social determinates, an individual constantly assesses his relationship to the social collective(s) to which he belongs and expresses his sense of relation through the way he accents his discourse. "Social multiaccentuality of the ideological sign" may sound like a corrected marxist version of "intonation," but is it? As I will show, Vološinov/Bakhtin simply repeat the pattern of argumentation, a pattern that ultimately reinstates the individual's power to determine her identity. In *Marxism*, when they move away from theory and turn to the analysis of specific discourse forms, they collapse the difference between "social-multiaccentuality" and "intonation," as they make the expression of social relations the task of one voice, of one speaker. They thus again reempower the individual, making his willingness to assume a social identity more a personal decision than an objective sociohistorical fact. In *Marxism*, however, this valorization of the individual is not simply a result of a shift in argumentative focus, a contradiction that is a result of the move from general theoretical claims to specific analysis of actual forms. It is a direct result of Vološinov/Bakhtin's attempt to make social

[30] Stewart argues that Bakhtin's revision of Marx effectively deemphasizes the "primacy of 'real man'" since the "socioeconomic base is seen as determining" but does not lock "ideology into a static and transcendent form. . . . Rather, ideology is seen as an area of conflict: one's speech both reveals *and produces* one's position in class society, in such a way, moreover, as to set into dialogue the relations among classes" ("Shouts," 276; Stewart's emphasis).

determinism less reductive, to rework marxism so it will include "refracted" ideological meaning, an endeavor that finally redefines ideology as a dynamic plurality of meaning which ultimately—and quite radically—deconstructs the base/superstructure dichotomy.

In their account of how an individual socially positions his discourse, Vološinov/Bakhtin begin by insisting on the social nature of even unspoken discourse. This time, in attempting to critique the idealist belief in the distinction between private and public, inner and outer, self and other, they stress that even unspoken words have an addressee, one that, according to Vološinov/Bakhtin, will usually be someone representative of the speaker's social group, someone, in other words, who is like the speaker:

> Each person's inner world and thought has its stabilized *social audience* that comprises the environment in which reasons, motives, values, and so on are fashioned. The more cultured a person, the more closely his inner audience will approximate the normal audience of ideological creativity. (*Marxism*, 86)

Here, stability has nothing to do with real political conditions; rather, it is a result of how "cultured," indeed, how "socialized," a person is, how successfully an individual has appropriated suitable forms of ideology. In other words, the more "public" the person, the more his inner world will resemble his outer world. Yet the identification between self and social audience, need not be singular. In fact, Vološinov/Bakhtin assert that the more socially identified an individual is, the more he will define himself in terms of what the theorists go on to call the "we-experience":

> The "we-experience" is not by any means a nebulous herd experience; it is differentiated. Moreover, ideological differentiation, the growth of consciousness, is in direct proportion to the firmness and reliability of the social orientation. The stronger, the more organized, the more differentiated the collective in which an individual orients himself, the more vivid and complex his inner world will be. (*Marxism*, 88)

If the individual is "stable," if his social orientation is "firm and reliable" even as it is "differentiated," then social identification will not threaten his inner world, but, on the contrary, will overcome the limited experience of a solitary individual to give him a plural identity. When internalized, social diversity undergoes a qualitative transformation, turning into the literary premiums of "vividness and complexity."

In contrast to the benefits offered through public identification, the opposite pole of orientation, what Vološinov/Bakhtin call the "I-experience," would in its extreme form "tend toward [the individual's] extermination":

> In its course toward this extreme, the experience relinquishes all its potentialities, all outcroppings of social orientation and, therefore, also loses its verbal delineation. Single experiences or whole groups of experiences can approach this extreme, relinquishing, in doing so, their ideological clarity and structuredness and testifying to the inability of the consciousness to strike social roots. (*Marxism*, 88)

Between the two poles of "I-experience" and "we-experience" are various degrees of "I/we" orientation that suggest the need to negotiate between a sense of "individuality" and a sense of social relatedness.

Although Vološinov/Bakhtin have criticized the "I-experience" for its detrimental effects, their terms nonetheless privilege the "I" in a way that makes it primary. In describing a dialogue as interaction between self and other, other is never anything more than what self is not. Communication is possible between speakers if they can establish a common language use, one that negotiates between meanings that Vološinov/Bakhtin describe as being different for different ideological communities. Insofar as society is a "we-orientation," it is the negotiation between the individual and a community; the individual must constantly situate herself in relation to social groups to which she always belongs in a partial way.

In this discussion of "we-orientation," Vološinov/Bakhtin refer to social groups rather than social classes. In this way they avoid articulating exactly how much their definition of the social as both chosen and plural conflicts not only with social determinism, but also with the marxist ideal of a classless society. As in their earlier description of capitalism's expansion of the "evaluative purview," its expansion of man's interest to "the remotest corners of the earth and even the most distant stars," Vološinov/Bakhtin find certain advantages in an economic system that they, as marxists, should criticize. Vološinov/Bakhtin like the dialectical struggle for meaning; they like the plurality that results from social difference. In trying to develop a marxist theory that will accommodate social pluralism, they instead have shown how their ideal of social plurality actually rationalizes capitalism. Yet, rather than engage this conclusion, Vološinov/Bakhtin, as we have seen, begin to shift their terms; they describe the value of social plurality not in terms of its economic or political consequences, but in terms of the literary values of "vividness and complexity." The literary becomes, as I will show, a way of defining social plurality to make it seem compatible with marxism.

As we have seen, given the barriers to understanding that social diversity entails, the fact that speakers can understand each other says more about the power of individuals to translate and interpolate meaning than about the determinacy of the economic base. Vološinov/Bakhtin in fact describe how every word that is exchanged actively engages a process of social unification:

> Each and every word expresses the "one" in relation to the "other." I give myself verbal shape from another's point of view, ultimately, from the point of view of the community to which I belong. A word is a bridge thrown between myself and another. If one end of the bridge depends on me, then the other depends on my addressee. A word is a territory shared by both addresser and addressee, by the speaker and his interlocutor. (*Marxism*, 86)

In this description, the speaker chooses his "verbal shape"; it does not choose him. Moreover, this verbal instantiation of an individual entails a complicated negotiation of identity; the self, the "I," must first distinguish between its identity and the identity of the "other's" point of view. He must then somehow form himself, adopt a "verbal shape" that will make him intelligible to his addressee. In other words, he must first regard his own identity through his imagined understanding of the addressee's values and then find a word that will contain this filtered identity. Again, Vološinov/Bakhtin's linguistic theory has moved from marxist notions of materialized ideology to idealist notions of individual autonomy. Language is still and always social for Vološinov/Bakhtin (the denotational meaning of language is, significantly, virtually ignored by their theory); but, in a way that is similar to their description in "Discourse" of how an art work serves as a locus for meaning, now words are places of encounter, "territories," where two individuals may meet. As Vološinov/Bakhtin stray from the power of the economic forms of production, their description of how meaning occurs switches from the material to the magical—despite the technological terms it is couched in: "It [meaning] is like an electric spark that occurs only when two different terminals are hooked together" (103). Meaning is no longer grounded in a place; it is a qualitative transformation.

Vološinov/Bakhtin do, however, attempt to convert, as it were, this magical language into socio-objective terms. They go on to inquire about the social character of this "electric" unification. Specifically they ask, "How, in fact, is another speaker's speech received? What is the mode of existence of another's utterance in the actual, inner-speech consciousness of the recipient? How is it manipulated there, and what proc-

ess of orientation will the subsequent speech of the recipient himself
have undergone in regard to it?" (*Marxism*, 117). The answer, according to these theorists, might best be found by analyzing a discourse form
that by its very nature expresses the relation of one individual to another: reported speech.

> What we have in the forms of reported speech is precisely an objective
> document of this reception. Once we have learned to decipher it, this docu-
> ment provides us with information, not about accidental and mercurial sub-
> jective psychological processes in the "soul" of the recipient, but about
> steadfast social tendencies in an active reception of other speakers' speech,
> tendencies that have crystallized into language forms. The mechanism of this
> process is located, not in the individual soul, but in society. It is the function
> of society to select and to make grammatical (adapt to the grammatical
> structure of its language) just those factors in the active and evaluative re-
> ception of utterances that are socially vital and constant and, hence, that are
> grounded in the economic existence of the particular community of speakers.
> (117)

At first the marxist invocation of materialized ideology may seem simply a restatement of the opening arguments in *Marxism*. But there has
been a subtle move away from the ideological sign: now economic
forces determine not just the necessary relation between signifier and
signified, but the grammatical structure of language. Ideological grammar here takes on a new importance as it metaphorically rematerializes
"we-orientation" by locating social value outside the individual's use of
language and back in the very forms of language itself.[31]

Grammar may be the "crystallization" of "steadfast social tendencies
in an active reception of other speakers' speech," but we find, in their
specific discursive forms like reported speech, these forms seem even
more concrete if they are *written*; in their analysis of syntax, Vološi-
nov/Bakhtin read written signifiers as the mimetic bodies of social subjects. They thus discover a utopian way of reconceiving their oral-cen-
trism as itself materialist. I want to argue that reported speech becomes
the ideal form for Vološinov/Bakhtin because, in their description of it,

---

[31] Dana B. Polan notes that such a move confuses the difference between base and
superstructure: "Without a theory of mediation, a curious inversion of the marxist
problematic takes place in Bakhtin's philosophy; communication ceases to be a mediation of other social practices and becomes instead the origin, the determining
center for these practices," which results in an "idealist philosophy that finally reifies language despite Bakhtin's declared attempts to restore the life of language
against all fixities" ("Text," 152).

it represents the perfect social self; its syntactical structure, which requires the speaker to relate his language to another speaker's, materializes the quality that they want to attribute to all language forms, a "we-orientation" that is a linguistic position activated to lesser or greater degrees by any speaking individual. As I will show, the most important feature of reported discourse is that, due to its self-referentiality, it seems not simply to signify but to instantiate the social orientation that is definitive of subjectivity. As we turn to the examples of reported discourse that they offer, we will see that they have made texts, specifically literary texts, into what is in fact the ideal mimetic body for subjectivity that is truly "we-oriented": the written form of reported discourse makes visible the speaker's necessary relation to a social other different from himself while preserving the autonomous discourse of both quoted and quoting speaker; this materialization of alterity stabilizes subjective difference and subjective relation to the point where each word can accommodate and make audible the *intonation* of each speaker, that which expresses not just the subjects' relation to each other but their more general social attitudes (and thus identities). Yet even Vološinov/Bakhtin can see that this logic leads to a valorization of the textual body over the social body; textual bodies are better because they are more mimetic: they can present a vivid picture of the multidirectionality of the "we-orientation" that defines human identity. In the conclusion to *Marxism* they back away from their argument and, in a surprising reversal, criticize the kinds of reported discourse that have so aptly embodied "we-orientation"; indeed, they seem to reject the fluid self-fashioning of we-orientation altogether as they move from description to prescription, calling for a language that expresses, not simply multivoicedness, but "responsible content," social values that coincide with a more orthodox marxist concept of objectivity.

VOLOŠINOV/BAKHTIN'S definition of reported speech is worth recalling: it is "speech within speech, utterance within utterance, and at the same time also *speech about speech, utterance about utterance*" (115; their emphasis). The theorists insist that a reported utterance cannot simply be something that is talked about; in an argument reminiscent of Genette's discussion of quotation, they maintain that language enjoys perfect mimesis; to represent it is to reproduce it:

> If its content is to be had to the full, it must be made part of a speech construction. When limited to the treatment of reported speech in thematic

terms, one can answer questions as to "how" and "about what" so-and-so spoke, but "what" he said could be disclosed only by way of reporting his words, if only in the form of indirect discourse. (115)

Reported speech is uniquely capable of reproducing its referent—the quoted words themselves—while simultaneously making the referent a signifier as the quotation becomes part of the new utterance.[32] But if the correlation of quotability and alterity is familiar from our study of the second wave theorists, for the Bakhtin Circle it is particularly the *form* of reported speech that expresses the relation between reporting and reported speech, of self to other and thus the form that, in their theory, makes legible "objective" social values: Vološinov/Bakhtin insist that "we are dealing here with words reacting on words" (*Marxism*, 116); the relationship between discourses is not described by the content of reported discourse but is enacted through the discourse form. To clarify their point, Vološinov/Bakhtin distinguish reported discourse from dialogue.

> In dialogue, the lines of the individual participants are grammatically disconnected; they are not integrated into one unified context. Indeed, how could they be? *There are no syntactic forms with which to build a unity of dialogue.* If, on the other had, a dialogue is presented as embedded in an authorial context, then we have a case of direct discourse, one of the variants of the phenomenon with which we are dealing in this inquiry. (116; their emphasis)

Dialogue, then, is actually less interactive than reported discourse because its structure keeps the utterances autonomous and therefore does not make legible their social relation. Reported discourse by contrast preserves the autonomy of the quoted language while making visible the speaker's relation to it:

> Reported speech is regarded by the speaker as an utterance belonging to *someone else*, an utterance that was originally totally independent, complete in its construction, and lying outside the given context. Now, it is from this independent existence that reported speech is transposed into an authorial context while retaining its own referential content and at least the rudiments of its own linguistic integrity, its original constructional independence. (116; their emphasis)

[32] As Steiner puts it, "For the Bachtinians, however, literature differs from other ideological domains not in failing to signify but in its mode of signifying. Literary signs, Medvedev claimed, are metasigns—representations of representations" (*Russian Formalism*, 262).

The syntactical structure thus expresses a social relation between quoter and quotee while it manifests each subjectivity separately through the words that "belong" respectively to each speaker. The quoter, even as he employs the quoted words, is conscious that they retain their independence. Because syntax materializes difference, Vološinov/Bakhtin can read verbal reproduction (quotation) as the image of the quotee's unmediated subjectivity; the quoted language goes so far as to become the palpable body of alterity: "the reported utterance perseveres as a construction—the body of the reported speech remains detectable as a self-sufficient unit" (116). Accordingly, sociopoetics need look no further than the forms of reported discourse to ascertain the character of societies and social selves: "the true object of inquiry ought to be precisely the dynamic inter-relationship of these two factors, the speech being reported (the other person's speech) and the speech doing the reporting (the author's speech)" (119).

Vološinov/Bakhtin so much believe in the ability of grammatical syntax to manifest objectively the socially objective identity of both reporter and reportee that, when they analyze the social relationships expressed by the varieties of reported discourse, they interpret them as different "styles" of materiality in terms that they significantly borrow not from linguistics, but from art history: the linear and the pictorial. On the one hand, discursive autonomy is preserved if reported speech is clearly set off from reporting speech and if both discourses seem homogeneous:

> The basic tendency of the linear style is to construct clear-cut, external contours for reported speech, whose own internal individuality is minimized. Wherever the entire context displays a complete stylistic homogeneity . . . the grammatical and compositional manipulation of reported speech achieves a maximal compactness and plastic relief. (*Marxism*, 120)

In their historical overview, the linear style is politicized as "authoritarian" and is said to characterize the Middle Ages and most of the seventeenth and eighteenth centuries. The "pictorial" style, on the other hand, "strives to break down the self-contained compactness of the reported speech, to resolve it, to obliterate its boundaries" (*Marxism*, 120). It "obliterate[s] the precise, external contours of reported speech" (120–21), and, at the same time, it individualizes the reported speech. This individuality is made "tangible" in that the "various facts of an utterance may be subtly differentiated" (121). In terms of historical development, the pictorial style is associated with individualistic relativism, which, in its extreme form, manifests itself in the "dissolution" of the reporting context. The Renaissance, late eighteenth century and all of the nineteenth century are characterized by this style.

If we stand back to consider the largest terms of the Bakhtin Circle's language theory, we discover, interestingly enough, that their commitment to marxist materialism has led them to a position akin to the second wave's decidedly nonmarxist understanding of novelistic discourse. The logic of linguistic intrinsicality—the notion that a person's identity can be authentically represented only through quotation—encourages Vološinov/Bakhtin to reproduce (or, more precisely, to anticipate) the second wave's belief that to report "what" someone says is to reproduce who that person is. But although it is key to note that the logic of social formalism leads its theorists to fetishize the forms of quoted speech, the philosophical differences between the second wave and the Bakhtin Circle—specifically the latter's commitment to marxist materialism—are registered in their different accounts of how quotation manifests identity. To begin with, Vološinov/Bakhtin's understanding of individuals as social subjects fundamentally revises the rivalrous relation between representer and represented that characterized Genette, Pascal, and Cohn's account of quotation: because they posit individual identity as essentially plural, as "we-oriented," reported discourse can seem the appropriate expression of that plurality: the mediated relation between the self and the other is, according to their social theory, the natural and inevitable condition of social identity. While the maximizing of "we-orientation" is, as it has always been in their theory, up to the individual, the importance of reported discourse for Vološinov/Bakhtin is that it prevents we-orientation from becoming merely a personal gesture: thanks to their belief that grammar materializes and objectifies social tendencies, one not need be a sympathetic genius or even a fiction writer to use language to express alterity; any speaker can display his we-orientation; indeed, their description of reported discourse goes so far as to suggest that the forms of grammar themselves promote a self-consciousness about we-orientation so that even less self-conscious speakers must reckon at those grammatical moments with their sociality.

Vološinov/Bakhtin's account of quotation thus differs from the second wave by attributing on the one hand more agency to the materiality of language forms per se and, on the other, a different ethical valence to the representation of alterity: as their social theory encourages them to argue, it is not altruism that enables an individual to represent the intrinsic identity of the other and it is not the operation of individual interest that initiates and sustains the representation of alterity; because reported discourse is a fact of socioeconomic change it cannot be interpreted exclusively as the index of more or less generous authors. The social relations expressed through quotation—be they linear or pictorial—are established by material realities beyond any single individual's control. Rather than describing intonation as the play of personal judgment—of the speaker's sympathy or irony toward the other she represents—Vološinov/Bakhtin define intonation as the speaker's self-conscious awareness of her own pluralized social identity.

Vološinov/Bakhtin make explicit their divergence from subjectivist theories in their critique of the pioneering studies of reported discourse:

> In the studies of both Lorck and Lerch, a consistent and emphatic individualistic subjectivism is pitted against Bally's hypostasizing objectivism. The individual, subjective critical awareness of speakers underlies the notion of linguistic psyche. Language in all its manifestations becomes expression of individual psychic forces and individual ideational intentions. The generation of language turns out to be the process of generation of mind and soul in individual speakers. (*Marxism*, 152)

In arguing against this subjectivist position, they reassert language's objective role in forming an individual personality:

> The fact is, after all, that the speaking personality, its subjective designs and intentions, and its conscious stylistic stratagems do not exist outside their material objectification in language. Without a way of revealing itself in language, be it only in inner speech, personality does not exist either for itself or for others; it can illuminate and take cognizance in itself of only that for which there is objective, illuminating material, the materialized light of consciousness in the form of established words, value judgments, and accents. The inner subjective personality with its own self-awareness does not exist as a material fact, usable as a basis for causal explanation, but it exists as an ideologeme. (152)

Once again, it is thanks to the correlation Vološinov/Bakhtin make between materiality per se and ideological objectivity that they are able to imagine that language makes legible the objective and authentic identity of subjectivity. It is the marxist roots of their theory that thus allows them to maintain their critique of subjectivists (like those of the second wave) while fetishizing the same linguistic forms.

We can see even in the summary I have given of Vološinov/Bakhtin's historio-materialist account of the development from the linear to the pictorial style that "we-orientation" is achieved at any particularly historical moment by navigating between the dominant tendencies of the two eras they identify: authoritarianism and individualistic relativism. But while this attempt to put reported discourse in a social and not just a literary context distinguishes Vološinov/Bakhtin from theorists like Genette, Pascal, and Cohn, the grossness of their "historical" categories reemphasizes their inability to nuance political and cultural identity. Rather than giving us a detailed picture of, say, the eighteenth century's use of quotation, Vološinov/Bakhtin instead describe for us the way reported discourse itself pictures alterity. And their criterion for interpreting this picture derives a politics based on an unusual ratio between plasticity and subjective individuality. As their art-historical terms reveal, they correlate a maximum of materiality—i.e. the "clear-cut, external contours" of the linear style—with a minimum of individual subjectivity: when reported speech "achieves a maximal compactness and plastic relief," when it is, in other words, most concretely distinguished from the reporting context, it is—for (presumably historical) reasons Vološinov/Bakhtin do not explain—least differentiated in terms of its style. This merely material difference between reported and reporting discourse is thus what leads them to characterize the linear style as authoritarian. By contrast, the pictorial style approaches the condition of FID: it breaks the rigid boundary of plasticizing quotational form; but materialized alterity is retained, seemingly, through the tangibility they now ascribe to style, the "facts of an utterance [that] may be subtly differentiated" (121). This shift from the plasticity of languages distinctly separated by quotation to the plasticity of style itself once again expresses the need Vološinov/Bakhtin have to imagine that identity can be objectified through the materiality of language rather than the convincing reasons why we should think of language as material in these ways. We can thus see the theoretical tensions that arise within their own attempt to develop an ethics of reported discourse that would have the social objectivity of a politics of quotation.

The ability of Vološinov/Bakhtin's social formalism to compromise their marxism is further evidenced by their untheorized tendency to conceive of reported discourse almost exclusively as a literary phenomenon, specifically a representational activity of fiction. In keeping with the ethics of linguistic intrinsicality that we saw elaborated in Chapter 2, for Vološinov/Bakhtin, the ontological status of the speaker is negated by the ontological status ascribed to quoted speech. In other words, it is unimportant whether a speaker is real or fictional because her words enjoy their own autonomy and rights. Although Vološinov/Bakhtin discuss at length theorists who try to account for the difference between real and fictional selves (the same theorists, in fact, that Pascal invokes in his overview of the development of FID), ultimately they dismiss these theories as "subjectivist" (*Marxism*, 152) and defend their own analysis by simply declaring that in the language of fiction as in all language, "we perceive the author's accents and intonations being interrupted by these value judgments of another person" (155).[33] Because Vološinov/Bakhtin have made the material form of language expressive of subjectivity, it does not matter whether the subjectivity expressed is fictional or real—each is equally represented and contained by forms of language. Their overvaluation of the material has preserved the social but ultimately dispensed with not just the forms of production, not just economic determinism, but with any important distinction between real, historical, and material people and products of the imagination, fictional characters.[34] By way of materialism they have justified idealism; they have given equal ontological status to the real and the imagined. Given how far removed they are from the marxist base that, at least in theory, allowed them to ascribe objective meaning to language forms, it is not surprising to find that, whether discussing discourse in "life" or discourse in "art," their analyses of reported speech become the highly subjective and unverifiable process of identifying selves with images of language, of finding both personal identity and social attitudes in the shape of the word.

Yet even though reported discourse has the potential to accomplish the utopian legibility of self and other, of language as self, as has already been suggested by their account of "individualistic relativism," some of the more "pictorial" forms of reported discourse dispense with this material image and, as in a form they call "quasi-indirect discourse" (an extreme form of FID), express an interpenetration of voices so complex that they can barely be identified. Vološinov/Bakhtin find themselves hard pressed to explain the subjective illegibility fostered by FID's syntactical ambiguity:

[33] See McHale, "Free Indirect Discourse," for an excellent early discussion of the connection between, on the one hand, Anglo-American and European and, on the other, Russian work on FID.

[34] Jefferson cites this lack of distinction with seeming approval: "Both literature and the reality which it represents are of the same order and, according to Bakhtin, this order is ideological" ("Russian Formalism," 43).

Especially in that area where quasi-direct discourse has become a massively used device—the area of modern prose fiction—transmission by voice of evaluative interference would be impossible. Furthermore, the very kind of development quasi-direct discourse has undergone is bound up with the transposition of the larger prose genres into a silent register, i.e., for silent reading. Only this "silencing" of prose could have made possible the multi-leveledness and voice-defying complexity of intonational structures that are so characteristic for modern literature. . . . The difficulty of evaluative, expressive intonation consists here in the constant shifting from the evaluative purview of the author to that of the character and back again. (*Marxism*, 156)

Although through quasi-indirect discourse the written, literary text seems to have achieved what Vološinov/Bakhtin presented as the social ideal—"we-orientation"—this ideal also makes clear how far the theorists have gone in replacing real social subjects with textual characters. Instead of following their argument to its conclusion, instead of embracing the success of quasi-indirect discourse's pluralized self—which would lead them to claim explicitly that texts are better social bodies than human bodies because they enjoy a polyvocality that exceeds the human body—their distress at FID's lack of legibility—its blurring of the lines of alterity—prompts them to reinvoke the human body as the more stable—if less mimetic—materialization of identity, even though this means abandoning their theoretical enterprise and exchanging it for moral didacticism. Vološinov/Bakhtin solve the problem of indistinguishability and thereby "save" their marxist theory by defending the logic of their social formalism through political critique: it is not grammar, or fiction, or texts that insufficiently represent human identity; it is modern society whose subjectivist relativism has "silenced" prose. In *Marxism*, this turn from theoretical inquiry to social critique is the only way they can reprivilege the oral voice of the nonfictional individual. Although they now find the "unspeakability" (i.e. the fact that no individual can render through oral delivery the text's vocal fluctuations) of the plural textual voice to be the sign of "the alarming instability of the ideological word," by reasserting the importance of the speaking subject they do not resocialize reported discourse, they do not return to a paradigm that would be more consistent with a marxist conception of persons; instead, they simply reassert the limitation of the organic body and, through metaphoric extension, the inevitability of unitary rather than radically mediated and plural personal identity. Vološinov/Bakhtin are left either with a limited speaking human subject, incapable of vocal plurality, or else textual images, capable of multivoicedness but possessing, at least in marxist terms, no meaningful social identity.

Rather than engage either of these unacceptable conclusions, Vološinov/Bakhtin ignore the relationship between reported discourse and their stated ideal of "we-orientation," and instead conclude *Marxism* by abandoning scientific description and developing instead their prescriptive suggestions for social reform. Condemning quasi-direct discourse on moral grounds, they deem the form to be "expressive of dangerous social tendency":

> The victory of extreme forms of the picturesque style in reported speech is not, of course, to be explained in terms either of psychological factors of the artist's own individual stylistic purposes, but is explainable in terms of the *general, far-reaching subjectivization of the ideological word-utterance.* No longer is it a monument, nor even a document, of a substantive ideational position; it makes itself felt only as expression of an adventitious, subjective state. (*Marxism,* 158; their emphasis)

> All this bespeaks an alarming instability and uncertainty of ideological word. Verbal expression in literature, rhetoric, philosophy, and humanistic studies has become the realm of "opinions," and out and out opinions, and even the paramount feature of these opinions is not *what* actually is "opined" in them but *how*—in what individual or typical way—the "opining" is done. This stage in the vicissitudes of the word in present-day bourgeois Europe and here in the Soviet Union . . . can be characterized as the stage of *transformation of the word into a thing,* the stage of *depression in the thematic value of the word.* (159; their emphasis)

Their proposed solution: "revive the ideological word"—"the word with its theme intact, the word permeated with confident and categorical social value judgment, the word that really means and takes responsibility for what it says" (*Marxism,* 159). In condemning the prevalence of quasi-direct discourse, the theorists simply condemn what has been their own consistent valorization of form over content, their own insistence in turning the "word into a thing." The solution that they offer here, the return to "confident and categorical social value judgment" through an act of will, shows how, in their attempt to make the relationship between base and superstructure more flexible, objective and necessary social value has turned into the individual's willingness to formulate consistent opinions. This conclusion, the turn from "scientific" analysis to emotional and didactic appeal, rather than being, as some critics have argued, a contradictory shift in Vološinov/Bakhtin's argumentative focus, is in fact the appropriate culmination to an argument that in its attempt to show the fallacy of subjectivism and idealism instead demonstrates the development of social formalism through marxism.[35]

[35] See Young, "Back to Bakhtin," 92.

4

Voice to Heteroglossia

'Problems of Dostoevsky's Poetics' and "Discourse in the Novel"

My voice goes after what my eyes cannot reach,
With the twirl of my tongue I encompass worlds and volumes
  of worlds.
　　　　　—Walt Whitman, "Song of Myself" (1855)

THE PLEA FOR stable ideological meaning that ends *Marxism and the Philosophy of Language* expresses the nostalgia that Vološinov/Bakhtin feel for the simple relation between belief and language that marxism seemed to give them and that their social pluralism deconstructed. Since "refraction," ideological pluralism, and "we-orientation" have made impossible the clear identification of ideology in language, Vološinov/Bakhtin now can only reassert stable social value by appealing to individual morality; they hope that the individual will voluntarily restore clear content to language. To do so, the individual would have to choose to limit his "we-orientation" to a stable identity that expresses itself through a discourse in which the word is "permeated with confident and categorical social judgment," the word "that really means and takes responsibility for what it says" (*Marxism*, 159). Yet even if it were possible to create these values willingly, even if the individual were to "revive the ideological word," how could she? Without the necessary social value posited by a strict connection between base and superstructure, and with no new basis for evaluating diverse ideologies, Vološinov/Bakhtin cannot explain why an individual would orient herself in one language over another, would "opine"—let alone believe—any kind of "categorical social value judgments." In their version of social pluralism, the "we-oriented" individual is not one who recognizes, say, the truth of economic materialism, nor is it even—as we have seen—the one who condemns capitalism's class society. Without strict economic determinism, Vološinov/Bakhtin are unable to assert not just orthodox

marxist values, but any values at all; they have no way of accounting
for either the fact or the substance of belief. The social self is simply that
which knows itself to be social and maximizes its social nature in being
"we-oriented." In Vološinov/Bakhtin's version of social pluralism, the
self is thus defined not by what it *is*, not by some static ontological content, and not by some specifiable ideological content, but by what it
does, how it performs the practice of social orientation.

Given the collapse of objective value and economic materialism that
takes place in *Marxism*, it is not really surprising to find that *Problems
of Dostoevsky's Poetics* and "Discourse in the Novel" continue the pursuit of sociopoetics without explicit reference to marxism. The absence
of marxist terminology is so conspicuous that, as I have mentioned,
some critics have argued that these two works represent an entirely new
system of thought, a system so complete as to be ascribable to a separate author, a nonmarxist author whom they would call "Bakhtin."[1] In
fact, the arguments advanced in *Problems of Dostoevsky's Poetics* and
"Discourse in the Novel"—whether or not they are written by Bakhtin
alone—continue the pattern of argumentation that I have been tracing.
These works should be termed post-marxist since they inherit the
groundless social pluralism that Vološinov/Bakhtin are left with after
their deconstruction of economic materialism. Indeed, given that so
many issues and ways of reasoning otherwise remain the same between
the two sets of texts, it is exactly this groundlessness that becomes the
definitive feature of the work that is commonly referred to as "Bakhtinian." What is most remarkable about *Problems* and "Discourse in the
Novel" is not the lack of marxist terminology, but that marxism has
been replaced by no other social theory that might provide a new basis
for positing necessary social value, an absence that is particularly glaring given the affinity of these Bakhtinian texts with *Marxism*'s most
"social" concepts: the explicit championship of a pluralized sociolinguistic subject and the implied valorization of a radical politics. Since
the attempt to make marxism accommodate social pluralism resulted in
the demise of necessary objective value, since the conflict between on
the one hand a pluralized and mediated subjectivity and on the other the
need for mimetic objectification of identity has made it impossible to
formulate "confident and categorical social value judgments," Bakhtin
simply tries to do without stable content—without relinquishing his
belief in the objective and objectifiable representation of subjectivity.

[1] See Titunik, "Translator's Introduction"; and Young, "Back to Bakhtin."

Determined to continue the project of "sociopoetics" and faced with the untenability of a marxist theory of objective ideology, in *Problems* and "Discourse in the Novel" he turns his attention to the problem of theorizing forms of social discourse that have not a necessary meaning, but a necessarily fluctuating meaning. And the novel is his prime example.

While Bakhtin's willingness to do without economic determinism allows him to embrace fluctuating meaning as a positive good, his attempt to theorize unstable meaning is no more successful than Vološinov/Bakhtin's attempts to theorize stable meaning. As I will show, Bakhtin's valorization of the subject in *Problems of Dostoevsky's Poetics* initially seems to suggest that he has reconciled the contradiction between materialism and idealism by eliminating the former and embracing the latter. His emphasis on the unique identity of the subject might even lead us to believe that his rejection of the material has also entailed the rejection of the social. Whereas Vološinov/Bakhtin repeatedly argued that there was no difference between consciousness and social identity because consciousness was simply introjected social identity, Bakhtin now seems to argue that there is no difference between consciousness and social identity because social identity is simply the externalization of consciousness, the exteriorization of a unique interior. Whereas for Vološinov/Bakhtin voice was vision, language was ideology, for Bakhtin vision and voice initially seem to denote the difference between interior and exterior, between private and public identity. Although vision, which in *Problems* and "Discourse in the Novel" he calls point of view, still has the potential to equal voice, the equality is accomplished only if consciousness is successfully externalized, if the subject is willing to translate his ideas into language.

Yet if we examine more closely Bakhtin's description of the subject, we find that, although Bakhtin is indeed doing without economic determinism, he has not in fact given up on the social subject. Bakhtin's apparent "subjectivist idealism" is best explained as the development of one of the lines of logic suggested in *Marxism*: that the social, severed from objective material value, is no more than an experience of the subject. But because Bakhtin still believes that this subject is if not ideologically then at least plurally constructed, the subject can have no intrinsic identity; its experience of the social has no positive content that could come from intrinsic or private experience. With no economically determined value and no intrinsically determined value, the social subject becomes in *Problems of Dostoevsky's Poetics* and "Discourse in the

Novel" not a person but a practice. The name Bakhtin gives to this contentless social subject is dialogics.

Although by defining the subject as an activity rather than an entity Bakhtin has indeed imagined a social subject that has no necessary social value, with no stable content, it—not surprisingly—becomes impossible to identify the "point" in the subject's unique "point of view." Bakhtin contradictorily insists, on the one hand, that individual identity is stable enough to be expressed and discerned as "voice," and, on the other hand, that individual identity is an active process of incorporating "other" voices. Since Bakhtin needs the "one" in order to have the "many," the best subject in *Problems* is ultimately that which can oscillate between an embodiment that is always partial and a disembodied unity that can be inferred but not apprehended. The author of the "polyphonic novel," whose dialogic consciousness is represented through—but is still greater than—the multiplicity of his characters' voices, becomes the new Bakhtinian ideal. And, as I will explain, it is what Bakhtin calls the "artistic logic" of the polyphonic novel that provides the author with that necessary component of the social formalist tradition: the objectifying material required for the objective representation of social subjects.

In tracing the logical development of Bakhtin's thought through *Problems* and "Discourse in the Novel," we will see how his career-long desire to understand literature as first and foremost a social discourse reinscribes his career-long temptation to valorize literature—in particular the novel—as the best kind of social discourse. If the privileging of reported discourse in *Marxism* allowed us to appreciate the social formalist connection between the Bakhtin Circle and the second wave's fetishization of FID, the valorization of the novel in the works signed by Bakhtin will enable us to understand the larger ways in which Bakhtin participates in the Jamesian social formalist tradition.

IN MANY SUPERFICIAL WAYS, it is easy to view *Problems of Dostoevsky's Poetics* as a continuation of Vološinov/Bakhtin's earlier arguments. Like "Discourse in Life and Discourse in Art" and *Marxism*, *Problems* argues for artistic discourse as a special form of social discourse. In *Marxism* a specific discourse form, reported discourse, served as an illustrative example of social discourse; in *Problems* a related form, double-voiced discourse and its generic literary counterpart, the polyphonic novel, are the topics of theoretical analysis. As with *Marxism*, *Problems* finds the historicization of discourse a necessary part of its theoretical project; indeed, rather than the vague generalities offered in *Marxism*, *Problems* attempts to make its historical focus more specific and thus more substantive. In the chapter "Characteristics of the Genre," Bakhtin finds the roots of the polyphonic novel in the ancient Greek sense of the serio-comical, what he will come to call the carnivalesque. Although this survey is as all-inclusive, and thus as generalized, as that provided in *Marxism*, it nevertheless does try to substantiate its claims with literary examples, and so provides, if not a more persuasive, than at least a more nuanced (though uneconomic) characterization of each historical period.

Both the similarity of argumentative structure and the continuity of general subject may, however, seem less striking to the reader of *Dostoevsky's Poetics* than the new set of terms introduced in the essay's opening pages and employed throughout Bakhtin's argument, terms that suggest a renunciation not just of marxism, but of the social itself. Seemingly, the "subjectivist-idealist" allegiances that undermined the explicitly marxist arguments that we have looked at are here allowed an independence of their own. They have moved, in other words, from subtext to text. Most obviously, this new emphasis is highlighted by Bakhtin's discussion of the social by means not of the material but of the literary; whereas in *Marxism* the overvaluation of the material led Vološinov/Bakhtin to collapse the distinction between real, historical material people and products of the imagination, in *Problems* Bakhtin simply assumes from the outset that human subjects and fictional subjects can be treated interchangeably and that the discourse of fictional characters can be read as paradigmatic of social discourse.

This seeming valorization of the autonomous subject—in life or art— is perhaps most startlingly highlighted in Bakhtin's initial description of Dostoevsky's novels, a description that he ultimately uses to define the genre that is the focus of this study, the polyphonic novel:

> *A plurality of independent and unmerged voices and consciousnesses, a genuine polyphony of fully valid voices* is in fact the chief characteristic of Dostoevsky's novels. What unfolds in his works is not a multitude of characters and fates in a single objective world, illuminated by a single authorial consciousness; rather a *plurality of consciousnesses, with equal rights and each with its own world*, combine but are not merged in the unity of the event. (*Problems*, 6; Bakhtin's emphasis)

Setting aside for the moment the question of authorial consciousness, of Dostoevsky's relation to polyphony, we can see that Bakhtin seems here

to define individual identity not in terms of ideology or "we-orientation" but rather as simply a "fully valid voice." What makes these
voices "valid" is, apparently, not their social identity, not their link to
the economic base, but their distinctive, "unmerged and independent"—
one might even say unique—features. This autonomy is, according to
Bakhtin, represented linguistically by the exteriorization of consciousness through "voice." Although these art-historical terms can no longer
apply to a system of representation that is not defined primarily by its
materiality, polyphony is more like the "linear" definition of individual
voices in reported discourse and not the "pictorial" merging of "we-
oriented" social identities. Pluralism's deconstruction of a "single objective world" seems at first to have altogether eliminated socially constructed identity. Without the correlation between economic materialism and ideology, Bakhtin seems to have given up on any form of "we-
orientation." He begins *Problems* talking instead about "autonomous
subjects" (7) and the plurality to which their "personal" (9) points of
view contribute. These subjects, rather than orienting themselves socially in language, are instead portrayed as battling to retain their individuality.

This new emphasis on the autonomous subject leads Bakhtin to focus
not on reported speech, not on syntactical structures that figure objectified social relations, but on internal discourse, the language of consciousness; in both literature and life a subject's thoughts are not just
the truth of what he believes, but are the truth of who he is:

> For Dostoevsky the verisimilitude of a character is verisimilitude of the char-
> acter's own internal discourse about himself in all its purity. . . .
>   . . . the "*truth*" at which the hero must and indeed ultimately does arrive
> through clarifying the events to himself, can essentially be for Dostoevsky,
> only *the truth of the hero's own consciousness*. It cannot be neutral toward
> his self-consciousness. In the mouth of another person, a word or a defini-
> tion identical in content would take on another meaning and tone, and
> would no longer be the truth. (*Problems*, 54–55; Bakhtin's emphasis)

This passage might at first glance seem to be taken from Dorrit Cohn; it
seems to be saying that because a person *is* what he thinks, fiction mi-
metically represents a character by representing his thoughts. But of
course Bakhtin is even more complicated than this. He argues that because the most internal form of internal discourse is introspective, self-
conscious discourse, discourse about the self, the truth of a subject is the
process, the fact, of his self-analysis. Whereas the materialist assump-

tions of *Marxism* led Vološinov/Bakhtin to claim that the self-reflexivity
of reported discourse ("speech about speech, utterance about utterance") did not simply reproduce but actually instantiated individual
identity, now Bakhtin's "subjectivist-idealist" biases lead him to argue
that internal discourse is not just a means for representing truth to oneself, but it *is* that truth. Taking the alterity of vocabulary that we saw in
Chapter 2 to an extreme, Bakhtin makes the authentic representation of
identity inseparable from self representation: someone else may be capable of representing the truth of your consciousness in the exact same
words, but because those words would not be *your* words, it cannot be
the truth which is always your truth.

By defining authentic representation in terms of individual perception
and personal language use, Bakhtin seems to eliminate the possibility of
not just socially determined but socially apprehended identity. To represent a character in terms of any external characteristics is now to misrepresent him, to present your view of the character and not his own
view of himself:

> The hero interests Dostoevsky not as some manifestation of reality that pos-
> sesses fixed and specific socially typical or individually characteristic traits,
> nor as a specific profile assembled out of unambiguous and objective fea-
> tures which, taken together, answer the question "Who is he?" No, the hero
> interests Dostoevsky as a *particular point of view on the world and on one-
> self*, as the position enabling a person to interpret and evaluate his own self
> and his surrounding reality. (*Problems*, 47; Bakhtin's emphasis)

Nothing could seem farther from a marxist argument. Now social position, far from constituting consciousness, cannot even represent consciousness accurately; nothing external can. No longer do the material
and concrete accurately represent the self; now the objective misrepre-
sents. In Bakhtin's new schema, no object or objective form can equal
consciousness because consciousness can always upset that equation by
making that object its subject. Simply put, a process (consciousness) can
never be equal to a thing (external, material traits). Whereas in his earlier marxist arguments individual identity was, as ideology, always beyond self-control, here self-consciousness has an infinite power to appropriate; it "absorb[s] into itself the entire world of objects" (49). In
imagining the objective as being swallowed by the personal and in describing truth as personal and thus private, Bakhtin seems to have effectively eliminated the individual's necessary relation to anything beyond
himself.

Yet for all Bakhtin's emphasis on consciousness, for all of his insistence on personal truths, the loss of economic determinism has not resulted in the unqualified triumph of subjectivist-idealist philosophy. In the same way that social pluralism deconstructed marxist monism, so now does his abiding commitment to social pluralism save Bakhtin from solipsism. In *Problems*, Bakhtin carefully defines his position against either marxist monism or traditional idealism. He begins by claiming that the two seemingly opposite approaches are equally reductive: "The monistic principle, that is, the affirmation of the unity of *existence*, is, in idealism, transformed into the unity of *consciousness*" (80; Bakhtin's emphasis). He then explains how, in his paradigm, existence and consciousness are in fact integrated into a larger unity by the constant flux of their relation:

> It is quite possible to imagine and postulate a unified truth that requires a plurality of consciousnesses, one that cannot in principle be fitted into the bounds of a single consciousness, one that is, so to speak, by its very nature *full of event potential* and is born at a point of contact among various consciousnesses. (81; Bakhtin's emphasis)

The "unified truth," the objective reality of existence, is the truth of social interaction. Thus the truth of personal consciousness is only a partial truth; the whole truth lies in the larger social relation between consciousnesses, specifically the "point of contact among various consciousnesses." Indeed, we find that the one constraint on the powers of incorporation that Bakhtin has attributed to the self-conscious is the existence not of objects, but of other subjects. Given his definition of self-consciousness as absorptive, we find that the Bakhtin of *Problems* formulates a relation between subjects that is more competitive than that theorized in *Marxism*. Whereas in *Marxism*, we-orientation could be postulated as a truth of social existence, one that might be more or less realized and represented by a particular speaker, in *Problems* a battle for hegemony takes place within the novel that is reminiscent of the struggle between novelistic subjects theorized by Lubbock and by the second wave of novel theorists: for Bakhtin, the consciousness of one subject is limited only by the objective reality of other subjects' consciousnesses: "To the all-devouring consciousness of the hero the author can juxtapose only a single objective world—a world of other consciousnesses with rights equal to those of the hero" (49–50). The point of contact between these consciousnesses is what gives rise to "events," to an externalization created by the interaction of one subject with another.

The polyphonic novel does not, then, simply represent a multiplicity of unique consciousnesses; it also enacts their interaction. In describing this interaction, Bakhtin replaces the now inapplicable materialist, art-historical terms "linear" and "pictorial," with terms that describe the degree of social contact achieved in any individual's discourse: "mon-ologic" and "dialogic." Dostoevsky's achievement, which is also the achievement of the polyphonic novel, is his capacity to be fully dialogic, to represent the objective truth of existence, the collective community of subjects who are themselves multiplicities:

> The uniqueness of Dostoevsky lies not in that he monologically proclaimed the value of personality (others had done that before him); it lies in the fact that he was able, in an objective and artistic way, to visualize and portray personality as another, as someone else's personality, without making it lyri-cal or merging it with his own voice—and at the same time without reducing it to a materialized psychic reality. (*Problems*, 12–13)

Dostoevsky is, in other words, able both to relate dialogically to his characters and to represent their own dialogic interaction. He does this without committing either an excess of subjectivism, i.e. turning the "other" into himself, or an excess of materialism, i.e. treating the psyche as object, as "body" and not voice. This capacity for dialogic interac-tion constitutes Dostoevsky's "uniqueness," which is at once his own special distinctiveness, his own identifiable individual reality, and his "objective" apprehension, his insight into the nonidiosyncratic, objec-tive truth of reality. This description of Dostoevsky begins to suggest how dialogics can simultaneously stress the importance of autonomous individuality and insist on social plurality:

> The author of a polyphonic novel is not required to renounce himself or his own consciousness, but he must to an extraordinary extent broaden, deepen and rearrange this consciousness (to be sure, in a specific direction) in order to accommodate the autonomous consciousnesses of others. (68)

Dostoevsky's ability to engage in dialogics is in part due to what in *Marxism* would have been called his personal capacity for "we-orientation"; and this description of the polyphonic author's capacity for appreciation—his ability to "broaden and deepen" his own con-sciousness in order to represent authentically the consciousness of oth-ers—certainly recapitulates the tension in *Marxism* between the social fact of alterity and an individual's personal genius for alterity. Bakhtin insists in *Problems* that an individual's capacity for dialogics is influ-enced by the objective conditions of existence. Although in *Problems* this objectivity is neither marxist nor material, it is historical. According to Bakhtin, within the necessary fact of dialogic interaction, some historical periods promote dialogism more than others. And interestingly, in the same way that Vološinov/Bakhtin found "we-orientation" to thrive under capitalism, so too does Bakhtin cite capitalist societies as the most congenial to polyphony:

> The polyphonic novel could indeed have been realized only in the capitalist era. The most favorable soil for it was moreover precisely in Russia, where capitalism set in almost catastrophically, and where it came upon an untouched multitude of diverse worlds and social groups which had not been weakened in their individual isolation, as in the West, by the gradual encroachment of capitalism. . . . In this way the objective preconditions were created for the multi-leveledness and multi-voicedness of the polyphonic novel. (*Problems*, 19–20)

For Bakhtin the unique development of capitalism in Russia has the positive power to hold social differences in suspension, to promote social simultaneity ("multi-leveledness and multi-voicedness"), a better good than either isolation ("an untouched multitude of diverse worlds") or similitude. Dostoevsky's "uniqueness" lies not simply in his own ability to express either his own voice or the voice of any one character, but rather in his ability to understand this social reality, the objective social conditions of his era, the very conditions that permit polyphony. Much like the description James gives of the successful novelist, Bakhtin praises Dostoevsky for making his individual point of view a representative point of view. But for Bakhtin this representation says as much about the age as it does about the author: Dostoevsky's insight into Russia's unique character becomes one of the extrinsic interests (what James would call the interesting object) that lends not only objectivity but also a public character to his own subjective point of view: "Dostoevsky as an artist does arrive at an *objective* mode for visualizing the life of consciousnesses and the forms of their living coexistence, and thus offers material that is valuable for the sociologist as well" (32; Bakhtin's emphasis).

BAKHTIN MAY SEEM to have thus resolved the contradiction between materialism and idealism by doing away with the former, but his desire to situate what he now calls the objective truth of unique personal consciousnesses in a historical context, his desire to show how the objective fact of dialogic interaction gave rise to a specific literary form, the polyphonic novel, indicates that his "subjectivist idealism" is still in tension with his belief that history itself is not only "objective" but creates the conditions that allow individual insight. Once we understand that the sociohistorical has not been eliminated from Bakhtin's theory, once we see that it is, on the contrary, central to his notion of dialogics, we need to reexamine his conception of consciousness as presented in *Problems*. Is consciousness really as private as it initially seemed? If the autonomous subject is defined as a unique point of view, a personal perspective, what has created this view point and how is it identified?

Bakhtin has, we have seen, established how internal discourse constitutes both the truth of what an individual believes and the truth of who he is. But when Bakhtin explains the way internal discourse operates, we find that, although this discourse may no longer be said to be socially determined, it still is *social*. Internal discourse is itself constituted by "ideas" that turn out to be little different from the "social material" that—in various versions—contained subjectivity in all the Vološinov/Bakhtin arguments:

> The idea—as it was *seen* by Dostoevsky the artist—is not a subjective individual-psychological formation with "permanent resident rights" in a person's head; no, the idea is inter-individual and inter-subjective—the realm of its existence is not individual consciousness but dialogic communion *between* consciousnesses. The idea is a *live event*, played out at the point of dialogic meeting between two or several consciousnesses. In this sense the idea is similar to the *word*, with which it is dialogically united. Like the word, the idea wants to be heard, understood, and "answered" by other voices from other positions. (*Problems*, 88; Bakhtin's emphasis)

The fact of consciousness may be personal, but the content is so social that Bakhtin can describe the idea (here figured as something internal) and the word (here, as in the earlier work, something external) as equally social; internal discourse is ultimately, as it was in the marxist arguments, simply internalized dialogue. It is an act, a "live event," of we-orientation.

Dostoevsky's understanding of the dialogic idea causes him to realize, according to Bakhtin, that the objective truth of existence is that there is no "impersonal truth" (*Problems*, 96). Dostoevsky's own understanding operates "not in thoughts but in points of view, consciousness, voices" (93). But Bakhtin goes on to argue that Dostoevsky also realizes a valid corollary notion, one that reinvokes an argumentative pattern that we saw in the marxist essays: because thoughts are objective and yet also embodied, they seem not so much to derive from persons but rather to entail them: he goes so far as to say, "there are no thoughts belonging to no one and every thought represents an entire person" (93). This means that, when a character like Raskolnikov thinks,

> his inner speech unfolds like a philosophical drama, where the *dramatis personae* are embodied points of view on life and on the world, realized in living situations.
>
> All the voices that Raskolnikov introduces into his inner speech come into a peculiar sort of contact, one that would be impossible among voices in an actual dialogue. Because they all sound within a single consciousness, they become, as it were, reciprocally permeable. They are brought close to one another, made to overlap; they partially intersect one another, creating the corresponding interruptions in areas of intersection. (*Problems*, 239)

In the same way that Bakhtin/Vološinov argued for a distinction between reported discourse and dialogue, claiming the latter to be less interactive than the former and thus less "we-oriented," so too does Bakhtin argue now that dialogic internal discourse is actually more social than actual dialogue. Consciousness may indeed be privileged in the work that is signed by Bakhtin, but only, it turns out, because it is the locus for the most socially diverse kind of contact. The dialogic subject may be defined by his internal discourse, but the content of that discourse is always the voices of others. While each subject is a unique point of view, "the position enabling a person to interpret and evaluate his own self and his surrounding reality" (47), that position is always "we-oriented." In fact, dialogic internal discourse is a more complete version of "we-orientation" because it accomplishes a more thoroughgoing merging; within the unity of a single consciousness, "voices" become "reciprocally permeable." But this achieved reciprocity reinscribes the enduring paradox of social formalist logic: the point of view of the representing subject possesses no identity but that of the relations it makes among the subjects it represents. In a pattern of logic familiar to us not only from the work of the Bakhtin Circle but from the novel theories discussed in Chapters 1 and 2, Bakhtin's thoroughly dialogic subject contains no content of its own; rather its own content is always constituted by the activity of social identification. This dialogic version of the deconstructed subject thus reproduces the negative capability that has characterized the social formalist tradition: the subject's moral ability to constitute his own identity through the accomplishment of alterity is enabled by the materializing power ascribed to the form of representation. In the case of *Problems*, inner speech enables the "embodiment" of points of view, and thus becomes the equivalent of Jamesian artistic form or Lubbockian noetic materialism. Indeed, like Lubbock, Bakhtin imagines inner speech as most effective when language becomes a place: specifically the stage where alterity can be dramatized and the autonomy of its multiple points of view "realized in living situations." And like *Marxism*'s analysis of the pictorial representation of reported discourse, the mimetic materiality of inner speech effects a social interaction—specifically a reciprocal permeability—that is, significantly, impossible in actual social life. Bakhtin's description of inner speech thus paves the way for an exceptionalist account of literature that is based on another familiar paradox from the social formalist tradition: the polyphonic novel is the best representation of sociality because it enacts an ideal sociality that can only be accomplished through the appreciation of alterity and the materializing power of artistic form.

Bakhtin uses his dialogic version of the social formalist subject to argue further for an intrinsicality based upon the subject's ultimate uncharacterizability; if a subject had a specifiable character, it would be possible to define her as an object and not a person, to delimit and thus limit who she is; it would be possible, in other words, to think about and represent the subject monologically:

> In a monologic design, the hero is closed and his semantic boundaries strictly defined: he acts, experiences, thinks, and is conscious within the limits of what he is, that is, within the limits of his image defined as reality; he cannot cease to be himself, that is, he cannot exceed the limits of his own character, typicality or temperament without violating the author's monologic design concerning him. (*Problems*, 52)

To have definable content, then, is to be static, to be limited to a singular identity, which thus allows you to become an object in someone else's monologic design.

In literature, a particular kind of internal discourse, self-analysis, not only thwarts the subject's objectification but, according to Bakhtin, reempowers the character by allowing him to have the same multiple viewpoint usually reserved for the author. By engaging in dialogic self-analysis, a character like Raskolnikov can regard himself from a multiplicity of "other" perspectives:

> What the author used to do is now done by the hero, who illuminates himself from all possible points of view; the author no longer illuminates the hero's reality but the hero's self-consciousness, as a reality of the second order. (*Problems*, 49)

Although Bakhtin seems to establish a difference between Dostoevsky and his characters, crediting Dostoevsky with the "purer" dialogic ability, saying that we "should learn not from Raskolnikov or Sonya, not from Ivan Karamazov or Zosima," but from "Dostoevsky himself as the creator of the polyphonic novel" (36), his analysis of the characters' discourse challenges, if not finally collapses, this distinction between the relative didactic benefits of character and author. If what we are to learn is the moral superiority of dialogic thought, then to the degree that these characters share their creator's capacity for dialogic activity, we learn from them as well. And, as we have seen, what we learn by examining both the author's and the characters' dialogic activities is that the best point of view is that which is plural and not singular. But to have a plural perspective is, as we have also seen, to have no identifiable point of view, a conclusion that is reflected in Bakhtin's praise for Dostoevsky's narration as "narration without perspective" (225). If the defining feature of the subject is that he is a specific, identifiable point of view on the world, and if the defining feature of dialogics is that it has no perspective, then the particular challenge of dialogics is, again, to accomplish the social formalist desideratum: to define one's own subjectivity by losing it.

The Bakhtinian ideal of "narration without perspective" shows us, then, that while there may be no "impersonal truth" there simultaneously can be no "personal" truth. The "point" in "point of view" that gives an individual her unique identity has, in the most thorough dialogic practice, no substance of its own; the locus, the point, becomes the activity of incorporation, an activity that ultimately allows for the subject to be constituted through the representation of the other's unmediated subjectivity. Yet although Bakhtin has deconstructed the individual to show that it is always already social, he still needs some kind of identifiable individual if he is to imagine any kind of meaningful plurality. The one may always be the many, but the many is necessarily constituted by a multiplicity of "ones."[2] Bakhtin does not seem to be bothered about the contradiction that lies at the heart of dialogics, mainly because he rarely focuses on the fully dialogized, unexternalizable sub-

[2] Although David Lodge does not engage this paradox in its largest sense, he does acknowledge a version of it when he begins his argument about Bakhtin by saying, "Here ... at the very heart of Bakhtin's thinking about language, we encounter a puzzle or paradox. If language is innately dialogic, how can there be monologic discourse?" ("After Bakhtin," 92). In my terms, how can there be a "one" to define the many?

ject; instead, he alternately describes the subject as *either* a unique individual *or* a social multiplicity. Although seemingly unaware of his own theoretical vacillation—the contradictory movement between subjectivist idealism and pluralistic objectivism—he tries, as we will see, to counter the deconstructive activity of dialogics by describing the subject as constantly engaged in a reconstructive activity: the dialogic subject ceaselessly seeks an embodiment that will give it a temporary coherence. Bakhtin in effect imagines the subject oscillating between an insufficient, partial material instantiation—a particularity that is necessary if the subject is to be thought of as an individual—and a disembodied unity that can only be implied since it is greater than any kind of instantiation.[3]

Bakhtin admits that limitation may actually be a psychological desire, the dialogic subject's longing to relinquish its constant activity, to rest in some fixed, monolithic social identity:

> The plot of the biographical novel is not adequate to Dostoevsky's hero, for such a plot relies wholly on the social and characterological definitiveness of the hero, on his full embodiment in life. . . . But Dostoevsky's hero in this sense is not embodied and cannot be embodied. He cannot have a normal biographical plot. The heroes themselves, it turns out, fervently dream of being embodied, they long to attach themselves to one of life's normal plots. (*Problems*, 101)

The plot that Bakhtin rejects here is another variety of the social objectification that he earlier dismissed; if a hero could embody a plot, one could, presumably, answer the question "Who is he?" The hero may desire this certainty, he may want to give up, on the one hand, his own point of view and, on the other, his own multiplicity in order to conform to some social type, but, Bakhtin asserts, this limitation can never be effected; the dialogic subject is compelled to sustain both his uniqueness and his multiplicity. For the same reason, a dialogic subject cannot be equated with his own personal body; even though that body might seem integral to his identity, it in fact falsely represents him:

> A man never coincides with himself. One cannot apply to him the formula of identity A = A. In Dostoevsky's artistic thinking, the genuine life of the personality takes place at the point of non-coincidence between a man and himself, at his point of departure beyond the limits of all that he is as a material

---

[3] Here I disagree with Arpad Kovacs, who criticizes Bakhtin for a purely idealist philosophy: "There is no personage—only his voice, there is no material sign—only its meaning" ("On the Methodology," 382).

being, a being that can be spied on, defined, predicted apart from its own will, "at second hand." The genuine life of the personality is made available only through a *dialogic* penetration of that personality, during which it freely and reciprocally reveals itself. (59; Bakhtin's emphasis)

This description might seem simply a reaffirmation of consciousness over materiality: in place of the constricting and unauthentic material body, a subject can fashion a better embodiment; she can choose to reveal her subjectivity, her internal discourse, by putting her "ideas" into words. Because a subject freely chooses to make her internal discourse external and because this language is *her* language, her words are not objectifications but are personal self-descriptions. Subjectivity is preserved as the subject's because the authentic word is the subject's own "word about herself." In the same way that internal discourse *is* the subject, so too is the subject's self-description her authentic social identity.

Problems thus arrives at the same conclusion as *Marxism*, but by way of opposite assumptions. For Bakhtin as for Vološinov/Bakhtin, language is the best body for subjectivity. Yet whereas for Vološinov/Bakhtin language had the virtue of being both body and material, the best container for multivoicedness, in *Problems* language is the best embodiment of subjectivity because it is the *least* material way of externalizing internal discourse. Words are simply the means by which a subject represents to others who she is; not for any intrinsic meaning or even social value it may have, but because the discourse is *hers*.

Yet Bakhtin simultaneously realizes that, even though a fluid, active embodiment through language might be the best possible embodiment, at some point even this externalized identity must be limited, must be defined as a "one" to which the "many" might respond, and that the subject's discourse will be treated not as an activity, not as the process of self-expression, but as an instantiation of the subject herself:

Dialogic relationships are reducible neither to logical relationships nor to relationships oriented semantically toward their referential object, relationships *in and of themselves* devoid of any dialogic element. They must clothe themselves in discourse, become utterances, become the positions of various subjects expressed in discourse in order that dialogic relationships might arise among them. . . . [J]udgments must be embodied, if a dialogic relationship is to arise between them and toward them. (*Problems*, 183)

Bakhtin here describes language in terms of clothes because the image makes language seem the least permanent and therefore least limiting body for subjectivity. But this metaphor reminds us that, while his social theory requires subjectivity to be in some way externalizable (if it is not embodied, dialogic subjects cannot encounter one another), his sense of the full plurality of the dialogic subject requires that embodiment always be partial and qualified; like clothing, the limitation taken on through discourse can be taken off and put back on. Even if the subject is willing to "freely and reciprocally reveal itself," it can only reveal itself through partial embodiment. Although Bakhtin does not seem to realize it, ultimately it is not the clothing—not the special nature of linguistic material—but the act of clothing, the temporary act of instantiation, that proves for him the "noncoincidence between a man and himself," which is in effect his oscillation between embodiment—either human or social or linguistic—and his nonembodiable dialogic plurality.

Bakhtin's inconsistent characterization of language as both a part of the subject and a container for subjectivity is reflected in the importance he places on the term "voice." When he moves from describing what I have been calling the subject's practice of oscillation to an author's practice of representing subjectivity in a literary text, when he moves, in other words, from the topic of subjective multiplicity to the topic of social interaction, Bakhtin uses the term "voice" to mediate between his contradictory characterization of subjectivity as both limited and unembodied. He first argues for the alterity of vocabulary: since the best externalization of subjectivity is the subject's own discourse, the best representation of the subject is the unmediated reproduction of that discourse:

> The author constructs the hero not out of words foreign to the hero, not out of neutral definitions; he constructs not a character, nor a type, nor a temperament, in fact he constructs no objectified image of the hero at all, but rather the hero's *discourse* about himself and his world.
>
> Dostoevsky's hero is not an objectified image but an autonomous discourse, *pure voice*; we do not see him, we hear him. (*Problems*, 53; Bakhtin's emphasis)

Given the complexity of Bakhtin's theory of identity, the alterity of vocabulary has stakes that were of no concern to Genette, Pascal, and Cohn. If discourse can be read as voice, then, so Bakhtin would have us believe, language has not distorted subjectivity through objectification—it has not imaged subjectivity—but has reproduced it. While Genette, Cohn, and Pascal focused on the mimesis of vocabulary, Bakhtin extends their notion of voice by stressing the importance of speaking itself:

the activity of verbalization is, for Bakhtin, as important to the authentic representation of identity as the words a character uses. He goes so far as to imply that any showing, any representation that realizes on visualization, compromises the autonomy of the represented other.

Yet when Bakhtin turns to the reader of the polyphonic novel, we find that the reader can only recognize a character's subjectivity by presuming it to be identifiable, that is to say limited, in language. Thus, in a move familiar from *Marxism*, voice becomes "reimaged"; voice is not the process of saying the word but is *in* the word:

> Dialogic relationships are possible not only among whole (relatively whole) utterances; a dialogic approach is possible toward any signifying part of an utterance, even toward an individual word, if that word is perceived not as the impersonal word of language but as a sign of someone else's semantic position, as the representative of another person's utterance; that is, if we hear in it someone else's voice. (184)

To hear someone else's voice in the word is, of course, to imagine the owner of that voice as singular and coherent. It is at moments like this, when he overvalues the subject's singularity, that Bakhtin can say admiringly, as he does at the conclusion of *Problems*, that "Dostoevsky's works are a word about a word addressed to a word" (266). But even when Bakhtin tries—as Vološinov/Bakhtin did in both "Discourse in Life and Discourse in Art" and *Marxism*—to allow for multiple voices within the word, he demands that each voice still be identifiable. In service of this endeavor, he includes in his analysis of the forms of Dostoevsky's discourse (a study that takes all of chapter 5) a chart that distinguishes the varieties of polyphony. Yet, as we have seen in both "Discourse in Life and Discourse in Art" and in *Marxism*, this chart simply creates the illusion of objectivity; in fact there is no definitive way of determining if a discourse form is, say, "uni-directional double-voiced discourse" or is actually "vari-directional double-voiced discourse." As with Vološinov/Bakhtin's attempts to codify the vocal content of discourse forms, the reader may ultimately be impressed more by the fictive character of the interpreter's vocal distinctions than by the real subjectivity expressed in language.

Of course in *Problems* Bakhtin does not expect the discourse form to do all the work of clear representation. As we have already amply seen, vocal clarity is dependent on the subject's ability to distinguish himself. In his analysis of *The Double*, for example, Bakhtin criticizes the "vacillating borders between the narration and the hero's discourse" (219) and asserts that this is not true polyphony:

> The whole work is constructed, therefore, entirely as an interior dialogue of three voices within the limits of a single dismantled consciousness. Every essential aspect of it lies at a point of intersection of these three voices, at a point where they abruptly, agonizingly interrupt one another. Invoking our image, we could say that this is not yet polyphony, but no longer homophony. (220)

Bakhtin explains that "these voices have not yet become fully independent real voices, they are not yet three autonomous consciousnesses" (220). Here we can vividly see how Bakhtin's own vacillation between a theory of autonomy and a theory of plurality causes him to criticize this extreme form of dialogic interpenetration, the very condition that at other moments he holds out as an ideal. In fact what Bakhtin does not like about "homophony" is that it "vacillates" when it should "oscillate"; that is, vacillation is here a weak form of oscillation. It fails to construct a coherent, partial instantiation that it can then discard; instead it allows a vocal "intersection" with no clear embodiment that would allow for even its temporary identification as a particular subject. Simply put, homophony obscures the "one" in the "many."

By contrast, successful polyphony in the form of the polyphonic novel seems to mediate—the way voice itself seemed to do—between subjectivity as one and many. While it represents the voices of more or less dialogic subjects, this multiplicity ultimately stands as the always partial instantiation of the implied unity of authorial consciousness. The voices of these dialogic subjects are, Bakhtin insists, truly other; he argues against the assertion that a character, a creation of the author's mind, can never be thought to be autonomous. In *Marxism* Vološinov/Bakhtin confronted this problem but never answered it directly; in that context a character's independence made sense only because they had argued for language's inherent ideological content, a content that would make all language express value whether the subjects were fictional or real. In *Problems* Bakhtin finds a nonsocial source for this objective meaning, "artistic logic":

> It might seem that the independence of a character contradicts the fact that he exists, entirely and solely, as an aspect of a work of art, and consequently is wholly created from beginning to end by the author. In fact there is no such contradiction. The characters' freedom we speak of here exists within the limits of the artistic design, and in that sense is just as much a created thing as is the unfreedom of the objectivized hero. But to create does not

mean to invent. Every creative act is bound by its own special laws, as well as by the laws of the material with which it works.

. . . Dostoevsky's hero is likewise not invented, just as the hero of the ordinary realistic novel, and the romantic hero, and the hero of the classicists are not invented. But each has his own order, his own logic, which enters into the realm of the author's artistic intention but is not infringed on by the author's whim. Once he has chosen a hero and the dominant of his hero's representation, the author is already bound by the inner logic of what he has chosen, and he must reveal it in his representation. (64–65)

Because Bakhtin cannot appeal to any objective social content that might grant the voices of characters real alterity, he tries to establish the difference between the subjects in novels by way of the abstraction "artistic logic." This new term allows Bakhtin to limit subjectivity— both the author's and the character's—without seeming to embody it. A force, a law, an objective condition of art and creativity dictates "the logic" of the author's creation; this "logic," this seemingly unembodied, wholly abstract system of distinguishing patterns of unity, thus seems to allow for the objective subjectivity that is a discernible but not a material difference.

In appealing to the law of artistic logic, Bakhtin is clearly reestablishing another important difference, that between life and art. If we grant that the creative act may be bound by its own special laws and generic requirements, we still might wonder where else in life such unembodied restraint, such controlled mediation, might be found. The author of the polyphonic novel has a special privilege in *Problems*. He can constitute his own singular identity through a social plurality; he can seem to imply the greater objective unity of his subjectivity through the partial representation of his consciousness as a vocal multiplicity that is read simultaneously as self and as other; and finally he can be bound by an abstract principle such as "artistic logic" that can limit his own subjectivity, his own unified consciousness, so that it makes sense to talk about the author as one point of view and his characters as other points of view.

We can thus—at long last—see that Bakhtin's final appeal in *Problems* to the special powers of novelistic representation is what makes him so attractive to a theorist like Booth who has consistently attributed to the art work a special communicative power. Booth, remember, praised *Problems* for emphasizing the importance of the author's imaginative gift: the author's vision of the (objectively) ideal condition of social plurality allowed him to restrain his novelistic voice in order to grant autonomy and equality to the voices of his characters. Booth's own formalist biases led him to ignore the many contradictions in Bakhtin's theory, especially Bakhtin's vexed definition of voice itself. But having read *Problems* in the context of the other work produced by the Bakhtin Circle, we can see that Bakhtin's appeal to the power of "artistic logic" is integrally related to the theoretical dilemma he inherits from *Marxism*: the need for a viable social theory that would account for the existence of subjectivities without having to derive them from either the reductive source of the economic or the mystified source of private consciousness. Insofar as Bakhtin's social subjectivities seem, then, both discrete and multiple, they must, he realizes, take specific forms; but if they are to retain their subjectivity, this formal manifestation must be contingent and temporary. And so Bakhtin's problem leads to Booth's social formalist solution—if not bodies, then texts.

IF THE EARLY "disputed" texts have deconstructed the marxist ground of objective meaning and if *Problems* has deconstructed the autonomous individual subject, then the two key terms that have shaped the theoretical enterprise of the Bakhtin Circle have both lost any particular force. In some ways, this mutual deconstruction might seem a happy condition. The tension between materialism and idealism that plagued the work of these theorists might thus be eased: reduced from ontologies to social activities, materialism and idealism come to seem more alike than opposite, as embodiments of meaning that are always provisional. In Bakhtin's next major work on social language, "Discourse in the Novel" (1934–35), he makes this similarity—the "process" of meaning that has collapsed any important difference between materialism and idealism—the organizing concept of what will prove to be the final important revision of his social theory. In an attempt to eliminate the debilitating dualisms—the conflicts between form and content, interior and exterior, consciousness and materiality, self and other—that reflected the Bakhtin Circle's inability to privilege consistently either materialism or idealism, Bakhtin replaces the "either/or" of the early marxist arguments by a theory of "both/and," a move that makes the paradoxes formulated in *Problems* more explicit—while trying also to make them beneficial.

Bakhtin begins "Discourse in the Novel" with the reassertion of one of his earliest arguments: discourse in art can only be understood as part of discourse in life. Although this claim has been the guiding principle of all the work done by the Bakhtin Circle, we have seen how the Circle's attempt to collapse the difference between discourse in art and discourse in life has repeatedly, if variously, reinscribed the difference between the two discourses, making it necessary for Bakhtin now to argue the point anew. In this latest formulation, he contends that those who have not recognized that discourse in the novel is social discourse misread the novel by overvaluing either its form or its content:

> The principal idea of this essay is that the study of verbal art can and must overcome the divorce between an abstract "formal" approach and an equally abstract "ideological" approach. Form and content in discourse are one, once we understand that verbal discourse is a social phenomenon—social throughout its entire range and in each and every of its factors, from the sound image to the furthest reaches of abstract meaning. ("Novel," 259)

We can see from the lengthy description that Bakhtin goes on to provide that both of these "abstract" approaches err in a similar overvaluation of the specific. Both the "formal" and the "ideological" approach mistake the part for the whole: the former mistakenly assumes that the study of verbal art is no more than the study of stylistic modifications, and the latter mistakenly assumes that the unitary "meaning" of the art work should be the exclusive interest of the scholar (260–65).[4] In contrast to either of these partial methods, Bakhtin claims that his "social" approach will not misrepresent the art work as one or another of its parts (form or content) but will instead show the art work itself to be one part of the larger whole that is a social language.

What distinguishes Bakhtin's language philosophy in "Discourse in the Novel" from that of *Problems* is his return to an ideological conception of social language, a difference marked by the supplementation of dialogism with the concept of heteroglossia. If in *Problems* Bakhtin could imagine social typification only as a reification of authentic subjective identity, in "Discourse in the Novel" he can't imagine individual identity without social typification: he now defines the novel as "a diversity of social speech types (sometimes even diversity of languages) and a diversity of individual voices, artistically organized" ("Novel," 262). Bakhtin's expanded sense of the one and the many leads him to

---

[4] Although Bakhtin does not specifically call "ideological critics" marxist critics, he leaves the term vague enough to include either scholars who read art as a reflection of an individual author's meaning (what he later calls "poetic" meaning) or scholars (like Georg Lukács) who read art for the social ideology reflected by the art work. (For a more extensive discussion of Bakhtin's critique of Lukács, see Corredor, "Lukács").

see ideology not as a threat to individual identity, but as another element in the fluctuation between specificity and undefinability that is now so all-encompassing in his theory as to seem its primary tenet. As Bakhtin describes it, "a social language . . . is a concrete socio-linguistic belief system that defines a distinct identity for itself within the boundaries of a language that is unitary only in the abstract" (356). In "Discourse in the Novel," not just the subject, but language and history are theorized as activities rather than entities; the individual subject, language, and history are now all part of a synergy created by the fluctuation between any form of specificity—a word or a person or an era— and the greater (always implied) whole that is now for Bakhtin the only kind of "objective" reality available to sociopoetics. The particular, in the form of an art work or a social language, is always, then, understood as and against a posited unity; without such unity there can be no specifiable boundaries. But any unity and any boundedness must always be provisional since either kind of completion by definition stays the irreducible flux of the social.

If in "Discourse in the Novel" we accept Bakhtin's assertion that discourse in art is social, that it should be related to "discourse outside the artist's study, discourse in the open spaces of public squares, streets, cities and villages, of social groups, generations and epochs" (259), we still might ask if this steadily enlarging movement (from study, to street, to epoch) means that the art work is endlessly social.[5] Bakhtin's proliferation of public contexts and identities extends the deconstructed subject of social formalism beyond the individual and to the social itself. Bakhtin has not replaced the ideological sign with the free play of the signifier: he still insists that there is something "concrete" called the social that eliminates the difference between form and content, between signifier and signified; yet, without the marxist base (or any other "concrete" understanding of the social) to provide a causal source for specific social difference, what but free play can his social discourse become?[6] After describing the steady enlargement of social discourse, Ba-

---

[5] For a superb account of the limitations of the public square as a social model, see Hirschkop, "Heteroglossia" and "Is Dialogism for Real?"

[6] The prescriptive methodology that concludes "Discourse in the Novel" shows Bakhtin to be so untroubled by the problem of limitlessness that he imagines literary studies can easily detect and assert real social borders:

> The real task of stylistic analysis consists in uncovering all the available orchestrating languages in the composition of the novel, grasping the precise degree of distancing that separates each language from its most immediate semantic in-

khtin notes the less obvious multiplicity of even an apparently unified
social language, its "internal stratification"

> into social dialects, characteristic group behavior, professional jargons, ge-
> neric languages, languages of generations and age groups, tendentious lan-
> guages, languages of the authorities, of various circles and of passing fash-
> ions, languages that serve the specific sociopolitical purposes of the day,
> even of the hour (each day has its own slogan, its own vocabulary, its own
> emphases). (262–63)

Although Bakhtin now unqualifiedly embraces the social pluralism
that deconstructed the marxist base/superstructure dichotomy, he still
needs (as we saw in *Problems*), if not a base, then at least some principle
by which he can distinguish these various and fluctuating social languages from one another. Since such multiplicity would be not only infinite but unintelligible without some way to limit it, in "Discourse in
the Novel" Bakhtin makes explicit what was implicit in *Problems*: the
existence of a larger principle of fluctuation that he now calls a "life
force."[7] "The realities of heteroglossia" are in fact dependent, Bakhtin
tells us, on other "generative forces of linguistic life, forces that struggle
to overcome the heteroglossia of language, forces that unite and centralize verbal-ideological thought, creating within a heteroglot national language the firm, stable linguistic nucleus of an officially recognized literary language, or else defending an already formed language from the
pressure of growing heteroglossia" ("Novel," 270–71). Bakhtin calls the
struggle between these two essential forces "centripetal" and "centrifugal." Although the centripetal is in his discussion frequently associated
with hegemonic social authorities who attempt to secure their own social power through the "processes of sociopolitical and cultural centrali-
zation," Bakhtin does not regret this tendency: it is simply a fact. Despite his clear political preference for a liberated and perhaps even subversive democratic populace, hegemony thus becomes, in this theoretical
account of language, like any other identifiable particularity: less a social evil than a social inevitability, merely one aspect of the larger cen-

---

stantiation in the work as a whole, and the varying angles of refraction of intentions within it, understanding their dialogic interrelationships and—finally—if
there *is* direct authorial discourse, determining the heteroglot background outside the work that dialogizes it. (416; Bakhtin's emphasis)

[7] David Patterson argues that this force is what specifically makes the novel like
life: "The dialogical dimensions of the novel are spiritual dimensions of the novel
and of life itself" ("Mikhail Bakhtin," 131).

tripetal unity that is the implied, but never achievable, unity without which heteroglossia would be incomprehensible.

The concepts of centripetal and centrifugal show, in short, how generalized Bakhtin's social theory has become. In "Discourse in Life and Discourse in Art," Vološinov/Bakhtin appealed to group identity in order to argue for the "assumed value" that was *in* language. In *Marxism*, Vološinov/Bakhtin still believed that this group identity, now called ideology, was in language, but they also realized that this identity could be dynamic and complex—and thus problematically related both to the forms of discourse and to the modes of production. Now, without economic materialism to root social difference in some objective source, social difference and the social languages that this difference produces become a general problem of social flux: how can the flux and multiplicity of the social be limited long enough to allow distinctions to be made? Under the pressure of such questions, Bakhtin is forced to describe his pluralism in terms whose necessary dualism—its yin and yang, as it were—becomes increasingly explicit even as its politics becomes occluded: the social either tends toward unity (the "centripetal") or away from it (the "centrifugal").[8]

Committed to the notion of social languages as limited and objective, and yet far removed from his own earlier notions of economic determinism, Bakhtin must reprise the move to linguistic materialism that dominated his explicitly marxist texts—a move that locates "Discourse in the Novel" clearly in the social formalist tradition that I have been tracing. He first imagines language as gaining a social identity from the people who use it, and then he makes that identity an objective feature of language itself:

> However varied the social forces doing the work of stratification—a profession, a genre, a particular tendency, an individual personality—the work itself everywhere comes down to the (relatively) protracted and socially meaningful (collective) saturation of language with specific (and consequently limiting) intentions and accents. . . . As a result of the work done by all these stratifying forces in language, there are no "neutral" words and forms—words and forms that can belong to "no one"; language has been completely

---

[8] Corredor rightly argues that Bakhtin's Platonism is what links him to Lukács and Hegel: "In all three, Bakhtin, Lukács and Hegel, we find an attack on mythical reality and a desire for objective truth similar to the demands of realism. In a modernist spirit, one could naturally argue that the truth behind Lukács' realism, Bakhtin's laughter, and Hegel's classicism are myths themselves, based on Platonic notions of totality and the whole" ("Lukács," 105).

taken over, shot through with intentions and accents. For any individual consciousness living in it, language is not an abstract system of normative forms but rather a concrete heteroglot conception of the world. ("Novel," 293)

Although without economic materialism the nature of these "social forces" remains vague, Bakhtin still assigns them a causal role in the "saturation" of language. And, despite the fact that Bakhtin now offers no explanation of how and why language should be regarded as material, he still asserts that it makes palpable the identity of the "intentions and accents" that have marked it. In this new description of social pluralism, the variety of social forces and the stratification they create may be endlessly various, yet Bakhtin, by reinvoking the materialization of ideology in language, is able to limit social identity by making it seem concrete, something *in* language. This materialized specificity is then passed on to the individual subject, who, through language, gains a "concrete" heteroglot conception of the world.

But the flimsiness of linguistic materiality at this point in Bakhtin's theorizing is made evident precisely in its inability to constrain the individual subject. The individual is now said to be free to "colonize" this already populated language, transforming it into her "private property," and thus making it serve her own particular "semantic and expressive intention" ("Novel," 293–94). Bakhtin even imagines that some subjects are so free that they transcend linguistic property relations altogether: for example, in the "dialogized heteroglossia" of the comic novel, authorial intention is "present" in every point of the work, but

> The author is not to be found in the language of the narrator, not in the normal literary language to which the story opposes itself (although a given story may be closer to a given language)—but rather, the author utilizes now one language, now another, in order to avoid giving himself up wholly to either of them. (314)

In other words, in a pattern that we saw in *Problems*, the author of the comic novel only "partially" "gives himself up" to a variety of social languages: he escapes the sheer flux of the social by engaging one "concrete" instantiation of it after another, while never having to sacrifice the unity of his own individuality.

Yet the apparent "variety" of heteroglossia in fact allows for only one real difference: for the self to feel "other"—even as it remains an implied unity:

Such forms open up the possibility of never having to define oneself in language, the possibility of translating one's own intentions from one linguistic
system to another, of fusing "the language of truth" with "the language of
everyday," of saying "I am me" in someone else's language, and in my own
language, "I am other." ("Novel," 315)

The dualisms of this description show that, from the point of view of
the subject, heteroglossia is not important for the "variety" of differences that theoretically constitutes it, but for the creation of one difference that is always the same: the subject's experience of the difference
between self and other.

Whereas the early marxist texts tried to explain substantively how it
might be possible and what it might mean to have and to bridge real
social differences, Bakhtin now makes social difference part of a general
problem of alterity and unity that is itself part of the larger paradox of
centripetal and centrifugal flux. It is the terms of this paradox that allow him to describe social reality alternately—and contradictorily—as
essentially and superficially various. For instance, while he claims on the
one hand that authors of novels know that "it is impossible to represent
an alien ideological world adequately without first permitting it to
sound, without having first revealed the special discourse peculiar to it"
("Novel," 335), he claims on the other hand that "there takes place
within the novel an ideological translation of another's language, and
an overcoming of otherness—an otherness that is only contingent, external, illusory" (365).

As we saw in *Problems*, then, Bakhtin characteristically collapses the
paradox of the one and the many into one extreme or another as he
vacillates between two contradictory descriptions of reality. His own
theoretical vacillation again finds its counterpart in—but should not be
confused with—the oscillation that he still describes as the subject's essential activity. As in *Problems*, oscillation remains the term Bakhtin
gives for the subject's variable animation of linguistic materiality. And
as it did in *Problems*, his discussion of oscillation inevitably reinvokes
the conflict between voice and image, between subjectivity and objectivity, between imperceptible unity and perceptible partialness. Bakhtin
now tries to mediate these conflicts through the concept of "image," a
term that denotes the least permanent and therefore least limiting body
for subjectivity, the kind of manipulatable linguistic materiality that
Bakhtin's theory can never do without. To "image" language is to make
its thingness tangible; it means putting discourse in "a new situation in

order to expose its weak sides, to get a feel for its boundaries, to experience it physically as an object" ("Novel," 348).[9]

According to Bakhtin, the novel is the kind of social discourse that can best "image" heteroglossia because it allows the subject to oscillate continuously and with the utmost variety. The novel can do this, Bakhtin says, because, unlike most social discourses, it does not simply *mean* but *represent*; in Bakhtin's terms, the novel allows the author to "display" languages without necessarily "transmitting" meaning through them. The novelist may "oscillate between the purely objective (the 'word on display') and the directly intentional, that is, the fully conceptualized philosophical dicta of the author himself (unconditional discourse spoken with no qualifications or distancing)" ("Novel," 322). The author does not simply objectify discourses into characterological images (although she may do this sometimes); she actively and variously engages these discourses as she experiments with "owning" them. It is the author's fluctuating "population" of the languages she employs, the degree to which she displays them or uses them to express her own intention, that makes all the novel's languages—no matter whom they seem to "belong to"—the image of heteroglossia.

It can no longer surprise us that Bakhtin would describe his ideal form of discourse in terms of not what it represents but how it represents. His theory of flux has excluded content so completely that the ideal social discourse is simply the form that allows the most (which is also the most temporary) limitation. The novelist's creation of linguistic borders thus participates in the larger impermanent embodiment of meaning that for Bakhtin

> signif[ies] a relativizing of linguistic consciousness in the perception of language borders—borders created by history and society, and even the most fundamental borders (i.e. those between languages as such)—and permit[s] expression of a feeling for the materiality of language that defines such a relativized consciousness. ("Novel," 323–24)[10]

[9] As Robert Seguin has said of Bakhtin, "novels do not 'reflect' social heteroglossia, they rather *are* social heteroglossia, filtered through such neutral containment devices as plot and character. These devices seem to operate only to the extent that they inscribe this heteroglossia in a manageable form, such that you can carry it around with you in your pocket or briefcase" ("Borders," 52; Seguin's emphasis).

[10] In his discussion of *Rabelais*, Dominick LaCapra approves of Bakhtin's emphasis on the border: "Dialogization heightened the importance of the border or the threshold where seeming opposites entered into an exchange and possibly coexisted, often in tensely charged relationships. It thus inserted the public square into language use itself" (*Rethinking*, 313).

Yet this approving description of relativity cannot be taken as Bakhtin's final theoretical statement. The relativized consciousness, despite its sense and even creation of materialized differences, is predicated on Bakhtin's nonrelativized description of reality that both informs the subject's activity of oscillation and unifies the vacillation of Bakhtin's own logic. Bakhtin himself insists that it is possible to speak objectively about relativity when he asserts that "this relativizing of linguistic consciousness in no way requires a corresponding relativizing in the semantic intentions themselves: even within a prose linguistic consciousness, intentions themselves can be unconditional" (324).

In "Discourse in the Novel," the real power of the novel lies, then, not in relativity but in relativization; through the oscillation it permits, the fluctuation between transmitting and displaying that it allows, the novel can, according to Bakhtin, express the author's knowledge of relativized meaning without preventing him from meaning. The novel can, in other words, both mean and not mean, be both subject and object:

> Thanks to the ability of a language to represent another language while still retaining the capacity to sound simultaneously both outside it and within it, to talk about it and at the same time to talk in and with it—and thanks to the ability of the language being represented simultaneously to serve as an object of representation while continuing to be able to speak to itself—thanks to all this, the creation of specific novelistic images of languages becomes possible. ("Novel," 358)

This familiar desideratum is, of course, what in *Marxism* attracted Vološinov/Bakhtin to the forms of reported discourse. In "Discourse in the Novel," Bakhtin's description of the novel's capacity to transmit and display meaning corresponds perfectly to the definition of reported speech as "speech within speech, utterance within utterance, and at the same time also *speech about speech, utterance about utterance*" (*Marxism*, 115; their emphasis).[11] While this persistent characterization of language as both subject and object, both intentional and material, may in fact perfectly describe the ideal condition of social identity and unrestricted subjectivity that Bakhtin desires, it ultimately tells us less about

---

[11] Although the novel has this special capacity, this does not mean that all verbal art both transmits and displays. On the contrary, and as I will discuss, Bakhtin calls "poetic" those art forms that try to stifle the natural heteroglossia of language, employing an "authoritative" discourse as if language communicated without mediation the author's "monologic" meaning.

real social discourses and more about the real problems of a language theory derived from social formalism.

THE FACT THAT BAKHTIN begins with philosophical assumptions about life and literature that are so removed from James's makes it all the more powerful to discover that the basis of similarity between James and Bakhtin lies in what seems to be a salient difference between them: their understanding of novelistic form. When we analyze Bakhtin's account of novelistic representation, we discover that Bakhtin's philosophy of social language shares striking characteristics with what is perhaps the most complicated aspect of James's aesthetic philosophy: his description of the artistic subject. By designating social *language* as the object of novelistic representation, Bakhtin conceptualizes alterity as more than characterological vocal diversity. For Bakhtin, if the novelist represents language accurately, then the social subjects constituted by language will, as a matter of course, be fully expressed; language itself, in other words, enjoys the respect that Lubbock, Cohn, and Booth accord to human subjects. Since Bakhtin describes language as possessing both the qualities of radical subjectivity and radical objectivity—on his view language materializes and thus both realizes and individuates the alterity of social subjects—Bakhtin's novelistic language possesses a strong resemblance to the hybridity of the Jamesian artistic subject.

First of all, for both James and Bakhtin novelistic representation is grounded in what they take to be the essential feature of authorial identity: the felt relation of the writer to the object of representation. The poet, for Bakhtin, is the writer who has no sense of language's alterity, who uses language as a means to an expressive end without realizing that it should also be a representational end in itself. Rather than distinguishing poetry from prose by any obvious formal differences—like short lines, rhythm, and rhyme—Bakhtin instead bases generic difference on the writer's *relation* to the language he employs: "The language of the poet is *his* language, he is utterly immersed in it, inseparable from it, he makes use of each form, each word, each expression according to its unmediated power to assign meaning (as it were, 'without quotation marks'), that is, as a pure and direct expression of his own intention" ("Discourse," 285, Bakhtin's emphasis). The poet's attempt to make language express only his own meaning denies what is for Bakhtin the true nature of language:

Actual social life and historical becoming create within an abstractly unitary national language a multitude of concrete worlds, a multitude of bounded verbal-ideological and social belief systems; within these various systems (identical in the abstract) are elements of language filled with various semantic and axiological content and each with its own different sound. ("Novel," 288)

The poet imagines—erroneously—that self-expression can be both private and unmediated. By trying to make language express only his own intention, he seeks to strip the social multiplicity from language; he attempts, in other words, to replace the socially and historically produced "verbal-ideological and social belief systems" that, according to Bakhtin, inhere in language, with his own personal meaning.

By contrast, the Bakhtinian prose writer both recognizes and welcomes the social diversity that constitutes language. He not only has a "sense of the boundedness, the historicity, the social determination and specificity of one's own language [that] is alien to poetic style" (285), but also is open to the alterity that inheres in language; he rejoices in expressing himself through languages not his own, is open to "alluding to alien languages, to the possibility of another vocabulary, another semantics, other syntactic forms and so forth, to the possibility of other linguistic points of view . . ." (285).

The Bakhtinian novelist, like the Jamesian artist, represents the self in and through its relation to an other: the Jamesian artist strives to represent the essential nature of the "thing" that interests him; the Bakhtinian novelist also strives to represent the essential nature of the thing that interests him, social language. Of course Bakhtin and James do diverge in their understanding of the kind of identity that can be ascribed to the interesting object (James seems to be able to manage difference serially, while Bakhtin embraces heterogeneity). But looked at another way, James's theory might be said to allow for more difference: for James the identity of the interesting object may be singular, but the potential sources of wonder are so various and unpredictable as to defy enumeration; for Bakhtin the object's identity may be multiplicitous, but the novelist's object of interest is always only one thing, social language. Whether singular or serial, the object's primary importance for both theorists is its latent subjectivity, called forth and made apparent only through the recognition of the artist/novelist. For both theorists, the artist/novelist's invested relation in the interesting object results in its objectivized representation of subjectivity: the Jamesian artist's wonder transforms the interesting object into a subject capable of self-expression; the Bakhtinian novelist's sensitivity to language as an end and not simply a means of representation unveils the social subjects that inhere in the linguistic body.

Bakhtin's theory seems even closer to James's when we discover why the Bakhtinian novelist is able to know and to practice the appreciation of alterity. The insight about language that distinguishes the Bakhtinian novelist from the poet is not garnered from any difference in social experience; Bakhtin instead invokes what we might call a generic essentialism: novelists are better able to know and represent the social nature of language, simply because they *are* novelists.

> [A]ll languages of heteroglossia, whatever the principle underlying them and making each unique, are specific points of view on the world, forms for conceptualizing the world in words, specific world views, each characterized by its own objects, meanings and values. As such they all may be juxtaposed to one another, mutually supplement one another, contradict one another and be interrelated dialogically. As such they encounter one another and co-exist in the consciousnesses of real people—first and foremost, in the creative consciousness of people who write novels. ("Novel," 291–92)

Bakhtin's "creative consciousness" thus seems indistinguishable from what James calls the artist's "responding imagination." In both cases, the quality that makes the appreciation of alterity possible is the sensibility of the artist. And in both cases, what begins as a seemingly democratic theory of representation evolves into a theory of artistic genius: James tells us that anyone can write a novel since everyone has a unique point of view to express, but his attachment to the appreciation of alterity leads him to distinguish the true artist as the person who can most sincerely express his own interests while simultaneously representing the intrinsic character of the object that interests him; Bakhtin tells us that any speaker has the capacity to know and represent the social identities that inhabit the language that she uses, but Bakhtin's attachment to the appreciation of alterity leads him to privilege the novelist, whose sole task is to accomplish through artistic representation an intensity and amount of dialogic interaction that supersedes the kinds of social interactions that are possible in daily life.

Like James, then, Bakhtin describes novelistic appreciation as essentially active and creative. The Bakhtinian novelist does not passively reflect the heterogeneous and dynamic social character of language; he imaginatively experiences what we might call a plethora of alterity: he identifies, occupies, and interrelates the "specific points of view" that inhere in language. This imaginative engagement makes the Bakhtinian novelist an agent as well as a recognizer of alterity: his participation in the juxtaposition, supplementation, contradiction, and dialogical interrelation among points of view creates, as it were, *more* alterity by establishing new ways for points of view to interrelate. For Bakhtin, then, as for James, the appreciation of alterity is indistinguishable from the production of subjective relationality, which both theorists take to be definitive of the novel as an art form. For James the appreciation of the interesting object results in a work of art, an expression of the relation between author and object that creates a new identity, that of the art work's artistic subject; while the "new" alterity, that produced by the relation between the author and the discourses he represents, is what, for Bakhtin, defines the novel as genre.

Bakhtin's social theory of the novel thus reinscribes an account of the appreciation of alterity that is compatible with James's; but it is Bakhtin's peculiar account of mimetic materiality that brings him closest to Jamesian formalism as I have been describing it. James's sense of the "objectness" of the artistic subject, we remember, helps him imagine that alterity inheres in form; the artist might express himself while retaining the integrity of the artistic subject thanks to the materializing power that he accords artistic form. Since Bakhtin does not define the novel as a form—much less a unified form—it would seem that his theory would be free from such mystification. But in Bakhtin's theory, the novelist could not represent social diversity at all if it were not for the materializing power that Bakhtin ascribes to language itself. The sociolinguistic appreciation of alterity that is staged in the novelist's creative consciousness depends upon the prior ability of language to instantiate social "points of view." When Bakhtin says that "elements of language" are "filled with various semantic and axiological content . . . each with its own different sound" (288), he means that language does not simply represent, but actually contains these different social identities. Linguistic form preserves the differences among points of view while allowing them to interrelate:

> At any given moment of its historical existence, language is heteroglot from top to bottom: it represents the co-existence of socio-ideological contradictions between the present and the past, between differing epochs of the past, between different socio-ideological groups in the present, between tendencies, schools, circles and so forth, all given a bodily form. ("Novel," 291)

Alterity can be manifested—points of view remain distinct, voices preserve their own "sound"—because linguistic form constitutes for Bakhtin an ideally self-expressive social "body": language becomes, in other words, the quarter that most completely expresses the multiple and
multiply-related social others who inhabit the novelist's creative consciousness. Like the Jamesian artist who is guided by his subject to an
objective assessment of the material within him, the Bakhtinian novelist
is led to discover the mimetic potentiality of linguistic forms that, when
"quarried," manifest the identity of the social subject even as they express the artist's own relation to it.

Thus for Bakhtin the language of the novelist never risks becoming
merely poetic language because he is not only attuned to language itself
as an other but also understands the expressive potential of linguistic
form. Novelistic representation, for Bakhtin as for James, is ultimately
as much about representing the other as an object as it is about representing it as a subject; indeed for Bakhtin the representation of the subjectivities that inhere in language can be accomplished only if social discourse is represented simultaneously as person and thing.

But having understood the specific kind of social formalism that
Bakhtin shares with James, we are also in a position to see why conceptualizing language in formalist terms leads Bakhtin to an ethics of alterity that differs from James's in crucial ways. For Bakhtin the novelist's
representation of language ultimately allows him a subjective freedom
that has no equivalent in James's aesthetic theory. James asserts that the
connection between representer and represented is determined, we remember, by the essential and inescapable quality of the artist's interests;
the art work represents the artistic subject in and through representing
this relation. By contrast, Bakhtin believes that, once the novelist learns
to objectify language, to display it and not simply to speak through it,
his relation to the object of representation becomes contingent: as a
novelist, he by definition will necessarily choose to represent language,
but he can, we remember, remain only partially identified with, and
thus expressed by, any particular languages he represents:

> The author does not speak in a given language (from which he distances
> himself to a greater or lesser degree), but he speaks, as it were, *through* lan-
> guage, a language that has somehow more or less materialized, become ob-
> jectivized, that he merely ventriloquates. ("Novel," 299; Bakhtin's emphasis)

Indeed, as we have seen, it is the process of instantiation and disinstan-
tiation that, for Bakhtin, becomes the novelist's defining creative experi-

ence: "He can make use of language without wholly giving himself up to it, he may treat it as semi-alien or completely alien to himself, while compelling language ultimately to serve all his own intentions" (299).

The Bakhtinian novelist thus might seem to have a more contingent and more selfish, even "poetic," relation to his subject than novelistic discourse should allow; but the novelist's self-expression through language distinguishes itself from poetic language precisely because of its embodied expression of its own contingency: the poet treats language as if it were his own; the novelist as if it were other—even while it expresses his intentions. The contingency of the novelist's relation to any particular language results in the experience of his own identity as inexhaustible. Ventriloquization, made possible by the "objectness" of language, allows, as we have seen, the Bakhtinian novelist to oscillate between I and thou and thereby to express himself constantly without ever fully expressing himself at all:

> Such forms open up the possibility of never having to define oneself in language, the possibility of translating one's own intentions from one linguistic system to another, of fusing "the language of truth" with "the language of everyday," of saying "I am me" in someone else's language, and in my own language, "I am other." ("Novel," 315)

A theoretical tradition that begins with the Jamesian appreciation of the other thus culminates in the Bakhtinian appreciation of the self as other. And the move to include authorial identity as the object of appreciation is predicated on what we might call a more cooperative version of the ethics of alterity, a difference from James that nonetheless is derived from the logic of social formalism. For James the artist wonders alone; the interesting object remains silent so he can speak for it. For Bakhtin the novelist who serves language is in turn served by language: language reciprocates by revealing to the artist the truth of his own alterity.

This Bakhtinian extension of the appreciation of alterity is made possible by a theoretical logic so enduring that I trust it now seems fully meaningful to call it novelistic, even in the context of a discipline, sociopoetics, whose explicit aims and values are so removed from James's: the hybrid quality James ascribes to the artistic subject—its ability to be author and other, person and thing, subjectivized object and objectifiable subject—becomes the definitive feature of Bakhtinian social formalism. James's emphasis on technique thus may have been the impetus for the Anglo-American theory of the novel, but his appreciation of the novel in terms of social formalism has outlived even the interest in narrative technique. What is more, the contemporary Anglo-American enthusiasm for Bakhtin shows that novel theorists are no longer content with arguing that the novel is as good as other art forms; they no longer feel a need to assert, as James did, that the novel's aesthetic success depends upon what it has in common with painting, music, and poetry. Rather, the appreciation of alterity has, through Bakhtin, become the generic feature that distinguishes the novel as a preeminent genre; to the degree that other genres and discourses achieve this ethical quality through formal means, they become novelized or novelistic. But, as we have seen, the current valorization of the novel by theory is predicated on an enduring social formalism that situates the novel's privileged achievement of alterity in a subjectivism that threatens the very theoretical grounding upon which that privilege rests.

5

Double Vision as Double Voice

The Social Formalism of Identity Studies

The strident, moral voice of the former slave recounting, exposing, appealing, apostrophizing and above all *remembering* his ordeal in bondage is the single most impressive feature of a slave narrative. This voice is striking because of what it relates, but even more so because the slave's acquisition of that voice is quite possibly his only permanent achievement once he escapes and casts himself upon a new and larger landscape.
　　　　　—Robert B. Stepto, *From Behind the Veil* (1979)

Rather than a rigidly personalized form, the blues offer a phylogenetic recapitulation—a nonlinear, freely associative, nonsequential meditation—of species experience. What emerges is not a filled subject, but an anonymous (nameless) voice issuing from the black (w)hole.
　　　　　—Houston A. Baker, Jr., *Blues, Ideology, and*
　　　　　Afro-American Literature (1984)

While the rest of us in the room struggled to find our voices, Alice Walker rose and claimed hers, insisting passionately that women did not have to speak when men thought they should, that they would choose when and where they wish to speak because while many women *had* found their own voices, they also knew when it was better not to use it.
　　　　　—Mary Helen Washington, "Foreword" to
　　　　　Their Eyes Were Watching God (1990)

WHAT DO WE CALL a subject who is both more and less than an individual and stronger and weaker than a free agent? For all three of the authors I have quoted, and for many cultural critics over the past two decades, the answer is a "voice." Voice has become the metaphor that best accommodates the conflicting desires of critics and theorists who want to have their cultural subject and de-essentialize it, too. Fluid and evanescent yet also substantial and distinct, voice appeals to scholars as a critical term because it seems to provide a way of eliding the paralyzing dualisms that plague philosophical accounts of subjectivity. Thanks to its metaphoric flexibility, the term can describe human identity as unproblematically both self-selected and socially determined, both individual and collective, natural and cultural, corporeal and mental, oral and textual. In this chapter I want to begin to theorize the conceptual role played by voice in recent cultural criticism by focusing on a line of argumentation that has its origin in African American studies but whose claims are currently influencing work in ethnic and gender studies generally: the move to make Du Boisian "double consciousness" synonymous with Bakhtinian "double voice."

W. E. B. Du Bois's theory that African Americans possess a "double" consciousness is the point of origin for much contemporary criticism of African American literature.[1] According to Bernard W. Bell, for example, the African American novel has

> from its inception . . . been concerned with illuminating the meaning of the black American experience and the complex double-consciousness, socialized ambivalence, and double vision which is the special burden and blessing of Afro-American identity. (*Afro-American Novel*, 35)

[1] Arnold Rampersad goes so far to say that, in describing "the irrevocable twoness of the black American, he [Du Bois] laid the foundation of all future literary renditions of the subject. True to his gift, he both analyzed and simultaneously provided the metaphor appropriate to his analysis" ("W. E. B. Du Bois," 60). Other critics who identify double consciousness as the central or motivating theme of African American literature include Michael Awkward, *Inspiriting Influences*; Houston A. Baker, Jr., *Long Black Song*, esp. 17, and *Modernism*, esp. 85; Paola Boi, "Moses"; Elliott Butler-Evans, *Race, Gender and Desire*; William E. Cain, "New Directions"; John F. Callahan, *In the African-American Grain*, esp. 25–27; Gates, "Afterword"; Gayl Jones, *Liberating Voices*; William Lyne, "Signifying Modernist"; Gwendolyn Mikell, "When Horses Talk"; Mary O'Connor, "Subject, Voice, and Women"; Stepto, *From Behind the Veil*; James B. Stewart, "Psychic Duality"; and Priscilla Wald, "Becoming 'Colored.'"

Most of these contemporary literary critics historicize double consciousness by showing its abiding importance to African American writers from James Weldon Johnson to Ralph Ellison to Toni Morrison. As Michael Cooke, in his *Afro-American Literature*, long ago documented, the Du Boisian term was immediately seized upon by members of the Harlem Renaissance who used fiction and poetry to dramatize what they took to be Du Bois's true description of African American identity. (For the origins of this tradition, see Stepto's reading of Johnson's *The Autobiography of an Ex-Colored Man, Beyond the Veil*, esp. 113.) While they chart the ways African American writers have attempted not just to represent but to resolve the Du Boisian dilemma, most of the African Americanists whom I have cited take for granted the fact that double consciousness still remains the constitutive feature of African American identity. See in particular Baker, *Long Black Song*, 17.

Yet if Du Boisian double consciousness has been hailed as the central theme of African American literature, another term and another theorist have often been invoked to explain how African American literature represents this theme. To a quite extraordinary extent, that is, African Americanists have glossed Du Bois by way of M. M. Bakhtin, and argued that double consciousness is most powerfully represented in African American literature by the Bakhtinian technique of "double voice." Michael Awkward, for example, has called "double-voicedness" the "discursive corollary" to the Du Boisian model of African American identity (*Inspiriting Influences*, 56). He discusses the role of double voice in texts like Toni Morrison's *The Bluest Eye* and Zora Neale Hurston's *Their Eyes Were Watching God* as a Bakhtinian "narrative strategy" for representing each author's revised version of Du Boisian double consciousness (54–56). Henry Louis Gates, Jr., declares double voice to be a "verbal analogue" for "double experience" ("Afterword," 214–15). So central is Bakhtin to Gates's own theoretical project that he prefaces his introduction to *"Race," Writing and Difference* with a quotation from "Discourse in the Novel"; *The Signifying Monkey* opens with two epigraphs, one from Frederick Douglass and another from Bakhtin. And Gates defines the key term of this later work, the African American activity of "signification," by quoting Bakhtin's definition of a "double-voiced word" (50).

For Gates and Awkward the relation between Du Boisian double consciousness and Bakhtinian double voice is even stronger than they often allow. When they describe double voice as a "verbal analogue" to or "discursive corollary" of double consciousness, Gates and Awkward imply that double voice is merely a literary technique, a mimetic strategy for representing double consciousness. Yet both critics believe, and elsewhere explicitly state, that the double-voicedness of African American literature is more than a literary convention. As a strategy of representation, double voice would be controlled and designed by the authors who employ it in their fiction; yet Gates and Awkward speak of double voice as if it were beyond authorial control, a property not just of literature but of language itself. They treat voice, in other words, as the language that constitutes consciousness—or rather, double voice as the languages that constitute double consciousness.[2]

---

[2] Gates's "signifyin(g)" and Awkward's "denigration" are first of all general linguistic practices and only secondarily literary techniques. See Awkward, *Inspiriting Influences*, esp. 8–10; and the "Introduction" to Gates's *Signifying Monkey*.

One might be tempted to blame this apparent confusion about Ba-khtinian double voice—the uncertainty whether it denotes a literary technique or linguistic identity—on the interpreters and not the concept; one might be tempted to say that the ambiguity comes either from mis-reading Bakhtin or from the inappropriateness of using Bakhtin's theory of language to gloss the nonlinguistic description of consciousness of-fered by Du Bois. Yet, while I will indeed show how influential theorists of African American identity have taken double voice out of context and how Bakhtin's language theory is not easily accommodated to a model of racial identity, my ultimate claim in this chapter is that the Af-rican Americanists who invoke Bakhtin have in fact been far truer to Bakhtin than they know. Their confusion about "voice" comes not from a misinterpretation of Bakhtin but from a mistake about language that they share with Bakhtin. This mistake is as crucial for Bakhtinian iden-tity theorists as it is for Bakhtin, because it seems to legitimate their shared attempt to theorize social identity by way of literary formalism—the procedure I have been calling social formalism.[3]

As I hope I have made clear, Bakhtin's critique of linguists who ab-stract language from its social matrix paradoxically leads him to treat the matrix as if it resided *within* language. Since Bakhtin believes that language specially objectifies and materializes both personal and social identity, it is perhaps not surprising that he ascribes to literature, as a form of language use that not only is especially self-conscious but also is *written*, the ability to objectify and materialize the nature and operation of social language. Yet in Bakhtin's theory, language and literature are not the sole agents of meaning and identity; he describes individuals as both "voiced" and able to "voice": a person's identity may be consti-tuted by the social languages that speak her, but she can nonetheless ex-ercise control over her social positioning by "inflecting" the social iden-tities manifested within the languages through which she is compelled to speak. If Bakhtin's social formalism leads him to describe social identity as materialized in and through language, it also encourages him to por-tray the people who use language as strangely immaterial, or rather ma-terialized only in and through their language use. The ideal human

---

[3] Here I am in agreement with the estimation of Bakhtin offered by Pecora, *Self*, esp. 20–21. Yet instead of seeing Bakhtin as simply contradictory, I would empha-size the logic by which Bakhtin believes he has reconciled his formalism and mate-rialism. It is precisely the relevance of this logic to contemporary debates about identity and not the a priori character of "pluralist, capitalist societies" that has made Bakhtin so important to African Americanists.

agent for Bakhtin is the novelist, who, as the master of linguistic mastery, is able to practice the appreciation of alterity: to realize his own identity by displaying the linguistic identity of others, by giving voice to the social voices in language.

Only with a full understanding of Bakhtinian social formalism can we appreciate all that is at stake in reading Du Bois through Bakhtin. In the discussion of Barbara Johnson and Mae Gwendolyn Henderson that concludes this chapter, I show how theorists of African American identity import the logic of Bakhtin's social formalism, but in the process make one important change: Johnson and Henderson attribute to the subaltern subject the linguistic mastery that Bakhtin reserved for the novelist. In reading Du Bois through Bakhtin, both Johnson and Henderson imply that the social discrimination that defines subaltern positionality is in fact the necessary condition for an epistemological privilege that in turn brings with it a new possibility for social and personal empowerment. The move from subaltern disempowerment to individual self-empowerment is accomplished in these arguments with the help of an idealized mediating term: voice is nothing less than the authentic de-essentialized self, made manifest.[4]

In glossing double consciousness as double voice, theorists thus attempt to transform the Du Boisian crisis of subaltern invisibility into a Bakhtinian triumph of self-articulation.[5] The pyrrhic victory of this conversion, I will argue, helps us appreciate the Du Boisian terms in which it fails. If instead of reading Du Bois in terms of Bakhtin we read Bakhtin in terms of Du Bois, the emptiness of not just the Bakhtinian triumph but the Bakhtinian subject is underscored. In the logic of social formalism, the "inflection" of social discourse may make individuality

[4] More than any other theorist, Henry Louis Gates has authorized the practice of describing African American identity in Bakhtinian terms. Awkward, Johnson, and Henderson—along with Lyne, O'Connor, and Wald—either cite Gates explicitly or else appear in collections of essays that he has edited. For a positive evaluation of the theoretical incorporation of Bakhtin into African American studies, especially as accomplished by Houston Baker and Gates, see Peterson, "Response."

[5] Lyne has trenchantly observed how Bakhtin has been used by recent critics to redefine double consciousness as a source of African American empowerment ("Signifying Modernist," esp. 319–20). Lyne tries to counter this theoretical trend by showing that writers such as Ralph Ellison felt, like the African American subject described by Du Bois, constrained by double consciousness. Lyne's practical criticism does, however, run into its own theoretical difficulties. Since he does not explicate the Du Boisian definition of double consciousness, he both oversimplifies the concept and makes the mistake of using voice and consciousness as interchangeable terms.

audible, but for all its tonal variety, inflection always signifies the same thing: a speaker's self-consciousness about the social identity expressed through his language. The Bakhtinian "heteroglot" novelist, like the silent Du Boisian African American, is defined by a negative capability: his self-consciousness about the social identities contained in language allows him to be more than the social languages that define him—but that greater identity, formulated through the activity of distanciation, possesses no positive content of its own.

ALTHOUGH DU BOIS has rightly been credited with providing an early account of socially constructed racial identity, if we look closely at the passage in which he introduces the term "double-consciousness," we can see that his formulation of the problem of African American identity is neither as self-evident nor as coherent as critics take it to be. In fact, the passage presents two distinct versions of socially constructed identity: an "ethnic" model that describes African Americans as defined by two (conflicting) cultural essences (African and American); and a "colonial" model that represents cultural identity not as something essential, but as the internalization of a subaltern social position dictated by hegemonic power relations. Du Bois's attitude toward the problem of socially constructed identity—whether ethnic or colonial—is complicated by yet a third model of identity also invoked in this passage: a version of transcendental individualism that expresses Du Bois's attachment to a more traditional—and romantic—American ideal of self-authorship.[6]

---

[6] Two recently published books have powerfully explored the complexity of Du Bois's notion of double consciousness. A collection of essays edited by Gerald Early (*Lure and Loathing: Essays on Race, Identity, and the Ambivalence of Assimilation*) marks the first concerted effort to reevaluate Du Boisian double consciousness. In his "Introduction" to this wide-ranging collection of essays that have been solicited especially to comment on Du Boisian double consciousness, Early, after quoting the famous passage in which Du Bois defines double consciousness, rightly asks, "Although this passage is endlessly quoted, have we ever been sure what it means?" (xviii). Early goes on to articulate the fissures of logic that characterize Du Bois's figurative language, but he concludes too hastily that the passage is not the "expression of a unified idea" but rather the "expression of a series of sentiments that are, more or less, rhetorically connected" (xx). Paul Gilroy, in *The Black Atlantic: Modernity and Double Consciousness*, performs the crucial task of relating Du Bois's sense of the particular crisis of African American identity to the African European experience of double consciousness. His rich contextualization of Du Bois's intellectual development enables him to illuminate the philosophical tensions underlying the Du Boisian definition of double consciousness. Du Boisian double

In the opening pages of *The Souls of Black Folk*, Du Bois describes the birth of his double consciousness as the moment when he first was made to feel his racial difference. A new (white) girl at school cuts him by refusing his visiting card, "peremptorily, with a glance" (8). The girl disdains him on the basis of what she can see (his skin color), and that refusal is itself expressed through a blind look that "rejects" Du Bois without knowing the person he believes he "really" is: someone who is no different from her or from anyone else, who is the same inside—alike, as he puts it, in "heart and life and longing" (8). Du Bois describes this experience of alienation from white society as the feeling of being "shut out from their world by a vast veil" (8). In this formative moment he comes to know, in other words, that he was wrong to think that there is simply a true inner world of experience—a soul—that constitutes personhood. His identity as an African American does not simply reside within; who he is depends upon how he is viewed by a racist society, a society that thinks it sees him even as it "veils" him. This personal experience of racial discrimination becomes, at least as he presents it in *Souls*, the basis for his adult generalizations about the truth of the "Negro" condition:

> After the Egyptian and Indian, the Greek and Roman, the Teuton and Mongolian, the Negro is a sort of seventh son, born with a veil, and gifted with

consciousness is for Gilroy "the unhappy symbiosis between three modes of thinking, being, and seeing" (127, see also 134).

Before Early and Gilroy, Cooke, Stepto, and, more recently, Dickson D. Bruce, Jr., illuminated if not the complexities of the passage then the complexities of the concept. See especially Cooke, *Afro-American Literature*, 35; Stepto, *From Behind the Veil*, 54; and Bruce, "W. E. B. Du Bois," 301. Although all of these critics perceive the general terms of the logical tension within Du Bois's definition, only Stepto keeps the full problematic in play. Cooke reduces the problem of double consciousness to a problem of self-possession (19–20). Bruce contextualizes the concept in terms of Romanticism and contemporary psychological theory, but he ultimately declares that Du Bois used double consciousness strategically to describe the conflict between African spirituality and American materialism set forth in *The Souls of Black Folk* (301). Awkward asserts the same point that Bruce argues for (*Inspiriting Influences*, 12). Double voice has otherwise been interpreted as "psychic duality" (Rampersad, *Art*, 74; and Stewart, "Psychic Duality"); "the struggle of self-consciousness" (O'Connor, "Subject," 202); "ambivalence" toward white culture (Bell, *Afro-American Novel*, 35; and Jones, *Liberating Voices*, 63); mediation by white culture (Wald, "Becoming 'Colored,'" 79–80); and "masking" (Callahan, *African-American Grain*, 26, and Baker, *Modernism*, 85). My reading of double consciousness attempts to show how these different meanings are invited by the passage and how Du Bois's figurative language both illuminates and works to make compatible the larger philosophical issues that inform his description.

second-sight in this American world,—a world which yields him no true self-consciousness, but only lets him see himself through the revelation of the other world. It is a peculiar sensation, this double-consciousness, this sense of always looking at one's self through the eyes of others, of measuring one's soul by the tape of a world that looks on in amused contempt and pity. One ever feels his two-ness—an American, a Negro; two souls, two thoughts, two unreconciled strivings; two warring ideals in one dark body, whose dogged strength alone keeps it from being torn asunder.

This history of the American Negro is the history of this strife,—this longing to attain self-conscious manhood, to merge his double self into a better and truer self. (8–9)

By defining African American identity in terms of a socially constructed consciousness, Du Bois implicitly combats the racist notion that the "Negro" is essentially different from the white. Yet racism nonetheless has such power over African Americans in this passage that it hides the "Negro" from the sight not only of history but of the "Negro" himself, who has yet to find his "better and truer self." The "veil" that white society has cast over the "Negro" does more than exclude him from white society: it creates a double consciousness within the "Negro," a split between his inner self and the self imposed by white society. If this outer self is false, it is, however, also the only self that the "Negro" can see: he is thus blind to himself, lacking any true self-consciousness.

And yet Du Bois says the veil also brings a gift and, what is more, a gift of sight, "second sight." Du Bois's motivating—and deliberately age-old—metaphor of "the veil" suggests that a position of social oppression has its compensations: what the subaltern lack in social power, they gain in knowledge. What can the "Negro" see that the white cannot?[7] He can see that the white cannot see him; he is behind a veil that the white mistakes for him. And he can also see that he cannot see himself. There is a special knowledge granted to the "Negro" by his second sight, then, and it is the knowledge that his true self is unknown, by both white and black. What's more, the "Negro" alone knows that this ignorance is created by his socially imposed identity, his veil; he alone knows, that is, just how constitutive of identity, or rather deconstitutive, social positionality can be. And finally, he knows that the white does

---

[7] Because Du Bois's project is definitional, his discussion of racial identity can best be explicated by retaining his terms. By putting Du Bois's *Negro* in quotation marks, I want to emphasize the term's constructedness.

not know he possesses this knowledge. The "Negro" does have a special identity, then, and it is kept special, private, by the veil.

As we have seen, however, this inner self is not safe or whole inside the body that white society pities or despises; rather, it is divided, conflicted, self-blind. While thwarting the racism that would reduce the "Negro" to the black body, Du Bois's account of double consciousness internalizes the veil of socially imposed difference that Du Bois might otherwise have restricted to the body. The visionary power of "second sight" that now distinguishes the "Negro" is thus a power only to see the veil that white society has imposed, not to see what is beneath the veil; for Du Bois, there is no alternative "Negro" identity that both escapes the encroachments of racism and remains visible to the "Negro" himself. Having refused to envision "Negro" identity as merely a physical property, Du Bois stops short, then, of characterizing the "Negro" spirit. Instead, he defines "Negro" identity—"this sense of always looking at one's self through the eyes of others"—as nothing more than a point of view.

In denoting both the loss and gain of sight, double consciousness thus first arises in *The Souls of Black Folk* to describe the consequences that subaltern positionality has for racial identity. But this complex description of an impenetrable soul on the one hand and an incoherent colonized soul on the other is, in fact, only one version of double consciousness suggested in this famous passage. In the second half of the passage the colonial model of mediated identity is itself broken into two. The African American is torn between two incompatible national affiliations, what we might call two ethnicities. Indeed, these ethnicities are at war; the African American experiences his interiority as a struggle between equally compelling—if only internally equal—"souls."[8]

Yet when Du Bois invokes a conventionally bifurcated ethnic model, not even this shift of paradigm can provide more solidity to "Negro"

---

[8] When Du Bois returns later in *Souls* to the concept of double consciousness, he imagines the problem of "Negro" identity in yet another distinct way, related, but not identical, to the dual and divided cultural identities he here describes. In this description, the veil now creates not divided consciousness but a division between authentic and inauthentic consciousness. The bifurcated social world produced in the South by the color line forces African Americans to live a double life, one whose duplicity cannot be sustained: "Such a double life, with double thoughts, double duties, and double social classes, must give rise to double words and double ideals, and tempt the mind to pretence or revolt, to hypocrisy or radicalism" (146).

identity. His rhetoric downplays the constitutive features of each rival social identity as it emphasizes the experience of struggle itself. In other words, the fact of conflict becomes more compelling—or at least more legible—than what is in contest. Rather than elaborating the content of each term, Du Bois instead proliferates appositives that describe the feeling of *division*: "two souls, two thoughts, two unreconciled strivings . . . two warring ideals." Moreover, since the opposing terms themselves, "Negro" and "American," are not clear logical opposites, the "twoness" of cultural essence seems not just deemphasized but actually deconstructed. Why do African and American identity seem unsynthesizable? Du Bois implies it is because American identity is another name for racism. The "Negro" is ultimately not allowed to become American not because of his heritage, not because he is an immigrant—not, that is, because of his hyphenated cultural identity—but because of his color. "Negro" is dichotomous with "American" not because America cannot accommodate a synthesis of African American culture, but because American identity is withheld from someone whose skin color is black. The ethnic model thus is ultimately implicated in the hegemonic model and the results are the same: in both cases the twoness of the African American is not more but less; his double social identity results in the empty internal activity of self-division.[9]

It is at this point that the term Du Bois originally attempts to exclude, the essentially black body, returns. If Du Bois has up to now suppressed the body to show that color is an arbitrary signifier, this does not mean that he imagines that "Negro" consciousness can exist apart from the "Negro" body. On the contrary, Du Bois's account of double consciousness culminates in a celebration of the "dark body" whose "dogged strength" keeps the "Negro" from being internally "torn asunder." This powerful body serves not only to "contain" a personal identity that otherwise threatens to explode but to compensate in some measure for the vulnerability to "Negro" consciousness. Yet Du Bois in this passage grants the "Negro" body only enough strength to suffer the pain of double consciousness, not to cure it. He offers the dark body not as a source of new meaning for "Negro" identity, but as at best a token of veiled in-

[9] See Coward and Ellis, *Language and Materialism*, for a critique of Althusser along the same lines. In arguing for the necessity of a psychoanalytic-materialist theory of the subject, Coward and Ellis reject the "empty subject" of traditional marxist theory, "which mechanically inhabits a specific ideological formation according to a distorted image of real relations produced by those relations" (71).

ner resources, like the knowledge of self-blindness. If "Negro" identity remains contingent on social positionality, if "Negro" consciousness cannot change apart from social change, at least bodily strength will insure the "Negro's" survival throughout his struggle for change.[10]

Through the figure of the veil and the metaphor of sight, Du Bois thus sets in motion, but leaves implicit, a variety of conflicting notions about how socially constructed identity might work and what its significance might be. For Du Bois, these ideas remain embedded in figurative language, I think, because the very idea of socialized interiority he briefly sketches here—in all its different versions—is itself in tension with an older model of identity that Du Bois takes for granted in *The Souls of Black Folk*, what we might call Emersonian transcendence. (Indeed, one of the sources of the term "double consciousness" seems to be Emerson's "Fate" [372]).[11] In the famous passage on double consciousness, Du Bois turns almost imperceptibly in his second paragraph away from a radical vision of socialized interiority and toward the familiar romantic ideal of what Du Bois calls "self-conscious manhood." Self-conscious manhood might be another name for "Man Thinking." Like the Emersonian scholar whose office it is "to cheer, to raise, and to guide men by showing them facts amidst appearances" (*Oration*, 19), Du Bois's race leaders begin with self-improvement. According to this model, social identity is something that is lived through, as it were, to ascend to a "better and truer self," a self that is presumably beyond either culture or body, that is, quite simply, a free spirit. Social identity

[10] The interest of Du Bois's position is, of course, that it attempts to fuse Romanticist and social-evolutionist paradigms of identity, despite their incompatibility. For example, even when he most explicitly entertains the notion of social evolution, he defines the "survival of the fittest" in terms of transcendentalist values: "It is, then, the strife of all honorable men of the twentieth century to see that in the future competition of races the survival of the fittest shall mean the triumph of the good, the beautiful and the true; that we may be able to preserve for future civilization all that is really fine and noble and strong" (119–20). This conflict is put in a larger context by Appiah in "Uncompleted Argument."

[11] For further discussion of the influence of Emerson on Du Bois, see Bernard Bell, *Folk Roots*, 16–31. Bruce cites "The Transcendentalist," an 1843 essay, as one of the first uses by Emerson of the term "double consciousness" ("W. E. B. Du Bois," 300). Because "Fate" gives a particularly bleak account of how socially constructed identity debilitates the power of the individual, and because Emerson poses creative and controlled self-alternation as an unconvincing solution to the problem of ontological dualism, that late essay seems particularly apposite to Du Bois's concerns.

may thus be necessary, but it is not final; as Emerson puts it, "the one thing in the world of value, is, [sic] the active soul,—the soul, free, sovereign, active" (*Oration*, 10). Du Bois uses these same terms in describing the most important goal of "Negro education":

> Above our modern socialism, and out of the worship of the mass, must persist and evolve that higher individualism which the centres of culture protect; there must come a loftier respect for the sovereign human soul that seeks to know itself and the world about it; that seeks a freedom for expansion and self-development; that will love and hate and labor in its own way, untrammelled alike by old and new. (*Souls*, 81–82)

Although much of *The Souls of Black Folk* is devoted to delineating the "physical, economic, and political" reform that will make these changes possible (203), social projects are thus subordinate for Du Bois to the goal of personal transformation—the dream, as he says, of merging "his double self into a better and truer self."[12] When society is changed, then the "Negro" can, like Emerson, feel that his individual identity is his own active creation, that he measures the world in terms of his "higher individualism," that rather than being a product of social positionality, his point of view defines the world in relation to himself.[13] "Double consciousness" thus may hold some consolations for the "Negro"—in a nation that institutionalizes social inequality it may offer a privileged kind of knowledge that compensates for lack of social power—but, in the best of all possible worlds, double consciousness itself would be replaced by Emersonian transcendence. The unifying body in Du Bois's account thus becomes a foretype for the transcendental consciousness to come: the "better and truer self" is that which can sustain the dynamic internal division of autonomous self-definition.

[12] The fact that Du Bois famously embraced a number of radical and radically different political positions suggests that it was by no means self-evident what kind of political activism would accomplish the betterment of material conditions. As Marable reminds us, Du Bois was at "various times a supporter of racial integration and voluntary racial segregation, an African nationalist, socialist, communist, and pacifist" (*W. E. B. Du Bois*, xiv).

[13] Porte's description of double consciousness in his "Emerson, Thoreau, and the Double Consciousness" reminds us that for Emerson self-consciousness actually is a source of self-alienation. "Reason" may allow man to define himself in relation to himself, but it is this very condition that effects his alienation from nature, the standard of ontological unity as well as the opposing "other" against which human identity is defined ("Emerson," 42–43).

IF FOR DU BOIS a divided identity is a specifically African American problem resulting from the particular social position of the "Negro" in America, for Bakhtin all identity is divided, and that division is produced in and through language.[14] This difference between Du Bois and Bakhtin is perhaps most easily grasped by way of a Bakhtinian parable concerned, as Du Bois's autobiographical anecdote is, with a coming into double consciousness. Bakhtin tells the story of an "illiterate peasant" who accepted his social position as simply a given. He failed to recognize the play of social forces that not only oppressed but divided him, forces that, for Bakhtin, were most noticeably manifested in the peasant's polyphony of languages, which he employed without even noticing how distinct and even rivalrous they were. As Bakhtin writes,

> Miles away from any urban center, naively immersed in an unmoving and for him unshakable everyday world, [the peasant] nevertheless lived in several language systems: he prayed to God in one language (Church Slavonic), sang songs in another, spoke to his family in a third and, when he began to dictate petitions to the local authorities through a scribe, he tried speaking yet a fourth language (the official-literate language, "paper" language). All these are *different languages*, even from the point of view of abstract socio-dialectological markers. ("Novel," 295–96; Bakhtin's emphasis)

Eventually, however, the peasant becomes radicalized; he learns that even his rural world is saturated with power struggles and ideologies in conflict.[15] This knowledge, it is crucial to note, does not come to the peasant through some economic disaster or political atrocity; as I have shown in Chapters 3 and 4, however much Bakhtin may, throughout his

---

[14] Du Bois, of course, did make statements about the character and function of African American language. He calls, for example, his own tendency to rely on figures rather than logic a "tropical—African" style (qtd. by Rampersad, "W. E. B. Du Bois," 64). Yet if Du Bois feels that his language expresses traits that he associates with African character, he does not feel that his identity is limited or defined by the character of his language. Du Bois seems far more concerned with using language as a tool to accomplish his representational ends. For a thorough discussion of Du Bois's move from naive realism—the attempt to represent, as Du Bois says in the "Note" to *The Quest of the Silver Fleece*, the truth of his own experience—to a sweeping definition of all art as propaganda, see Rampersad, *Art*, 196.

[15] For a theorist like Graham Pechey, the peasant's step into relativization would be politically significant. The peasant knows what Pechey says the Bakhtinian novelist shows: "The truth that no rule is absolute." Pechey concludes that the "radicalism" of Bakhtin's position is that it reveals the "necessity of politics, of dialogical struggle, of power as struggle" ("On the Borders," 66).

work, declare his interest in concrete historical and social realities, these materialist specifics are conspicuously absent from his writings. Rather, the social forces that shape the peasant's identity are so fully rendered in the peasant's language use that he only needs to feel the friction created by his competing language systems in order to recognize his own dividedness:

> As soon as a critical interanimation of languages began to occur in the consciousness of our peasant, as soon as it became clear that these were not only various different languages but even internally variegated languages, that the ideological systems and approaches to the world that were indissolubly connected with these languages contradicted each other and in no way could live in peace and quiet with one another—then the inviolability and predetermined quality of these languages came to an end, and the necessity of actively choosing one's orientation among them began. (296)

In other words, the peasant learns to distinguish among the ideological systems to which he belongs thanks to the different linguistic forms they take. The identity of Bakhtin's peasant may be as constructed and divided as that of Du Bois's "Negro," but, far from being hidden behind a "veil," every fragment of his identity can become fully visible, as it were, in language.

If this theory seems at first far more radically constructivist than any proposed by Du Bois, the parable of the peasant nevertheless reminds us that Bakhtin believes the incorporation of voice within language actually liberates individual agency. Rather than lurking undiscernibly beneath the Du Boisian veil of social objectification, the identity or identities imposed on the peasant are themselves so thoroughly objectifiable in language that the peasant can not only comprehend them but "actively" choose his "orientation" among them. In other words, just as the voices of competing ideologies reside within the form or body of language, so individuality can itself be expressed through these voices. As we have seen in Chapters 3 and 4, Bakhtin's vagueness about how this individuality manifests itself within the more primary forms of sociolinguistic identity is signaled by the abundance of figures he uses to describe it: the "orientation" practiced by the knowing peasant is elsewhere called "inflection," "refraction," "accent," or "ventriloquization." His particular reliance on vocal metaphors, however, suggests a model of communication based on an ideal of spoken exchange that is immediate, responsive, and active. For Bakhtin the "passive" interpenetration of consciousness that Du Bois describes is transformed through

self-consciousness into a linguistic activity. What Du Bois regarded as
the obliteration of individual point of view—having to "look at one's
self through the eyes of others"—Bakhtin formulates as a liberating
ideological mobility—"looking at one social language through the eyes
of another." By making point of view a property of language and not
individuals, by making looking the same as speaking, Bakhtin stresses
that identity is never a matter of private interiority, but, on the contrary, is always a matter of social relation. In Bakhtin's model, African
American identity might always be possible to manifest, even if it were
materialized "only" through mediation, through the inflection of hegemonic discourse rather than through its own autonomous social language.

If Bakhtin imagines that a form so localizable as a single utterance
can embody the multiplicity of individual and social subjectivity, it is
not surprising that he also imagines that this isolatable linguistic form
facilitates cultural understanding by making subjectivity specially legible
and thus optimally interpretable. That this dynamic meaning is not expressed by conventionally formal compositional markers does not deter
Bakhtin. On the contrary, as I have shown, he imagines that the complex inner life of the utterance is evinced by the linguistic palpability of
features like "refraction" and "voice"—even if these traces of subjectivity are so subtle as to seem nonexistent, made visible or audible only by
Bakhtin's highly original analysis of discourse. So attuned to the nuances of language does Bakhtin claim to be that he can even tell when
one language, by drawing attention to the materiality rather than the in-
tentionality of discourse, reifies another.[16]

Unsurprisingly, then, despite the metaphorics of voice in which it is
expressed, Bakhtin's social formalism has directed attention to the language of texts, especially literary texts, rather than spoken discourse. Although the example of the peasant might suggest that, like Du Bois,
Bakhtin wants to correlate linguistic power with class position, Bakhtin
does not explore the ramifications of social position, choosing instead to
create a continuum of linguistic self-consciousness in which the illiterate

---

[16] As I have suggested in Chapters 3 and 4, although Bakhtin's inquiry seems to
rely on a systematic classification of discourse types, his interpretative method is so
idiosyncratic and so dependent on metaphoric terms that it has spawned countless
unresolved debates among critics who attempt to chart Bakhtinian voice patterns
through the microanalyses of specific texts. Michael André Bernstein notes this
problem as early as 1983 ("When the Carnival Turns Bitter," esp. 288–89).

peasant marks one extreme.[17] As I have shown in Chapter 4, the other extreme is marked not by the czar or general secretary but by the novel-ist—the language user most sensitive to the voices in the languages he uses.

The term "double-voiced discourse" is introduced in "Discourse in the Novel" as one of the complicated techniques employed by the novel-ist to represent this linguistic encounter:

> Heteroglossia, once incorporated into the novel (whatever the forms for its incorporation), is *another's speech in another's language,* serving to express authorial intentions but in a refracted way. Such speech constitutes a special type of *double-voiced discourse.* It serves two speakers at the same time and expresses simultaneously two different intentions: the direct intention of the character who is speaking, and the refracted intention of the author. In such discourse there are two voices, two meanings and two expressions. And all the while these two voices are dialogically interrelated, they—as it were—know about each other (just as two exchanges in a dialogue know of each other and are structured in this mutual knowledge of each other); it is as if they actually hold a conversation with each other. (324; Bakhtin's emphasis)

Because language is for Bakhtin an ideal social body, double voice can seem to solve the problem of double consciousness: it can equalize power relations simply through self-expression. In Du Bois's description of double consciousness, hegemonic mediation sunders the ideal unity of African American identity: the social conditions of racial discrimination turn even the positive content of ethnic affiliation into a negative self-relation—"two souls, two thoughts, two unreconciled strivings, two warring ideals"—resulting in the experience of internal division rather than the manifestation of double identity. By contrast, in Bakhtin's model, the unequal power relations between author and character are mediated, and thus transformed, in and through the capacious social body of language; language manifests two different subjectivities—"two voices, two meanings, and two expressions"—and even allows them a new relation to each other, a dynamic unity that preserves individual identity while promoting not just intersubjective relation but, more powerfully, intersubjective communion.

Author and character, like hegemonic and subaltern subjects, are ini-tially characterized in this description of double voice by their unequal manifestation within the language body: the character's intention is di-

---

[17] See Hirschkop, "Heteroglossia" and "Is Dialogism for Real?" for a critique of Bakhtinian populism.

rectly expressed, while the author's is refracted. But unlike Du Bois's description of social power relations in which social subjects are mediated only through each other, in Bakhtin's account of the novel, mediated subjects preserve their autonomy because they are equally mediated by language. Thanks to the materializing power of language, the difference between "direct" and "refracted" intentions is less important than the visibility of each. In, as Bakhtin puts it, "serving" two speakers equally, language thus not only expresses two different intentions, but ultimately converts these two intentions into a single shared intention. If character and author initially used the same language to say two different things, their cohabitation within the same language body leads them to speak equally to each other about only one thing: each other. The subjective difference between character and author is simultaneously preserved and overcome by the dialogue within the language body; but the ontological difference between a real author and her fictional characters is, like the difference between subaltern and hegemonic subjects, nullified by the special representational power that Bakhtin accords to language, the power to convert the realities of social stratification into a linguistic utopia of intellectual and conversational community.[18]

For Bakhtin, then, the novelist possesses two extraordinary capabilities—but ones that are commonplace to the social formalist tradition: a godlike ability to represent the self through the other, to occupy but not violate the autonomy of the "other," as well as a negative capability to manifest himself through language while always being more than language. Like the sovereign transcendental soul that Du Bois describes, Bakhtin's novelist seeks "a freedom for expansion and self-development"; but whereas for Du Bois this freedom would create a more unified self, the "better and truer self" of the Bakhtinian novelist might be said to "seek to know itself and the world around about it" through the activity of alteration, the "oscillation" (322) between I and thou that I

---

[18] For Bakhtin, ultimately even political power is no more than a matter of linguistic form. The particular social conditions of any time or nation may make each individual's diverse cultural membership more or less problematic, depending on the ebb and flow of hegemonic forces that attempt "to preserve the socially sealed-off quality of a privileged community ('the language of respectable society'), or to preserve local interests at the national level" ("Discourse," 382). For Bakhtin, in other words, political structures preserve their power by using language to centralize authority and suppress the diversity of one's social affiliations. Thus, even the most multifarious cultural identities are finally politicized by one's participation in either of two dichotomous linguistic activities: hegemonic consolidation or subversive dispersal.

have discussed in Chapter 4. Indeed, as I have shown, the Bakhtinian novelist fulfills his subjectivity through a rhythm of regulation; self and other are distinguished less by any particular social attributes than by the fruitful division of phenomenological noncoincidence.

WHAT MAKES BAKHTINIAN theory immediately inviting for African Americanists are the points of connection between Bakhtin's and Du Bois's descriptions of the socially constructed subject. They each imagine personal identity to be determined by social identity, which both critics define as membership in an identifiable cultural group. Because they believe that social identity is prior to and constitutive of personal identity, each describes individual consciousness as point of view, a concept that stresses the nonessential "content" of consciousness and emphasizes the integral relation between a person's thought and the ideology of her subject position. In addressing the crisis of African American identity expounded by Du Bois, theorists rely in particular on two concepts from Bakhtin: the notion that social identity is embodied in language; and the belief that an individual can manifest those social identities through his or her own language use. By adding Bakhtin's account of language to Du Bois's model of the socially constructed racial subject, these theorists thus turn the "empty" identity of Du Bois's "Negro" into a negative capability produced by subaltern positionality.

As we have seen, Du Bois assumes that consciousness is the ideal site of identity. In his account, the catastrophe of hegemonic power relations is that they violate the inner sanctum of consciousness. Yet paradoxically, this very invasion gives the "Negro" a certain power over his colonizers, the power to represent, if only to himself, the limitations of hegemony as an objectifiable point of view. Since the "Negro" internalizes not just the white view of himself but also the hegemonic power relations that create the difference between "Negro" and white identity, the "Negro" cannot, by definition, see himself as whites see him, even when the white point of view resides within. This internal alienation from hegemonic vision allows him to know that he is more than the point of view that defines him but not to know the precise content of this hidden self. Thus "Negro" consciousness produces a "Negro" beyond hegemonic knowledge and control, even if it is only the activity of negative relation that constitutes an "authentic" "Negro" point of view.

Theorists like Gates, Awkward, Henderson, and Johnson accept Du Bois's account of African American consciousness as divided, but they employ Bakhtin's theory of double-voiced discourse to transform the social conditions of self-alienation into the linguistic condition of self-articulation. In reinterpreting Du Bois's model of African American consciousness through Bakhtin's sociolinguistic definition of point of view, these African Americanists conclude that there is more than one kind of container for socially constructed identity. The dark body contains within it a form that manifests rather than veils social identity: the linguistic body. Bakhtin's description of language as a container for multiple social identities means that the invasion of the African American's physical body can be countered by the African American's own invasion of the hegemonic linguistic body. The activity of negative relation that defines African American identity can thus be expressed in and through language. And because language is externalizable, because the language that constitutes consciousness can be formed outside of the mind, African Americans have a way of making their own point of view visible— even if this point of view is no more than the process of negative relation, the inflection of hegemonic language. In reading Du Bois through Bakhtin, then, theorists discover a source of empowerment for the African American: he controls, if not the terms of his identity, then at least his own linguistic expression of that identity. Bakhtin's social formalism encourages theorists to declare, moreover, that the African American's externalization of negative identity has political consequences. The articulation of subaltern identity can subvert hegemony by making visible its limitations.[19]

A pivotal moment in Mae Gwendolyn Henderson's "Speaking in

---

[19] The political consequences of heteroglossia are implied throughout "Novel," but they are treated most directly in the section entitled "The Two Stylistic Lines of Development in the European Novel" (366–422). Hegemony for Bakhtin is the attempt of a ruling faction to consolidate power by creating a "single unitary language." Subversion of this power can be achieved through the expression of linguistic diversity. This "decentering" reveals the constructedness of hegemonic rule, exposing as arbitrary and self-serving what had been taken to be impersonal and necessary. As Bakhtin puts it:

> This verbal-ideological decentering will occur only when a national culture loses its sealed-off and self-sufficient character, when it becomes conscious of itself as only one among *other* cultures and languages. It is this knowledge that will sap the roots of a mythological feeling for language, based as it is on an absolute fusion of ideological meaning with language; there will arise an acute feeling for language boundaries (social, national and semantic), and only then will language reveal its essential *human* character; from behind its words, forms, styles, nationally characteristic and socially typical faces begin to emerge, the images of speaking human beings. (370; Bakhtin's emphasis)

Tongues: Dialogics, Dialectics, and the Black Woman Writer's Literary Tradition" reveals how the capacity for linguistic alterity that, for Bakhtin, is the source of the novelist's power is now equated with the subaltern condition of internal division:

> It is the process by which these heteroglossic voices of the other(s) "encounter one another and coexist in the consciousness of real people—first and foremost in the creative consciousness of people who write novels," that speaks to the situation of black women writers in particular, "privileged" by a social positionality that enables them to speak dialogically racial and gendered voices to the other(s) both within and without. (118)[20]

Significantly, Henderson has made Bakhtin's agent at once more specific and more general. On the one hand, the position of creative supremacy ("first and foremost") that Bakhtin accords the novelist is expanded to include all writers; but, on the other hand, this creative capacity is explicitly linked—in a way that it is not limited in Bakhtin—to a particular social positionality. Henderson's modification of Bakhtin thus raises a question she never answers: is the black woman's identity as a writer part of her subject position? Or is her subject position defined by race and gender and her creative consciousness attributable to some inherent talent that belongs to writers? It is this ambiguity that allows Henderson to imply that "social positionality" actually creates creative consciousness. She is thus able to accomplish the startling conversion of social disempowerment into vocal privilege.[21]

In her influential essay "Metaphor, Metonymy and Voice in *Their Eyes Were Watching God*" (1987), Barbara Johnson's use of Bakhtin is more implicit, but it is nonetheless crucial for her account of subaltern language and its political consequences. Like Bakhtin, Johnson believes that some people are specially capable of understanding, and thus ex-

---

[20] The larger goal of Henderson's project is to modify Bakhtin's theory of sociolinguistic identity by refashioning it through Gadamer's insights about dialectical relation.

[21] Wald and O'Connor also imagine that double consciousness can be glossed as double voice in order to describe the special problem of woman's social construction and the special power of woman's self-consciousness. Wald declares that double voice opens " 'fixed and indisputable' language to inspection," allowing a "self-authorization that marks the subject's continuous efforts to choose consciously and actively among an interplay of differences" ("Becoming 'Colored,'" 80–81). O'Connor similarly concludes: "The more voices that are ferreted out, the more discourses that a woman can find herself an intersection of, the freer she is from one dominating voice, from one stereotypical and sexist position" ("Subject," 202).

pressing, the truth of self-division. Like Henderson, she believes that social position, specifically that entailed by race and gender, allows some social groups more than others, "blacks" more than "whites" and black women more than black men, to be especially self-conscious of the socially constructed division that constitutes their identity.[22] Because this social condition of alienation is expressed in and through subaltern language, the subaltern voice must, "to be authentic" in literature as in life, "incorporate and articulate division and self-difference" (166).

To argue this thesis, Johnson quotes the Du Bois passage on double consciousness. Significantly, she introduces it by way of a quotation from Henry Louis Gates in which he describes the "writer of African descent" as belonging to "at least two traditions—the individual's European or American literary tradition, and one of the three related but distinct black traditions."[23] While Gates here seems willing to admit that the cultural heritage of the African American writer is complex—he belongs to "at least" two traditions and one of these traditions can itself be divided into three—he proceeds, in the passage quoted by Johnson, to reduce the intricacies of ethnic relation to a simple dichotomy. In Gates's description the African American writer's cultural heritage is reified in language, a division that is instantiated, Gates ultimately asserts, through the "double-voiced" literary "utterance."[24]

Johnson is certainly right to recognize that Gates's description of *literary* doubleness has in mind the Du Bois quotation, but she does not see that Gates has also rewritten Du Bois through Bakhtin. Without analyzing the Du Bois quotation itself, she seems to accept Gates's as-

[22] That Henderson and Johnson regard African American women as particularly privileged by their social position should come as no surprise given the logic I have been tracing. If the subaltern position of all African Americans bestows upon them a double consciousness and a double voice, then the subaltern position of African American women, a group who are doubly excluded on the grounds of race and gender, results, according to Johnson and Henderson, in the doubling of double consciousness and double voice. Although in such arguments race and gender are taken to be the primary categories that define subaltern groups, Johnson's essay does briefly envision an endless field of social affiliation, one structured by an endless variety of significant hierarchical relations that might produce in turn an endlessly divided self ("Metaphor," 169). See Clive Thomas, "Mikhail Bakhtin and Contemporary Anglo-American Feminist Theory," for an early account of Bakhtin's adoption by feminist theory. For a stunning analysis of the relation of Johnson to other contemporary white feminists who theorize fiction written by African American women, see Elizabeth Abel, "Black Writing."

[23] Johnson, "Metaphor," 166, quoting Gates, "Criticism," 4.

[24] Johnson, "Metaphor," 166, quoting Gates, "Criticism," 8.

sumption that Du Boisian double consciousness is defined only in terms of what I am calling the "ethnic" model: the division between what Gates glosses as African and Euro-American cultural identities. Johnson does not see how Du Bois problematizes the category of cultural heritage by obscuring the "essential" characteristics of each group identity, nor does she see how Du Bois's use of the term "Negro" further destabilizes the notion of what might be termed cultural essence.[25] Although Johnson's own argument is interested in how identity is constructed in and against hegemonic social forces, she also does not see in the Du Bois quotation the complexities raised by his invocation of the "colonial model": his definition of "Negro" identity not simply as divided but as mediated by the hegemonic point of view. In other words, all Johnson sees in Du Bois is confirmation of the familiar deconstructionist paradox: that knowledge about the truth of self-division is empowering. And she sees in Gates's Bakhtinian gloss of Du Bois a way of making this knowledge inseparable from the sociolinguistic identity of African Americans. That this buried allusion to Bakhtin seems hidden from Johnson herself, even as it plays such a crucial role in the development of her argument, shows exactly how much the Bakhtinian notion of voice is taken for granted by theorists of African American identity.

In reading Du Boisian double consciousness through Gates through Bakhtin, Johnson not only makes consciousness indistinguishable from language, but makes a certain kind of language use—"double-voicedness"—synonymous not just with the positionality of African American literary texts (Gates's equation), but with all of African American identity. African Americans can know better and express more fully the truth of self-division because their divided social position allows them a privileged insight that is perfectly represented by their use in life and literature of double-voiced discourse. Like the Bakhtinian novelist, Johnson's African American can both resist and expose hegemonic appropriation simply through linguistic self-expression.

Through the concept of "voice," then, critics like Gates, Awkward, Henderson, and Johnson can describe African American identity as constituted by a social positionality that does not simply divide but splinters

---

[25] More recently, in her "Response" to Gates's "Canon-Formation, Literary History, and the Afro-American Tradition: From the Seen to the Told," Johnson has shown that she does not always accept Gates's position uncritically. She notes, for example, the doubleness of his own critical discourse, describing him as "driven by an empowering desire to have it both ways, to have his western theory and his vernacular theory too" (40).

identity; indeed, according to these theorists, African American identity is so fragmented that neither any single piece nor any combination of pieces can accurately represent the whole. These critics thus imply that the best way to define African American identity is as an activity rather than an entity: African American identity is not fragmented but the very process of fragmentation. The category of race is thus retained but also redefined: instead of restricting African American identity by limiting it to either one kind of body or even one kind of social division, "race" now allows African American identity to be conceived of as infinitely fluid.[26]

While this redefinition of African American identity may thus discover a freedom within social determination, it also risks making African American identity illegible and perhaps even imperceptible.[27] As I have tried to demonstrate, the social formalism that these identity theorists share with Bakhtin leads them to believe that Bakhtin's theory of language provides an answer to this problem. They imagine that language as Bakhtin describes it both preserves and reconciles what I have shown to be the two different models of African American identity—the "ethnic" and the "colonial"—that inform Du Bois's description of double consciousness. According to the logic of social formalism, the uniquely "two-toned" heritage of African American identity is instantiated in African American language, while African Americans as subalterns are dialogically empowered within the hegemonic language through which they speak. These two models of double identity coincide for social formalists because the doubleness of "ethnic" African American identity derives not from any positive cultural content but from the negative capability inherent in subaltern positionality: the capacity of the African American not simply to accommodate but to know, practice, and instantiate linguistic self-division.

[26] See Fuss, *Essentially Speaking*, esp. 73–96. While I would quarrel with Fuss's reading of theorists like Houston Baker and Henry Louis Gates, Jr., her discussion provides an important overview of the antiessentialist debate, both within and beyond African American theory. See Homans, "'Women of Color,'" for a critique of Fuss (84) and, more generally, of white feminists for whom, as Homans puts it, the "embodied black woman tends to become part of the machinery for validating disembodiment" (87).

[27] We can see this danger in O'Connor's formulation of what she sees as the happy Bakhtinian solution to the Du Boisian problem: "Although consciousness may seem to be the ultimate goal—one single definition of self by which to live—this self must be one in constant transition because it is always in dialogue with other personalities who represent other social forces" ("Subject," 202).

Yet this influential account of African American double-voicedness may leave us wondering exactly what kind of distinguishing "gift" it bestows in compensation for the pain of racial discrimination, the grounding assumption in the Bakhtinian revision of Du Bois. In fact, it seems that, by interpreting the "gift" of second sight as self-conscious language use (double vision as double voice), the logic of social formalism introduces a new kind of crisis for African American identity: by reading Du Bois through Bakhtin, theorists have imagined a way that subaltern identity can distinguish itself from the hegemonic identity that defines it, but it has won African American self-definition at the price of making all subaltern difference the same.[28] Since social formalists define African American identity not as positive content but only as linguistic oscillation, how can they distinguish African American expression from the similarly oscillatory discourse of any other subaltern group? Johnson's suggestion that some groups are more oppressed and thus more linguistically divided than others is one attempt to grant different subaltern groups a discursive autonomy. But even if Johnson is right that the subaltern position of black women, say, makes them "more divided" than black men, how are we to differentiate between languages that are both expressive only of an "ever-differing self difference" ("Metaphor," 170)? African Americanists initially turn to Bakhtin because double voice seems to hold a special relation to African American identity; yet Bakhtinian social formalism ultimately works to divest African American identity from any privileged relation to double consciousness. When double vision is read as double voice, the distinguishing feature of African American identity comes to define all subaltern identity. Reading double consciousness as double voice thus may free the African American from any particular crisis of inexpressibility, but in doing so the particularity of African American identity is also lost: the African American is free to speak, but can utter only the subaltern language of empty self-expression.

[28] See Hitchcock, *Dialogics of the Oppressed*, for a theory of subaltern identity that avoids social formalism through a sophisticated and critical account of Bakhtinian dialogism. Hitchcock and Hirschkop both profitably question the ability of minority discourses to speak "miraculously or narcissistically" for themselves (Hitchcock, *Dialogics*, 2; Hirschkop, "Is Dialogism for Real?").

Conclusion

THE EVOLUTION OF social formalism—the move from privileged artists to disempowered minorities and from novels to social discourse—is accomplished by what we might call a reversal in the point of view from which point of view is theorized, a shift from that of the representer to that of the represented. For James the foundational characteristic of individual identity, the idiosyncratic interests that make one point of view different from another, is also the potential solution to the problem of mediated knowledge: the capacity to be interested solves the problem of interestedness; "wonder" leads the artist beyond the self and to the other. But Jamesian wonder makes the successful representation of the interesting other wholly dependent upon the sensibility of the representer. The Jamesian artist struggles to represent the subject in its own terms, but this intrinsic representation is predicated on the assumption that the difference between viewer and viewed is precisely what enables the viewer to know the identity of the other as different, and thus know the other more completely than she can know herself. Lubbock's novel theory ostensibly imagines a way for the other to speak for herself. In conceptualizing the other as a novelistic character, Lubbock accords to fictional constructs what he takes to be the definitive attribute of human subjects, the power for authentic self-representation through direct expression. But the autonomy that Lubbock grants novelistic characters is, as we have seen, indistinguishable from supremely successful authorial co-optation; for Lubbock the novel's signal accomplishment is the illusion rather than the actuality of characterological autonomy. By defining language as a body for rather than a commodity of identity, linguistic and semiotic theory gave novel theorists a way to describe the speaking other as a reality not just of fiction but of social life. For the theorists of the second wave, the subjectivities expressed in language are still dependent upon novelists for public recognition, but there is an increasing sense of the expressive rights that belong to the represented other. In Bakhtin's model, the represented other may still be dependent upon the novelist for her fullest representation, but the novelist's altruism is less invidious because it is more passive: unveiling the identity of the other through amplification rather than Jamesian penetration, the Bakhtinian novelist strives to present not "the secret" (to use James's expression) of an identity that he alone can appreciate, but the voices of social identity whose dialogic self-expression only needs artistic intensification to be properly heard. However, the Bakhtinian novelist's appreciation still depends upon his ability to control the social identities he depicts. For theorists of minority identity, the altruism of the representer is simply a veil for his own self-interest. From the point of view of the oppressed, alterity is not the someone else whose difference should be appreciated, but the self-alienation created by social discrimination.

Yet as I have been arguing, the attempt to derive a theory of minority self-empowerment from an aesthetic tradition results not in a politicization of the aesthetic but in an aestheticization of the political. In trying either to dismiss the special claims that Bakhtin makes for the novel—in ignoring not just his genre distinctions but his more general sense of art's special powers—those looking to Bakhtin for a way of conceptualizing the literary as the social end up with a description of the subaltern subject theorized through the representational privilege that Bakhtin bestows upon literary agents: novels and novelists.

It might be argued that the search for a "vernacular" theory of representation, a project that has been respectively pursued by Henry Louis Gates, Michael Awkward, and Houston Baker, stands as an important alternative to the social formalism that I have been describing. *The Signifying Monkey*, for example, understands the African American literary tradition through a historical methodology that in its detail alone distinguishes itself from Bakhtin's cursory summaries of social trends. But to recognize Gates's formidable accomplishments as a literary historian and to see in his work a real alternative to social formalism is simply to say that social formalism is not the only position he holds.[1] *The Signifying Monkey* in fact moves between a literary historical account of the African American literary tradition and a social formalist account of black identity; although Gates interrelates the positions, they are in fact usefully and easily detached from each other.

Gates's literary historical account of the development of African American literature documents the social attitudes that made authorship

---

[1] *Figures in Black*, for instance, is a literary history that does not rely on social formalism to discuss the issues of black literacy and self-representation.

nothing less than a proof of humanity for African Americans. As Gates puts the problem:

> The very proliferation of black written voices, and the concomitant political import of them, led fairly rapidly in our literary history to demands both for the coming of a "black Shakespeare or Dante," as one critic put it in 1925, and for an authentic black printed voice of deliverance, whose presence would by definition, put an end to all claims of the black person's subhumanity. (*Signifying*, 132)

But given the politics of alterity that Gates describes, to prove black humanity by reproducing white literary voices was to gain recognition as a "speaking subject" at the expense of leaving African American experience unvoiced. The project for African American authors became, according to Gates, the creation of "a collective black voice through the sublime example of an individual text, and thereby to register a black presence in letters, that most clearly motivated black writers, from the Augustan Age to the Harlem Renaissance" (131). On Gates's view, the registration of "a black presence in letters" is accomplished, we know, through signifyin(g): "Whatever is black about black American literature is to be found in this identifiable black Signifyin(g) difference" (xxiv). Because signifyin(g) is paradoxically the vernacular of the black literary tradition, black experience can be registered in literary texts even when it seems unvoiced: "The originality of so much of the black tradition emphasizes refiguration, or repetition and difference, or troping, underscoring the foregrounding of the chain of signifiers, rather than the mimetic representation of a novel content" (79).

But the interest and power of signifyin(g) as a historical concept and as a literary strategy becomes confused in *The Signifying Monkey* with a language theory that makes the mimetic representation of the chain of signifiers not only a positive good but an imperative for the authentic expression of any black identity. We can see Gates's investment in signifyin(g) change when he moves from a description of the literary tradition itself to a description of his critical methodology. Gates initially defines his own role as a literary critic in terms that are compatible with Bakhtinian amplification. Gates strives to be an appreciative mediator, to present the tradition he studies in its own terms:

> My desire has been to allow the black tradition to speak for itself about its nature and various functions, rather than to read it, or analyze it, in terms of literary theories borrowed whole from other traditions, appropriated from without. (*Signifying*, xix)

As formulated here, the critic's identity is irrelevant to the study of a vernacular literary tradition. Gates makes this point explicitly in another essay that responds to an attack by Tzvetan Todorov; in "Talkin' That Talk," he argues against the racialization of interpretation, stressing his own encouragement of "students and critics of all ethnic and cultural groups to write about black literature" ("Talkin'," 405). Since the tradition is textual, he argues, vernacular theory is there to be heard by anyone who takes the trouble to listen: "Within African and Afro-American literature, there can be no question that the *texts* that comprise these traditions repeat, refute, and revise key, canonical tropes and topoi peculiar to those *literary* traditions" (405; Gates's emphasis). Yet in a familiar pattern of logic, the critic turns out to represent the indigenous tradition authentically by representing it better than it could represent itself: the vernacular tradition expresses itself, it turns out, with the help of Gates's altruistic mediation. Gates says that in *The Signifying Monkey* he attempts to make explicit "that which is implicit in what we might think of as the logic of tradition" and thus "enhance the reader's experience of black texts by identifying levels of meaning and expression that might otherwise remain mediated, or buried beneath the surface" (*Signifying*, xx). The attempt to represent the black tradition in its own terms, in other words, is not only guided by Jamesian wonder but results, furthermore, in the construction of a Jamesian point of view for the outsider/reader, a vantage point that allows her to appreciate the "other" without compromising its alterity.

The appreciation of the vernacular tradition is thus not, after all, simply a matter of listening. For Gates as for James, the intrinsic or indigenous representation of the subject is accomplished through altruistic mediation. But in the Gatesian version of Jamesian "wonder," the critic's felt similarity to rather than his felt difference from his object of interest enables him to voice it as voice. Gates can represent the vernacular because he himself speaks the vernacular. Signifyin(g) is not, as Gates stresses throughout *The Signifying Monkey*, only a literary practice accomplished in response to certain historical conditions; it is the definitive linguistic practice of African American identity: "Signifyin(g), of course, is a principle of language use and is not in any way the exclusive province of black people, although blacks named the term and invented its rituals" (90). Gates thus feels that not just novelists, not just authors working in a literary tradition, but any African American utterance represents black identity most authentically when practicing signification. Thus the voicing of the literary tradition of signification is inseparable for Gates from the voicing of contemporary African American identity. In "Talkin' That Talk," Gates makes an argument not just for the importance of the indigenous study of the African American literary tradition, but for the intrinsic expression of contemporary black identity through the vernacular theorization of this tradition. African American theory, he argues, should express African American identity "in our own images, in our own voices"; he asks rhetorically, "how *else* are we to define theories of our own literatures but to step out of the discourse of the white masters and speak in the critical language of the black vernacular?" ("Talkin'," 408; Gates's emphasis). A tradition that begins in the effort to create a science of fiction thus fulfills itself in the theorization of theory itself as the objective expression of subjective identity.

If literary theory thus becomes, in Gates's account, the same as "talkin' that talk," and if "talkin' that talk" means "underscoring the foregrounding of the chain of signifiers, rather than the mimetic representation of a novel content," then minority discourse once again risks becoming the empty language of self-expression. In this formulation of the literary theoretical project, mimetic reproduction creates an echo chamber: the only thing worth saying is the vernacular and the only thing that the vernacular can say is the vernacular. Houston Baker, in an essay that is part of an ongoing dialogue with Gates about vernacular theory, is willing to make a strong case for contentless discourse. Baker exhorts minority speakers to "sound racial poetry in the courts of the civilized" ("Caliban's," 395), a "guerilla action" that he maintains will clear "the (U.S.) bases in Third World geographies, providing space for poetry, a song, a sound, rather than a sight, cite, or site for further Western duels—and dualities" (395).[2] On this view, the most efficacious expression of minority social identity is a discourse that is outside of social identity: an utterance whose signifier is so "foregrounded" as to turn the social word into pure sound. That Baker can call this discourse "poetry" suggests that the rise of social formalism in and out of the novel leads finally to a revalorization of the novel's generic other: the social formalism that is produced in the attempt to raise the aesthetic prestige of the novel fulfills itself by finding political efficacy in a discourse of social unintelligibility, the purely poetical.

[2] See Houston Baker's *Blues*, esp. 5 (qtd. as an epigraph to Chapter 5) for a more extended definition of the African American vernacular. For a full articulation of his concept of guerilla action, see *Modernism*, esp. 49.

Reference Matter

Works Cited

Abel, Elizabeth. "Black Writing, White Reading: Race and the Politics of Feminist Interpretation." *Critical Inquiry* 19 (1993): 470–98.

Abrams, M. H. *The Mirror and the Lamp: Romantic Theory and the Critical Tradition.* New York: Oxford Univ. Press, 1953.

Aldridge, John W., ed. *Critiques and Essays on Modern Fiction, 1920–1951.* New York: Roland, 1952.

Althusser, Louis. "Ideology and Ideological Apparatuses (Notes Toward an Investigation)." In *Lenin and Philosophy.* Ed. Ben Brewster. London: New Left Books, 1971. 121–73.

Anderson, Perry. *Considerations on Western Marxism.* London: New Left Books, 1976.

Anesko, Michael. *"Friction with the Market": Henry James and the Profession of Authorship.* New York: Oxford Univ. Press, 1986.

Appiah, Anthony. "The Uncompleted Argument: Du Bois and the Illusion of Race." In Gates, ed., *"Race," Writing and Difference,* 21–37.

Arac, Jonathan. "Rhetoric and Realism; or Marxism, Deconstruction, and the Novel." In *Criticism Without Boundaries: Directions and Crosscurrents in Postmodern Critical Theory.* Ed. Joseph A. Buttigieg. Notre Dame: Univ. of Notre Dame Press, 1987. 160–76.

Armstrong, Nancy. *Desire and Domestic Fiction: A Political History of the Novel.* New York: Oxford Univ. Press, 1987.

Asthana, Rama Kant. *Henry James: A Study in the Aesthetics of the Novel.* Atlantic Highlands, N.J.: Humanities Press, 1980.

Auerbach, Erich. *Mimesis: The Representation of Reality in Western Literature.* Trans. Willard R. Trask. Princeton: Princeton Univ. Press, 1953.

Awkward, Michael. *Inspiriting Influences: Tradition, Revision, and Afro-American Women's Novels.* New York: Columbia Univ. Press, 1989.

Baker, Houston A., Jr. *Blues, Ideology, and Afro-American Literature: A Vernacular Theory.* Chicago: Univ. of Chicago Press, 1984.

———. "Caliban's Triple Play." In Gates, ed., *"Race," Writing, and Difference,* 381–95.

———. *Long Black Song: Essays in Black American Literature and Culture.* Charlottesville: Univ. Press of Virginia, 1972.

———. *Modernism and the Harlem Renaissance.* Chicago: Univ. of Chicago Press, 1987.

Bakhtin, M. M. *The Dialogic Imagination.* Ed. Michael Holquist. Trans. Caryl
Emerson and Michael Holquist. Austin: Univ. of Texas Press, 1981.

———. "Discourse in the Novel." 1934–35. In *The Dialogic Imagination,*
259–422.

———. *Problems of Dostoevsky's Poetics.* 1929. Ed. and trans. Caryl Emerson. Minneapolis: Univ. of Minnesota Press, 1984.

———/P. N. Medvedev. *The Formal Method in Literary Scholarship: A Critical Introduction to Sociological Poetics.* 1928. Trans. Albert J. Wehrle.
Cambridge, Mass.: Harvard Univ. Press, 1985.

Bal, Mieke. "The Narrating and the Focalizing: A Theory of Agents in Narrative." *Style* 17 (1983): 234–69.

———. *Narratology: Introduction to the Theory of Narrative.* Trans. Christine
van Boheemen. Toronto: Univ. of Toronto Press, 1985.

Banfield, Ann. *Unspeakable Sentences: Narration and Representation in the
Language of Fiction.* Boston: Routledge and Kegan Paul, 1982.

Barker, Francis, John Coombes, Peter Hulme, David Musselwhite, and Richard
Osborne, eds. *Literature, Society, and the Sociology of Literature.* Colches-
ter: Univ. of Essex Press, 1977.

Barthes, Roland. *S/Z.* Paris: Éditions du Seuil, 1970.

———. *S/Z: An Essay.* Trans. Richard Miller. New York: Hill and Wang,
1974.

Bašić, Sonja. "From James's Figures to Genette's *Figures*: Point of View and
Narratology." *Revue Française d'Études Américaines* 17 (1983): 201–15.

Baym, Nina. *Novels, Readers, and Reviewers: Responses to Fiction in Antebellum America.* Ithaca: Cornell Univ. Press, 1984.

Beach, Joseph Warren. *The Method of Henry James.* 1918. Philadelphia: Albert
Saifer, 1954.

Bell, Bernard W. *The Afro-American Novel and Its Tradition.* Amherst: Univ.
of Massachusetts Press, 1987.

———. *The Folk Roots of Contemporary Afro-American Poetry.* Detroit:
Broadside, 1974.

Bell, Michael Davitt. *The Problem of American Realism: Studies in the Cultural
History of a Literary Idea.* Chicago: Univ. of Chicago Press, 1993.

Bell, Millicent. *Edith Wharton and Henry James: The Story of Their Friendship.*
New York: George Braziller, 1965.

Bennett, Tony. *Formalism and Marxism.* New York: Methuen, 1979.

Bentley, Phyllis. *Some Observations on the Art of Narrative.* New York:
Macmillan, 1947.

Bernard-Donals, Michael F. *Mikhail Bakhtin: Between Phenomenology and
Marxism.* New York: Cambridge Univ. Press, 1994.

Bernstein, J. M. *The Philosophy of the Novel: Lukács, Marxism, and the Dialectics of Form.* Minneapolis: Univ. of Minnesota Press, 1984.

Bernstein, Michael André. "When the Carnival Turns Bitter: Preliminary Reflections upon the Abject Hero." *Critical Inquiry* 10 (1983): 283–305.

Bersani, Leo. *A Future for Astyanax: Character and Desire in Literature.* New
York: Columbia Univ. Press, 1984.

Bialostosky, Don H. "Bakhtin Versus Chatman on Narrative: The Habilitation of the Hero." *Revue de l'Université d'Ottawa* 53 (1983): 109–16.

——. "Booth's Rhetoric, Bakhtin's Dialogics and the Future of Novel Criticism." *Novel* 18 (1985): 209–16.

——. "Dialogics as an Art of Discourse in Literary Criticism." *PMLA* 101 (1986): 788–97.

——. "Dialogics, Narratology and the Virtual Space of Discourse." *Journal of Narrative Technique* 19 (1989): 167–73.

Blair, Sara. "Henry James and the Paradox of Literary Mastery." *Philosophy and Literature* 15 (1991): 89–102.

Blanchard, Marc E. "The Sound of Songs: The Voice in the Text." In *Hermeneutics and Deconstruction*. Ed. Hugh J. Silverman and Don Ihde. Albany: State Univ. of New York Press, 1985. 122–35.

Blanchot, Maurice. *The Gaze of Orpheus, and Other Literary Essays*. Ed. P. Adams Sitney. Trans. Lydia Davis. Barrytown, N.Y.: Station Hill Press, 1981.

Boi, Paola. "Moses, Man of Power, Man of Knowledge: A 'Signifying' Reading of Zora Neale Hurston (Between a Laugh and a Song)." In *Women and War: The Changing Status of American Women from the 1930s to the 1950s*. Ed. Maria Diedrich and Dorothea Fischer-Hornung. New York: St. Martins, 1990. 107–25.

Booth, Wayne C. *The Company We Keep: An Ethics of Fiction*. Berkeley: Univ. of California Press, 1988.

——. *Critical Understanding: The Powers and Limits of Pluralism*. Chicago: Univ. of Chicago Press, 1979.

——. "Freedom of Interpretation: Bakhtin and the Challenge of Feminist Criticism." In *The Politics of Interpretation*. Ed. W. J. T. Mitchell. Chicago: Univ. of Chicago Press, 1983. 51–82.

——. "Introduction." In Bakhtin, *Problems*, xiii–xxvii.

——. *The Rhetoric of Fiction*. Rev. ed. Chicago: Univ. of Chicago Press, 1983.

——. "Rhetorical Critics Old and New: The Case of Gérard Genette." In Lerner, ed., *Reconstructing Literature*, 123–41.

Bowden, Edwin T. *The Themes of Henry James: A System of Observation Through the Visual Arts*. New Haven: Yale Univ. Press, 1956.

Brodhead, Richard H. *Cultures of Letters: Scenes of Reading and Writing in Nineteenth-Century America*. Chicago: Univ. of Chicago Press, 1993.

——. *The School of Hawthorne*. New York: Oxford Univ. Press, 1986.

Brodsky, Claudia J. *The Imposition of Form: Studies in Narrative Representation and Knowledge*. Princeton: Princeton Univ. Press, 1987.

Brooks, Cleanth, and Robert Penn Warren. *Understanding Fiction*. 1943. 3d ed. Englewood Cliffs, N.J.: Prentice Hall, 1979.

Bruce, Dickson D., Jr. "W. E. B. Du Bois and the Idea of Double Consciousness." *American Literature* 64 (1992): 299–309.

Bush, Ronald. "Paul de Man, Modernist." In *Theoretical Issues in Literary History*. Harvard English Studies 16. Ed. David Perkins. Cambridge, Mass.: Harvard Univ. Press, 1991. 35–51.

Butler, Judith. *Gender Trouble: Feminism and the Subversion of Identity.* New York: Routledge, 1990.

Butler-Evans, Elliott. *Race, Gender and Desire: Narrative Strategies in the Fiction of Toni Cade Bambara, Toni Morrison, and Alice Walker.* Philadelphia: Temple Univ. Press, 1989.

Cain, William E. "New Directions in Afro-American Literary Criticism: *The Signifying Monkey.*" *American Quarterly* 42 (1990): 657–63.

Callahan, John F. *In the African-American Grain: Call-and-Response in Twentieth-Century Black Fiction.* Middletown: Wesleyan Univ. Press, 1988.

Calvet, Louis-Jean. *Roland Barthes: A Biography.* 1990. Trans. Sarah Wykes. Bloomington: Indiana Univ. Press, 1995.

Cameron, Sharon. *Thinking in Henry James.* Chicago: Univ. of Chicago Press, 1989.

Carroll, David. "The Alterity of Discourse: Form, History, and the Question of the Political in M. M. Bakhtin." *Diacritics* 13 (1983): 65–83.

———. *The Subject in Question: The Language of Theory and the Strategies of Fiction.* Chicago: Univ. of Chicago Press, 1982.

Caserio, Robert L. *Plot, Story, and the Novel from Dickens and Poe to the Modern Period.* Princeton: Princeton Univ. Press, 1979.

Chatman, Seymour. *Coming to Terms: The Rhetoric of Narrative in Fiction and Film.* Ithaca: Cornell Univ. Press, 1990.

———. *Story and Discourse: Narrative Structure in Fiction and Film.* Ithaca: Cornell Univ. Press, 1978.

Clark, Katerina, and Michael Holquist. *Mikhail Bakhtin.* Cambridge, Mass.: Harvard Univ. Press, 1984.

Clarke, Simon, Victor Jeleniewski Seidler, Kevin McDonnell and Kevin Robins, and Terry Lovell, eds. *One-Dimensional Marxism: Althusser and the Politics of Culture.* New York: Allison and Busby, 1980.

Cohn, Dorrit. "The Encirclement of Narrative: On Franz Stanzel's *Theorie des Erzählens.*" *Poetics Today* 2 (1981): 157–82.

———. "Signposts of Fictionality: A Narratological Perspective." *Poetics Today* 11 (1990): 775–804.

———. *Transparent Minds: Narrative Modes for Presenting Consciousness in Fiction.* Princeton: Princeton Univ. Press, 1978.

Cooke, Michael. *Afro-American Literature in the Twentieth Century: The Achievement of Intimacy.* New Haven: Yale Univ. Press, 1984.

Corredor, Eva. "Lukács and Bakhtin: A Dialogue on Fiction." *Revue de l'Université d'Ottawa* 53 (1983): 97–107.

Coward, Rosalind, and John Ellis. *Language and Materialism: Developments in Semiology and the Theory of the Subject.* London: Routledge and Kegan Paul, 1977.

Culler, Jonathan. *Barthes.* London: Fontana Press, 1983.

———. "Foreword." In Genette, *Narrative Discourse,* 7–13.

———. "Problems in the Theory of Fiction." *Diacritics* (1984): 2–11.

Danow, David K. "M. M. Bakhtin in Life and Art." *American Journal of Semiotics* 3 (1985): 131–41.

Davidson, Cathy N. *Revolution and the Word: The Rise of the Novel in America.* New York: Oxford Univ. Press, 1986.

Davis, Lennard J. *Resisting Novels: Ideology and Fiction.* New York: Methuen, 1987.

de Man, Paul. "Dialogue and Dialogism." *Poetics Today* 4 (1983): 99–107.

Dews, Peter. "Althusser, Structuralism and the French Epistemological Tradition." In Elliott, ed., *Althusser,* 104–41.

Diengott, Nilli. "The Mimetic Language Game and Two Typologies of Narrators." *Modern Fiction Studies* 33 (1987): 523–34.

Donoghue, Denis. "Reading Bakhtin." *Raritan* 5 (1985): 107–19.

Dowling, William C. *Jameson, Althusser, Marx: An Introduction to* The Political Unconscious. Ithaca: Cornell Univ. Press, 1984.

Du Bois, W. E. B. *The Quest of the Silver Fleece.* 1911. Boston: Northeastern Univ. Press, 1989.

———. *The Souls of Black Folk.* 1903. New York: Vintage, 1990.

Eagleton, Terry. "Introduction Part I." In Eagleton and Milne, eds., *Marxist Literary Theory,* 1–15.

———. *Literary Theory: An Introduction.* Minneapolis: Univ. of Minnesota Press, 1983.

———, and Drew Milne, eds. *Marxist Literary Theory.* Oxford: Blackwell, 1996.

Early, Gerald. "Introduction." In *Lure and Loathing: Essays on Race, Identity, and the Ambivalence of Assimilation.* Ed. Gerald Early. New York: Penguin, 1993. xi–xxiv.

Edel, Leon. *Henry James.* Vol. 5: *The Master: 1901–1916.* 1972. New York: Avon, 1978.

———. "Introduction: Colloquies with His Good Angel." In James, *Complete Notebooks,* ix–xvii.

Edgar, Pelham. *The Art of the Novel: From 1700 to the Present Time.* New York: Macmillan, 1933.

Elliott, Gregory, ed. *Althusser: A Critical Reader.* Oxford: Blackwell, 1994.

Emerson, Caryl. "The Outer Word and Inner Speech: Bakhtin, Vygotsky and the Internalization of Language." In Morson, ed., "Forum," 245–64.

———. "Problems with Baxtin's Poetics." *Slavic and East European Journal* 32 (1988): 503–25.

Emerson, Ralph Waldo. "The American Scholar." 1837. Published as *An Oration, Delivered Before the Phi Beta Kappa Society at Cambridge, August 31, 1837.* Boston: James Munroe, 1838.

———. "Fate." 1860. *The Portable Emerson.* Ed. Carl Bode in collaboration with Malcolm Cowley. Rev. ed. New York: Penguin, 1981. 346–74.

Erlich, Victor. *Russian Formalism: History, Doctrine.* 3d ed. New Haven: Yale Univ. Press, 1965.

Feidelson, Charles. "James and the 'Man of Imagination.'" In *Literary Theory and Structure.* Ed. Frank Brady, John Palmer, and Martin Price. New Haven: Yale Univ. Press, 1973. 331–53.

Fisher, Philip. *Hard Facts: Setting and Form in the American Novel.* New York: Oxford Univ. Press, 1985.

Fogel, Daniel Mark. *Covert Relations: James Joyce, Virginia Woolf, and Henry James.* Charlottesville: Univ. Press of Virginia, 1990.

Forgacs, David. "Marxist Literary Theories." In *Modern Literary Theory: A Comparative Introduction.* Ed. Ann Jefferson and David Robey. 2d ed. Totowa, N.J.: Barnes & Noble, 1986. 166–203.

Forster, E. M. *Aspects of the Novel.* New York: Harcourt, Brace and World, 1927.

Freedman, Jonathan. *Professions of Taste: Henry James, British Aestheticism, and Commodity Culture.* Stanford: Stanford Univ. Press, 1990.

Friedman, Norman. "Point of View in Fiction: The Development of a Critical Concept." In Scholes, ed., *Approaches,* 113–42.

Fuss, Diana. *Essentially Speaking: Feminism, Nature, and Difference.* New York: Routledge, 1989.

Gallagher, Catherine. "The New Materialism in Marxist Aesthetics." *Theory and Society: Renewal and Critique in Social Theory* 9 (1980): 633–46.

———. *Nobody's Story: The Vanishing Acts of Women Writers in the Marketplace, 1670–1820.* Berkeley: Univ. of California Press, 1994.

Gardiner, Michael. *The Dialogics of Critique: M. M. Bakhtin and the Theory of Ideology.* New York: Routledge, 1992.

Gates, Henry Louis. "Afterword." In *Jonah's Gourd Vine.* By Zora Neale Hurston. New York: Harper & Row, 1990. 207–17.

———. *Figures in Black: Signs and the "Racial" Self.* Oxford: Oxford Univ. Press, 1987.

———. *The Signifying Monkey: A Theory of African-American Literary Criticism.* New York: Oxford Univ. Press, 1988.

———. "Talkin' That Talk." In Gates, ed., *"Race," Writing and Difference,* 402–9.

———, ed. *"Race," Writing and Difference.* 1985. Chicago: Univ. of Chicago Press, 1986.

Genette, Gérard. "Fictional Narrative, Factual Narrative." *Poetics Today* 11 (1990): 755–74.

———. *Narrative Discourse.* 1977. Trans. Jane E. Lewin. Ithaca: Cornell Univ. Press, 1980.

———. *Narrative Discourse Revisited.* 1983. Trans. Jane E. Lewin. Ithaca: Cornell Univ. Press, 1988.

Gerould, Gordon Hall. *How to Read Fiction.* Princeton: Princeton Univ. Press, 1937.

Gilbert, Sandra M., and Susan Gubar. *The Madwoman in the Attic: The Woman Writer and the Nineteenth-Century Literary Imagination.* New Haven: Yale Univ. Press, 1979.

Gilmore, Michael T. "The Book Marketplace I." In *The Columbia History of the American Novel.* Ed. Emory Elliott. New York: Columbia Univ. Press, 1991. 46–71.

Gilroy, Paul. *The Black Atlantic, Modernity and Double Consciousness.* Cambridge: Harvard Univ. Press, 1993.

Girard, René. "Theory and Its Terrors." In *The Limits of Theory*. Ed. Thomas M. Kavanagh. Stanford: Stanford Univ. Press, 1989. 225–54.

Godzich, Wlad. "Foreword." In Medvedev/Bakhtin, *Formal Method*. vii–xiv.

Goldmann, Lucien. "Introduction to the Problems of a Sociology of the Novel." In Eagleton and Milne, eds. *Marxist Literary Theory*, 204–20.

Goodson, A. C. "Structuralism and Critical History in the Moment of Bakhtin." In Natoli, ed., *Tracing Literary Theory*, 27–53.

Gossman, Lionel. Review essay. *Comparative Literature* 38 (1986): 337–49.

Grabo, Carl H. *The Technique of the Novel*. New York: Scribner, 1928.

Haddad, Lahcen. "Bakhtin's Imaginary Utopia." *Cultural Critique* 22 (1992): 143–64.

Hamilton, Clayton. *Materials and Methods of Fiction*. New York: Baker and Taylor, 1908.

Hartman, Geoffrey H. *Beyond Formalism: Literary Essays, 1958–1970*. New Haven: Yale Univ. Press, 1970.

Hawkes, Terence. *Structuralism and Semiotics*. Berkeley: Univ. of California Press, 1977.

Henderson, Mae Gwendolyn. "Speaking in Tongues: Dialogics, Dialectics, and the Black Woman Writer's Literary Tradition." In *Reading Black, Reading Feminist: A Critical Anthology*. Ed. Henry Louis Gates, Jr. New York: Meridian, 1990. 116–42.

Hernadi, Paul. *Beyond Genre: New Directions in Literary Classification*. Ithaca: Cornell Univ. Press, 1972.

Hirschkop, Ken. "The Author, the Novel, and the Everyday." *Times Higher Education Supplement*, May 1, 1992, 27.

———. "Heteroglossia and Civil Society: Bakhtin's Public Square and the Politics of Modernity." *Studies in the Literary Imagination* 23 (1990): 65–75.

———. "Introduction: Bakhtin and Cultural Theory." In *Bakhtin and Cultural Theory*. Ed. Ken Hirschkop and David Shepherd. Manchester: Manchester Univ. Press, 1989. 1–38.

———. "Is Dialogism for Real?" *Social Text* 30 (1992): 102–13.

———. "On Value and Responsibility." *Critical Studies* 2 (1990): 13–27.

Hitchcock, Peter. *Dialogics of the Oppressed*. Minneapolis: Univ. of Minnesota Press, 1993.

Holland, Laurence. *The Expense of Vision: Essays on the Craft of Henry James*. Princeton: Princeton Univ. Press, 1964.

Holloway, John. "Language, Realism, Subjectivity, Objectivity." In Lerner, ed., *Reconstructing Literature*, 60–80.

Holquist, Michael. "Answering as Authoring: Mikhail Bakhtin's Trans-Linguistics." *Critical Inquiry* 2 (1983): 307–19.

———. "Introduction." In Bakhtin, *Dialogic Imagination*, xv–xxxiv.

Homans, Margaret. "'Women of Color' Writers and Feminist Theory." *New Literary History* 25 (1994): 73–94.

Hopkins, Mary Frances. "Interview: With Wayne C. Booth." *Literature in Performance* 2 (1982): 46–63.

Horne, Philip. *Henry James and Revision: The New York Edition.* Oxford: Clarendon Press, 1990.

Hughes, Herbert L. *Theory and Practice in Henry James.* Ann Arbor, Mich.: Edwards Brothers, 1926.

Jakobson, Roman. "On Realism in Art." In *Readings in Russian Poetics: Formalist and Structuralist Views.* Ed. Ladislav Matejka and Krystyna Pomorska. Cambridge, Mass.: MIT Press, 1971.

James, Henry. "The Art of Fiction." 1888. In *The Future of the Novel,* 3–27.

———. *The Art of the Novel: Critical Prefaces.* Ed. R. P. Blackmur. 1934. New York: Scribner, 1962.

———. *The Complete Notebooks of Henry James.* Ed. Leon Edel and Lyall H. Powers. Oxford: Oxford Univ. Press, 1987.

———. *The Future of the Novel: Essays on the Art of Fiction.* Ed. Leon Edel. New York: Vintage, 1956.

———. Henry James to the Deerfield Summer School. 1889. In *The Future of the Novel,* 28–29.

Jameson, Fredric. *The Political Unconscious: Narrative as a Socially Symbolic Act.* Ithaca: Cornell Univ. Press, 1981.

Jay, Martin. *Downcast Eyes: The Denigration of Vision in Twentieth-Century Thought.* Berkeley: Univ. of California Press, 1994.

Jefferson, Ann. "Realism Reconsidered: Bakhtin's Dialogism and the 'Will to Reference.'" *Australian Journal of French Studies* 23 (1986): 169–84.

———. "Russian Formalism." In *Modern Literary Theory: A Comparative Introduction.* Ed. Ann Jefferson and David Robey. 2d ed. Totowa, N.J.: Barnes & Noble, 1986. 24–45.

Jha, Prabhakara. "Lukács, Bakhtin and the Sociology of the Novel." *Diogenes* 129 (1985): 63–90.

Johnson, Barbara. *The Critical Difference.* Baltimore: Johns Hopkins Univ. Press, 1980.

———. "Metaphor, Metonymy, and Voice in *Their Eyes Were Watching God.*" In *A World of Difference.* Baltimore: Johns Hopkins Univ. Press, 1987. 160–83.

———. "Response." In *Afro-American Literary Study in the 1990s.* Ed. Houston A. Baker, Jr., and Patricia Redmond. Chicago: Univ. of Chicago Press, 1989. 39–44.

Jones, Gayl. *Liberating Voices: Oral Tradition in African American Literature.* Cambridge, Mass.: Harvard Univ. Press, 1991.

Juhl, P. D. *Interpretation: An Essay in the Philosophy of Literary Criticism.* Princeton: Princeton Univ. Press, 1980.

Knight, Diana. "Roland Barthes: The *Corpus* and the *Corps.*" *Poetics Today* 5 (1984): 831–37.

Kovacs, Arpad. "On the Methodology of the Theory of the Novel: Bachtin, Lukács, Pospelov." *Studia Slavica Academiae Scientiarum Hungaricae* 26 (1980): 377–93.

Kristeva, Julia. "How Does One Speak to Literature?" In *Desire in Language: A Semiotic Approach to Literature and Art.* Ed. Leon S. Roudiez. Trans.

Thomas Gora, Alice Jardine, and Leon S. Roudiez. New York: Columbia Univ. Press, 1980. 92–123.

———. "The Speaking Subject." In *On Signs*. Ed. Marshall Blonsky. Baltimore: Johns Hopkins Univ. Press, 1985. 210–20.

LaCapra, Dominick. *Rethinking Intellectual History: Texts, Contexts, Language*. Ithaca: Cornell Univ. Press, 1983.

Lanser, Susan Sniader. *The Narrative Act: Point of View in Prose Fiction*. Princeton: Princeton Univ. Press, 1981.

———. "Sexing the Narrative: Propriety, Desire, and the Engendering of Narratology." *Narrative* 3 (1995): 85–94.

———. "Shifting the Paradigm: Feminism and Narratology." *Style* 22 (1988): 52–60.

———. "Toward a Feminist Narratology." In *Feminisms: An Anthology of Literary Theory and Criticism*. Ed. Robyn R. Warhol and Diane Price Herndl. New Brunswick, N.J.: Rutgers Univ. Press, 1991. 610–29.

Lentricchia, Frank. *After the New Criticism*. Chicago: Univ. of Chicago Press, 1980.

———. *Ariel and the Police: Michel Foucault, William James, Wallace Stevens*. Madison: Univ. of Wisconsin Press, 1988.

Lerner, Laurence, ed. *Reconstructing Literature*. Oxford: Blackwell, 1983.

Lodge, David. "After Bakhtin." In *The Linguistics of Writing: Arguments Between Language and Literature*. Ed. Nigel Fabb, Derek Attridge, Alan Durant, and Colin MacCabe. Manchester: Manchester Univ. Press, 1987. 89–102.

Lovell, Terry. "The Social Relations of Culture Production." In Clarke et al., eds., *One-Dimensional Marxism*, 232–56.

Lubbock, Percy. *The Craft of Fiction*. 1921. New York: Peter Smith, 1931.

Lukács, Georg. *Studies in European Realism*. 1948. Trans. Edith Bone. London: Merlin, 1950.

Lyne, William. "The Signifying Modernist: Ralph Ellison and the Limits of the Double Consciousness." *PMLA* 107 (1992): 319–30.

MacCannell, Juliet Flower. "The Temporality of Textuality: Bakhtin and Derrida." *MLN* 100 (1985): 968–88.

McDonnell, Kevin, and Kevin Robins. "Marxist Cultural Theory." In Clarke et al., eds., *One-Dimensional Marxism*, 157–231.

McGann, Jerome. "Revision, Rewriting, Rereading; or, An Error [Not] in *The Ambassadors*." *American Literature* 64 (1992): 95–109.

McHale, Brian. "Free Indirect Discourse: A Survey of Recent Accounts." *PTL* 3 (1978): 249–87.

———. "Islands in the Stream of Consciousness: Dorrit Cohn's *Transparent Minds*." *Poetics Today* 2 (1981): 183–91.

McKeon, Michael. "A Defense of Dialectical Method in Literary History." *Diacritics* 19 (1989): 83–95.

———. *The Origins of the English Novel, 1600–1740*. Baltimore: Johns Hopkins Univ. Press, 1987.

———. "Reply to Ralph Rader." *Narrative* 1 (1993): 84–90.

Macherey, Pierre. *A Theory of Literary Production*. 1966. Trans. Geoffrey Wall. Boston: Routledge & Kegan Paul, 1978.

Marable, Manning. *W. E. B. Du Bois: Black Radical Democrat*. Boston: Twayne, 1986.

Martin, Wallace. *Recent Theories of Narrative*. Ithaca: Cornell Univ. Press, 1986.

Marx, Karl. *Capital: Volume One*. 1867. Trans. Ben Fowkes. New York: Vintage, 1976.

Medvedev, P. N. / M. M. Bakhtin. *The Formal Method in Literary Scholarship: A Critical Introduction to Sociological Poetics*. 1928. Trans. Albert J. Wehrle. Cambridge, Mass.: Harvard Univ. Press, 1985.

Mikell, Gwendolyn. "When Horses Talk: Reflections on Zora Neale Hurston's Haitian Anthropology." *Phylon* 43 (1982): 218–30.

Miller, D. A. *Bringing Out Roland Barthes*. Berkeley: Univ. of California Press, 1992.

———. *Narrative and Its Discontents: Problems of Closure in the Traditional Novel*. Princeton: Princeton Univ. Press, 1981.

———. *The Novel and the Police*. Berkeley: Univ. of California Press, 1988.

Miller, J. Hillis. *The Ethics of Reading: Kant, de Man, Eliot, Trollope, James, and Benjamin*. New York: Columbia Univ. Press, 1987.

Miller, James E., ed. *Theory of Fiction: Henry James*. Lincoln: Univ. of Nebraska Press, 1972.

Milne, Drew. "Introduction Part II: Reading Marxist Literary Theory." In Eagleton and Milne, eds., *Marxist Literary Theory*, 16–29.

Minter, David. *A Cultural History of the American Novel: Henry James to William Faulkner*. New York: Cambridge Univ. Press, 1994.

Mitzener, Arthur. "The Novel of Manners in America." *Kenyon Review* 12 (1950): 1–19.

Mocnik, Rastko. "Toward a Materialist Concept of Literature." *Cultural Critique* 4 (1986): 171–89.

Moriarty, Michael. "The Longest Cultural Journey." In Prendergast, ed., *Cultural Materialism*, 91–116.

———. *Roland Barthes*. Stanford: Stanford Univ. Press, 1991.

Morson, Gary Saul. "Introduction: Rethinking Bakhtin." In *Rethinking Bakhtin: Extensions and Challenges*. Ed. Gary Saul Morson and Caryl Emerson. Evanston: Northwestern Univ. Press, 1989. 1–60.

———. "Who Speaks for Bakhtin? A Dialogic Introduction." *Critical Inquiry* 10 (1983): 225–43.

———, ed. "Forum on Mikhail Bakhtin." *Critical Inquiry* 10 (1983): 225–319.

———, and Caryl Emerson. *Mikhail Bakhtin: Creation of a Prosaics*. Stanford: Stanford Univ. Press, 1990.

Mosher, Harold F., Jr., and William Nelles. "Guides to Narratology." *Poetics Today* 11 (1990): 419–27.

Muir, Edwin. *The Structure of the Novel*. London: Hogarth, 1928.

Mulhern, Francis. "Althusser in Literary Studies." In Elliott, ed., *Althusser*, 159–76.

Musselwhite, David. "Towards a Political Aesthetics." In Barker et al., eds., *Literature, Society, and the Sociology of Literature*, 8–17.

Natoli, Joseph, ed. *Tracing Literary Theory*. Urbana: Univ. of Illinois Press, 1987.

Nelson, Cary, and Lawrence Grossberg. "Introduction: The Territory of Marxism." In *Marxism and the Interpretation of Culture*. Urbana: Univ. of Illinois Press, 1988. 1–13.

Nussbaum, Martha C. *Love's Knowledge: Essays on Philosophy and Literature*. New York: Oxford Univ. Press, 1990.

O'Connor, Mary. "Subject, Voice, and Women in Some Contemporary Black American Women's Writing." In *Feminism, Bakhtin, and the Dialogic*. Ed. Dale M. Bauer and S. Jaret McKinstry. Albany: State Univ. of New York Press, 1991. 199–217.

Pascal, Roy. *The Dual Voice: Free Indirect Discourse and Its Function in the Nineteenth-Century European Novel*. Manchester: Manchester Univ. Press, 1977.

Patterson, David. "Mikhail Bakhtin and the Dialogical Dimensions of the Novel." *Journal of Aesthetics and Art Criticism* 44 (1985): 131–39.

Pechey, Graham. "On the Borders of Bakhtin: Dialogisation, Decolonisation." In *Bakhtin and Cultural Theory*. Ed. Ken Hirschkop and David Shepherd. Manchester: Manchester Univ. Press, 1989. 39–67.

Pecora, Vincent P. *Self and Form in Modern Narrative*. Baltimore: Johns Hopkins Univ. Press, 1989.

Peterson, Dale E. "Response and Call: The African American Dialogue with Bakhtin." *American Literature* 65 (1993): 761–75.

Phelan, James. *Worlds from Words: A Theory of Language in Fiction*. Chicago: Univ. of Chicago Press, 1981.

———, ed. *Reading Narrative: Form, Ethics, Ideology*. Columbus: Ohio State Univ. Press, 1989.

Polan, Dana B. "The Text Between Monologue and Dialogue." *Poetics Today* 4 (1983): 145–52.

Porte, Joel. "Emerson, Thoreau, and the Double Consciousness." *New England Quarterly* 41 (1968): 40–50.

Porter, Carolyn. "Gender and Value in *The American*." In *Henry James: A Collection of Critical Essays*. Ed. Ruth Bernard Yeazell. Englewood Cliffs, N.J.: Prentice Hall, 1994.

———. "History and Literature: 'After the New Historicism.'" *New Literary History* 21 (1990): 253–72.

———. *Seeing and Being: The Plight of the Participant Observer in Emerson, James, Adams, and Faulkner*. Middletown, Conn.: Wesleyan Univ. Press, 1981.

Posnock, Ross. *The Trial of Curiosity: Henry James, William James, and the Challenge of Modernity*. New York: Oxford Univ. Press, 1991.

Poulet, Georges. *The Metamorphoses of the Circle*. 1961. Trans. Carley Dawson and Elliott Coleman in collaboration with the author. Baltimore: Johns Hopkins Univ. Press, 1966.

Prendergast, Christopher, ed. *Cultural Materialism: On Raymond Williams.* Minneapolis: Univ. of Minnesota Press, 1995.

Prince, Gerald. "On Narrative Studies and Narrative Genres." *Poetics Today* 11 (1990): 271–82.

———. "On Narratology: Criteria, Corpus, Context." *Narrative* 3 (1995): 73–84.

———. "On Narratology (Past, Present, Future)." In *Narratology and Narrative.* Ed. A. Maynor Hardee and Freeman G. Henry. Columbia, S.C.: Univ. of South Carolina Press, 1990. 1–14.

Rader, Ralph W. "Defoe, Richardson, Joyce and the Concept of Form in the Novel." In *Autobiography, Biography, and the Novel.* Ed. William Matthews and Ralph W. Rader. Los Angeles: Univ. of California Press, 1973. 31–72.

———. "The Emergence of the Novel in England: Genre in History vs. History of Genre." *Narrative* 1 (1993): 69–83.

———. "From Richardson to Austen: 'Johnson's Rule' and the Development of the Eighteenth-Century Novel of Moral Action." In *Johnson and His Age.* Ed. James Engell. Cambridge, Mass.: Harvard Univ. Press, 1984. 461–83.

———. "The Novel and History Once More: A Response to Michael McKeon's 'Reply.'" *Narrative* 1 (1993): 173–83.

———. "On the Literary Theoretical Contribution of Sheldon Sacks." *Critical Inquiry* 6 (1979): 183–92.

Rampersad, Arnold. *The Art and Imagination of W. E. B. Du Bois.* 2d ed. New York: Schocken, 1990.

———. "W. E. B. Du Bois as a Man of Literature." In *Critical Essays on W. E. B. Du Bois.* Ed. William L. Andrews. Boston: G. K. Hall, 1985. 57–72.

Ricoeur, Paul. "Althusser's Theory of Ideology." In Elliott, ed., *Althusser,* 44–72.

Rimmon-Kenan, Shlomith. *Narrative Fiction, Contemporary Poetics.* New York: Methuen, 1983.

Roberts, Morris. *Henry James's Criticism.* Cambridge, Mass.: Harvard Univ. Press, 1929.

Rowe, John Carlos. *Theoretical Dimensions of Henry James.* Madison: Univ. of Wisconsin Press, 1984.

Rylance, Rick. *Roland Barthes.* New York: Harvester, 1994.

Sartre, Jean-Paul. "Why Write?" In *"What Is Literature?" and Other Essays.* Cambridge, Mass.: Harvard Univ. Press, 1988. 48–69.

Scholes, Robert, ed. *Approaches to the Novel: Materials for a Poetics.* San Francisco: Chandler, 1961.

———, and Robert Kellogg. *The Nature of Narrative.* New York: Oxford Univ. Press, 1966.

Schorer, Mark. "Foreword." In Aldridge, ed., *Critiques and Essays,* xi–xx.

———. *The World We Imagine: Selected Essays.* New York: Farrar, Straus and Giroux, 1968.

Schwartz, Daniel R. *The Humanistic Heritage: Critical Theories of the English Novel from James to Hillis Miller.* Philadelphia: Univ. of Pennsylvania Press, 1986.

Sedgwick, Eve Kosofsky. *Between Men: English Literature and Male Homoso-cial Desire.* New York: Columbia Univ. Press, 1985.

———. "Queer Performativity: Henry James's *The Art of the Novel.*" *GLQ* 1 (1993): 1–16.

Seguin, Robert. "Borders, Contexts, Politics: Mikhail Bakhtin." *Signature* 2 (1989): 42–59.

Selden, Ray. "Russian Formalism and Marxism: An Unconcluded Dialogue." In Barker et al., eds., *Literature, Society, and the Sociology of Literature,* 93–104.

Shevtsova, Maria. "Dialogism in the Novel and Bakhtin's Theory of Culture." *New Literary History* 23 (1992): 747–63.

Simpson, David. "Feeling for Structures, Voicing 'History.'" In Prendergast, ed., *Cultural Materialism,* 29–50.

Singer, Alan. "The Ventriloquism of History: Voice, Parody, Dialogue." In *Intertextuality and Contemporary American Fiction.* Ed. Patrick O'Donnell and Robert Con Davis. Baltimore: Johns Hopkins Univ. Press, 1989. 72–99.

Spilka, Mark, and Caroline McCracken-Flesher, eds. *Why the Novel Matters: A Postmodern Perplex.* Bloomington: Indiana Univ. Press, 1990.

Steiner, Peter. *Russian Formalism: A Metapoetics.* Ithaca: Cornell Univ. Press, 1984.

Stepto, Robert. *From Behind the Veil: A Study of Afro-American Narrative.* 2d ed. Urbana: Univ. of Illinois Press, 1991.

Stewart, James B. "Psychic Duality of Afro-Americans in the Novels of W. E. B. Du Bois." *Phylon* 44 (2) (1983): 93–107.

Stewart, Susan. "Shouts on the Street: Bakhtin's Anti-Linguistics." In Morson, ed., "Forum," 265–81.

Strickland, Geoffrey. *Structuralism or Criticism? Thoughts on How We Read.* New York: Cambridge Univ. Press, 1981.

Tate, Allen. "Techniques of Fiction." 1944. In Aldridge, ed., *Critiques and Essays,* 31–42.

Thomas, Clive. "Mikhail Bakhtin and Contemporary Anglo-American Feminist Theory." *Critical Studies* 1 (1989): 141–61.

Thompson, E. P. *The Poverty of Theory and Other Essays.* New York: Monthly Review Press, 1978.

Tillotson, Kathleen. *The Tale and the Teller.* London: Rupert Hart-Davis, 1959.

Titunik, I. R. "Translator's Introduction." In Vološinov[/Bakhtin], *Freudianism,* xv–xxv.

Todorov, Tzvetan. "A Dialogic Criticism?" Trans. Richard Howard. *Raritan* 4 (1984): 64–76.

———. *Mikhail Bakhtin: The Dialogical Principle.* Trans. Wlad Godzich. Minneapolis: Univ. of Minnesota Press, 1984.

Tompkins, Jane P. *Sensational Designs: The Cultural Work of American Fiction, 1790–1860.* New York: Oxford Univ. Press, 1985.

Tonkin, Boyd. "Between Difference and Doctrine: *S/Z* and the Construction of 'Classic Realism.'" *Literature and History* 10 (1984): 95–104.

Torgovnick, Marianna. "Still Towards a Humanist Poetics? A Largely Positive Panel." Part of "'The Present and Future States of Novel Criticism': A Hopeful Overview." *Novel* 18 (1985): 199–202.

Van Ghent, Dorothy. *The English Novel: Form and Function.* 1953. New York: Harper, 1961.

Veeder, William. *Henry James—The Lessons of the Master: Popular Fiction and Personal Style in the Nineteenth Century.* Chicago: Univ. of Chicago Press, 1975.

Vološinov, V. N. [/ M. M. Bakhtin]. "Discourse in Life and Discourse in Art." 1926. In *Freudianism*, 93–116.

——— [/ M. M. Bakhtin]. *Freudianism: A Critical Sketch.* 1927. Trans. I. R. Titunik and ed. with Neal H. Bruss. 1976. Bloomington: Indiana Univ. Press, 1987.

——— [/ M. M. Bakhtin]. *Marxism and the Philosophy of Language.* 1929. Trans. Ladislav Matejka and I. R. Titunik. Cambridge, Mass.: Harvard Univ. Press, 1986.

Wald, Priscilla. "Becoming 'Colored': The Self-Authorized Language of Difference in Zora Neale Hurston." *American Literary History* 2: 79–100.

Ward, J. A. *The Search for Form: Studies in the Structure of James's Fiction.* Chapel Hill: Univ. of North Carolina Press, 1967.

Warhol, Robyn R. *Gendered Interventions: Narrative Discourse in the Victorian Novel.* New Brunswick, N.J.: Rutgers Univ. Press, 1989.

Warner, William B. "Realist Literary History: McKeon's New Origins of the Novel." *Diacritics* 19 (1989): 62–81.

Washington, Mary Helen. "Foreword." In *Their Eyes Were Watching God.* By Zora Neale Hurston. 1937. New York: Harper & Row, 1990. vii–xiv.

Watt, Ian. *The Rise of the Novel.* Berkeley: Univ. of California Press, 1957.

Watts, Cedric. "Bottom's Children: The Fallacies of Structuralist and Deconstructionist Literary Theory." In Lerner, ed., *Reconstructing Literature*, 20–35.

Wehrle, Albert J. "Introduction." In Bakhtin/Medvedev, *Formal Method*, xv–xxix.

Weinstein, Philip M. *Henry James and the Requirements of the Imagination.* Cambridge, Mass.: Harvard Univ. Press, 1971.

Wellek, René. "Henry James's Literary Theory and Criticism." *American Literature* 30 (1958): 293–321.

Wiesenfarth, Joseph. *Henry James and the Dramatic Analogy: A Study of the Major Novels.* New York: Fordham Univ. Press, 1963.

Williams, Raymond. *Marxism and Literature.* New York: Oxford Univ. Press, 1977.

———. *Problems in Materialism and Culture.* London: New Left Books, 1980.

Wright, Elizabeth. "An Ideological Reading of Narrative." *Poetics Today* 11 (1990): 437–42.

Wright, Walter F. *The Madness of Art: A Study of Henry James.* Lincoln: Univ. of Nebraska Press, 1962.

Yeazell, Ruth Bernard, ed. *Sex, Politics, and Science in the Nineteenth-Century Novel.* Baltimore: Johns Hopkins Univ. Press, 1986.

Young, Robert. "Back to Bakhtin." *Cultural Critique* 2 (1985–86): 71–92.

Index

In this index an "f" after a number indicates a separate reference on the next page and an "ff" indicates separate references on the next two pages. A continuous discussion over two or more pages is indicated by a span of page numbers, e.g., "57–59." *Passim* is used for a cluster of references in close but not consecutive sequence.

Sincerity, *see* Novelistic sincerity
Small Boy and Others, A (James), 51
Social discourse, 114n3, 115f, 127, 163, 181–83, 188–93 *passim*
Social formalism: cultural criticism and, 4–5, 8, 14–15, 200, 220–25 *passim*; James's founding of, 4, 22n5, 65, 195–96; as link between many theories, 4–6, 15; valorization of alterity, 7–10, 14, 18–19, 63; Bakhtin and, 13–17 *passim*, 115, 124–27, 164, 172–73, 185–96 *passim*, 213, 221–22; Lubbock and, 52–53, 61–63, 77; Booth and, 69, 75, 77, 122; Barthes and, 70–71, 99, 100–109 *passim*; Gates and, 15, 18, 219, 222–25; Genette and, 70, 85–87; logic of, 100; Vološinov/Bakhtin and, 160; African American criticism and, 219
Social subject, 163
Sociality: novel as representative of, 5, 13f; novel as agent of, 9n, 10; novel's social nature, 76, 113; characterizations of, 14; as formal property, 14; discourse as, 68, 147, 151f; second wave and, 68, 71; Bakhtin and, 125, 162–64, 168, 171, 181–87 *passim*, 192–93. *See also* Social discourse; Social formalism; Social subject; Socio-poetics
Socio-poetics, 129, 153, 163, 195
"Song of Myself" (Whitman), 161
Souls of Black Folk, The (Du Bois), 203–8
Sound and the Fury, The (Faulkner), 74
"Speaking in Tongues: Dialogics, Dialectics, and the Black Woman Writer's Tradition" (Henderson), 215–16
Spoils of Poynton, The (James): artistic sensibility, 31; on artistic process, 32, 39–40, 42n36; materialization, 33; value of artistic object, 36–37, 42; novel as relational, 41; value of "the interesting," 44; authorial presence, 48
Stepto, Robert, 197, 202n
Structuralism, 66, 70

Subaltern identity, 14
Subaltern point of view: and subaltern subject, 18; nature of, 202, 205; privilege of, 204–5, 215–18, 222; as negative capability, 214, 219; limits of, 220n, 225
Subject, *see* Artistic subject; Social subject
Subjectivism, 24–25, 51n
Subjectivist idealism, 163–71 *passim*, 180
Subjectivity: in Genette, 70, 83; in Barthes, 103, 111n, 108–9; transcendence of, 125; social nature, 151. *See also* Consciousness
Sympathy, *see* Novelistic sympathy
Syntax, 153
S/Z: An Essay (Barthes), 99–112 *passim*; critique of novel theory, 64, 99; critique of structuralism, 70; valorization of interpretation, 71; debt to Jamesian tradition, 100f, 107, 109; critique of phenomenology, 101; and point of view, 102; critique of objectivism, 104. *See also* Vocal codes

"Talkin' That Talk" (Gates), 224f
Telling, 16, 65–69 *passim*, 86–88
Thackeray, William Makepeace, 56, 58–59
Their Eyes Were Watching God (Hurston), 197, 199
Third-person narration, 90, 92, 98
Thoreau, Henry David, 64
Tillotson, Kathleen, 22n5
Titunik, I. R., 128
Tolstoy, 53, 58–59, 121
Tompkins, Jane, 6–7
"Toward a Feminist Narratology" (Lanser), 3n
Transparent Minds: Narrative Modes for Presenting Consciousness in Fiction (Cohn), 96
Trollope, Frances, 55–56
Turgenev, Ivan, 121

Understanding Fiction (Brooks and Warren), 64

Library of Congress Cataloging-in-Publication Data

Hale, Dorothy J.
    Social formalism : the novel in theory from Henry James to the
present / Dorothy J. Hale.
        p.   cm.
    Includes bibliographical references and index.
    ISBN 0-8047-3355-4 (alk. paper). —
    ISBN 0-8047-3356-2 (pbk. : alk. paper)
    1. Fiction—History and criticism—Theory, etc. 2. Fiction—
Social aspects. 3. James, Henry, 1843–1916. I. Title.

PN3365.H33   1998
809.3—dc21   97-47426
                                                      CIP

Original printing 1998
Last figure below indicates year of this printing:
07 06 05 04 03 02 01 00 99 98

Printed and bound by CPI Group (UK) Ltd, Croydon, CR0 4YY

09/06/2025

14685746-0003